## YOU CAN OVERCOME

PRESENTED TO: _Roger A Pelletier_

ON: _____

MESSAGE: _____ 2 - 10 - 88 _____

PRESENTED BY: _____

*"He who overcomes, I will grant to him to sit down with Me on My throne, as I also overcame and sat down with My Father on His throne."*

**—Jesus Christ**

# YOU CAN OVERCOME

## by Jim McKeever

Omega Publications
P.O. Box 4130
Medford, Oregon 97501

The painting on the front cover of this book is by Andy Zito and is copyrighted by him. It is used with his permission.

The painting on the back cover is by R. S. Riddick and is copyrighted by him. It is used with his permission, which was obtained by Richard Casey.

YOU CAN OVERCOME

Omega Publications
P.O. Box 4130
Medford, Oregon 97501

Printed in the United States of America
First printing—June, 1981
Second printing—February, 1982

ISBN 0-86694-091-X (Hardbound)
ISBN 0-86694-092-8 (Softbound)
UNILIT # 782052 (Hardbound)
UNILIT # 782210 (Softbound)

# TABLE OF CONTENTS

This book is dedicated first and foremost to the
glory of God and His Son, Jesus Christ.


This book is further dedicated to
all those in centuries past who were overcomers
and to those Christians, both present
and future,
who will become overcomers
to the glory of God.

# FOREWORD

Great books are few and far between, but this book, *You Can Overcome* is a gold mine of knowledge and wisdom. It sheds light on major questions that have nagged at the minds of thinking Christians for years.

It deals with issues like: Are the overcomers a unique group of Christians? What is God's purpose for our existence? Why did God not want His children to know the difference between good and evil? Who is Satan and where did he come from? Are demons fallen angels? and many other questions of this nature.

*You Can Overcome,* though dealing in heretofore uncharted areas of biblical understanding, lifts up Jesus and honors God. It deals with some of the sacred cows of theology and strips away the fog of theory and assumption and presents its Bible-based truth in a forceful but loving way. It challenges believers to become overcomers and conquer evil, the world and Satan.

I heartily recommend this truly great book.

Giff Claiborne, Pastor
Faith Community Church

# ACKNOWLEDGEMENTS

I would like to start off by acknowledging the role of the Holy Spirit in creating this book. Many fresh and exciting insights have been gained directly from the Holy Spirit as He revealed some deep things of Jesus Christ from the Scriptures. Perhaps this is some of the "hidden manna" that is promised to the overcomers.

On the human level I am deeply appreciative of those who are in our Bible study group, who contributed support, inspiration and interaction as we developed some of these concepts. I am especially indebted to:

Jim and Tina Andrews
Al and Sheri Dinardi
Bud and Maxine Eastman
Joe and Marge Robinson

Without the prayers, the concern and the undergirding of these precious couples, this book might never have been written.

I am also indebted to Richard Casey who contacted Ron Riddick, who did the painting of Christ, and got permission for us to use this outstanding painting on our back cover.

I also appreciate the prayers and support of the board of directors of our ministry, Ministries of Vision:

Ed Gruman
Roger Minor
Harry Stiritz

In addition, I would like to express my appreciation to Gifford Clairborne and the many others who heard the tapes from the cassette album "Become an Overcomer" and encouraged me to put that message into book form.

On the human level, however, more than anyone else, my wife, Jeani, is responsible for the existence of this book. Not only did she provide the usual loving functions of a writer's wife, such as giving gentle encouragement and inspiration, but she served officially as editor, proofreader, contributor of ideas, critic and best friend. I praise the Lord for her and her valuable contribution to this book. I cannot imagine a more perfect wife and co-laborer. I am grateful to the Lord for giving me such a wonderful lady for my wife.

Yet, above all, the driving force that caused me to write this book, that motivated and inspired me, is the love that God has given me for Himself and His Son, Jesus Christ.

Jim McKeever
P.O. Box 4636
Medford, Oregon 97501

# INTRODUCTION

Since I dislike long introductions, this one will be very brief.

Most Christians tend to think of all Christians as being equal for all eternity. Unfortunately the Bible does not teach this. As you will see in this book, the Bible teaches that there is a subset of Christians called the overcomers. These overcomers are promised special positions and special privileges throughout eternity, Yet the average born-again Christian knows little, if anything, about the overcomers.

After learning what rewards the overcomers will have, people almost always ask: "How can I become an overcomer? What do I overcome?  How do I overcome?"

After examing the rewards given to the overcomers, this book discusses what we overcome and how we overcome it. I believe, without any hesitation, that this is the most important work that I have ever written and likely will be the most important work that I will ever write.

I honestly believe that if you read this book with an open heart, the Holy Spirit can use it to transform your life. He will make you into a Christian who lives for the glory of Christ.

I would personally appreciate your prayers that this book would glorify God and His Son, Jesus Christ, and that God could use the information in this book to help prepare Christians spiritually for the hard times that are ahead of us.

May the Lord bless you and enrich your spiritual life as you read this volume.

Jim McKeever

# DETAILED OUTLINE

# 1

# REWARDS OF THE OVERCOMERS

This entire book is going to deal with an exciting subject and yet one that might be new to most Christians. We tend to think of Christians as all of one class and having equal rewards in eternity. What most Christians do not realize is that Christ Himself clearly taught that there are at least two classes of Christians and that they have varying degrees of rewards in eternity.

When I used the word "Christian," I mean someone who has personally acknowledged Jesus Christ as the divine Son of God and the only way to heaven, and who has received Him as Savior and Lord. If you are not absolutely sure that if you were to die in bed tonight with a heart attack that you would go immediately to be with the Lord, I would ask you to stop here and read Appendix A, entitled "How To Become A Christian," before proceeding with this book.

Therefore, I am going to assume that anyone who is reading the remainder of this book knows Jesus Christ as his personal Savior. We Christians can all rejoice in the fact that when we stand before the judgment seat of God (usually referred to as the Great White Throne Judgment), we will be covered by the blood of Jesus Christ and God will see us as perfect and sinless.

However, what many Christians do not realize is that when Christians die, they must first stand before the judgment seat of Jesus Christ to receive varying degrees of rewards (and possibly punishment). This judgment of Christians by Christ precedes the White Throne Judgment. One of the Scriptures that deals with Christians standing before the judgment seat of Christ is found in 2 Corinthians 5:

> **10 For we must all appear before the judgment seat of Christ, that each one may be recompensed for his deeds in the body, according to what he has done, whether good or bad.**

It is clear in this verse that "we," referring to Christians, will indeed stand before the judgment seat of Christ. Each Christian is going to be paid back (recompensed) for what he has done in his body, whether it be "good or bad." Evidently we can be paid back "good" or "bad."

This is further amplified in 1 Corinthians 3:

> **10 According to the grace of God which was given to me, as a wise master builder I laid a foundation, and another is building upon it. But let each man be careful how he builds upon it.**
> **11 For no man can lay a foundation other than the one which is laid, which is Jesus Christ.**
> **12 Now if any man builds upon the foundation with gold, silver, precious stones, wood, hay, straw,**
> **13 each man's work will become evident; for the day will show it, because it is *to be* revealed with fire; and the fire itself will test the quality of each man's work.**
> **14 If any man's work which he has built upon it remains, he shall receive a reward.**
> **15 If any man's work is burned up, he shall suffer loss; but he himself shall be saved, yet so as through fire.**

I believe this is speaking of the same judgment, wherein Christians will stand before Christ. We see that what we build upon the foundation, which is Jesus Christ, is going to be tried by fire. If our work is pure and precious, it will endure, but if it is not, it will be burned up. Verse 14 says that *if our work remains,* we will receive a reward. Paul goes on to say, in verse 15, that if a man's work is burned up, he is going to suffer loss, but he himself will barely be saved, as though by fire.

To further substantiate that at the judgment seat of Christ we are going to be receiving either good or bad rewards, consider this: whose tears is God going to wipe away in Revelation 21? We know that it will not be the tears of the unsaved because they will be in the lake of fire where there will be weeping and wailing and gnashing of teeth day and night forever. Therefore, it must be the Christians (all or perhaps just some) whose tears God wipes away. Where do the tears come from in the new heaven and new earth? I suspect, although I cannot prove it from the Bible, that it is the tears of those of us who have suffered loss at the judgment seat of Christ, because our work was made out of wood, hay, and stubble rather than precious stones, gold, and silver.

So already we can see that as Christians stand before the judgment seat of Christ, which precedes the Great White Throne Judgment, they are going to be judged based on what they have done since receiving Christ as Savior and they are going to be rewarded, *good or bad,* according to what they have done. Thus, there are going to be varying degrees of reward (and possibly punishment), based on how much or how little we have truly lived for Jesus Christ.

No one can ever become a Christian or gain salvation by doing good works. However, as soon as one becomes a Christian, works become very important. It is on our works that we will be judged, as we stand before the judgment seat of Christ. This distinction is clearly shown in Ephesians 2:

> 8 **For by grace you have been saved through faith; and that not of yourselves,** *it is* **the gift of God;**
> 9 **not as a result of works, that no one should boast.**
> 10 **For we are His workmanship, created in Christ Jesus for good works, which God prepared beforehand, that we should walk in them.**
>
> —Ephesians 2

Here we see that our salvation is not a result of works. However, this also makes it clear that once one becomes a Christian, then God wants us to walk in good works.

## THE THREE SPIRITUAL R's

We are going to be getting into some things that may seem new and perhaps different to you, but before we do that, I would like to discuss the three spiritual R's. I am sure that you remember the three R's of education—readin', writin' and 'rithmetic. (Obviously spelling was not one of them.)

Did you know that there are also three spiritual R's? I believe that these three spiritual R's are even more important than the three educational R's. Let's take a look at them:

> 10 And the brethren immediately sent Paul and Silas away by night to Berea; and when they arrived, they went into the synagogue of the Jews.
>
> 11 Now these were more noble-minded than those in Thessalonica, for they received the word with great eagerness, examining the Scriptures daily, *to see* whether these things were so.
>
> 12 Many of them therefore believed, along with a number of prominent Greek women and men.
>
> —Acts 17

As you can see from these verses, the Christians in Berea did three things:

1.  They received the word with great eagerness.

2.  They examined the Scriptures daily to see if what was being taught matched with the Scriptures.

3.  Many of them believed.

So first to enumerate the three spiritual R's, we see three things that were true about these Christians:

1.  They were RECEPTIVE.

2.  They did RESEARCH.

3.  They RESPONDED with their lives.

What happens if one of these three characteristics is absent from a Christian's life? What if a Christian is not *receptive* to new teaching? I'm sure that you have all seen the "closed mind" type of Christian, the kind who has all the answers and does not even want to discuss anything that might be different from the way he believes. It is as though he has locked his mind and thrown away the key. This is very sad because God cannot teach such people anything. I believe that all Christians should be continually *open* to new things, so that God can teach them. I don't believe exactly today as I did ten years ago and, if the Lord tarries, I hope that ten years from now I won't believe exactly as I do today. I want to continue to learn and to be open to new things that God might have for me.

However, if a person is *receptive* but doesn't take time to do *research* in the Scriptures to see if what he is learning matches the Scriptures, then he is like a feather blown to and fro by the wind or a cork tossed about on the ocean.

A person who does not take the time to do research has no stability in his life. He hears someone speak on the radio and he is off in that direction; then he hears a television minister and he is off in another direction; he reads a book or attends a Christian conference and he is off in still another direction. Such a person tends to be so gullible that he will fall for anything new that comes along.

We must take the time to do the *research* in the Scriptures to see if what our pastor, or any other teacher, is teaching us really matches with God's word.

If we are receptive and take the time to do research, but it doesn't affect our lives, we are in some ways worse off than we were at the beginning. I knew one lady in Dallas who could put prophecy together backwards and forwards and yet she had no love and warmth in her life. In fact, her harshness and coldness was actually driving her own teenage daughter away from home and away from Christ. Certainly, if what we hear matches with the Scriptures, then God wants us to *respond* with our lives.

I am going to ask you to do only one thing through the remainder of this book, and that is to be *receptive*. Hopefully, even right now, you will breathe a prayer such as this: "Dear God, open up my heart and mind and help me to receive the things out of this book that are from You." After you have completed reading the book, go back to the Bible and take the time to do the research to see if the Bible does indeed support what we will be teaching in this book.

After you do your research, between you and God I trust that you will respond with your life.

My prayer is that the things that I share that are the truth of God will be made very real and alive to your heart and will minister to you, and if there is any area wherein I have missed the mark, that God will eradicate those things from your memory. But for now, all I am asking you to do is be receptive to some new things, because only when you are receptive can the Holy Spirit teach you.

## REJOICE–CHRIST IS PREACHED

Back in 1954–1957, I was president of a Christian Businessmen's Luncheon in Dallas, Texas, which met at the First Baptist Church. Normally I had various speakers come in and I rarely did the speaking myself. However, there began to be some dissension among those who attended regularly. The Baptists believed strongly in one particular form of water baptism, and some of the other brethren did not agree. The Pentecostals believed strongly in the baptism of the Spirit and gifts of the Spirit, and others did not agree. Some felt strongly that once we were saved, we were always saved, while others did not agree. It looked like some of these disagreements were about to ruin the luncheon.

The Lord then led me to personally do the speaking at one of our weekly meetings and He led me to speak out of Philippians 1:

> **15 Some, to be sure, are preaching Christ even from envy and strife, but some also from good will;**
> **16 the latter *do it* out of love, knowing that I am appointed for the defense of the gospel;**
> **17 the former proclaim Christ out of selfish ambition, rather than from pure motives, thinking to cause me distress in my imprisonment.**
> **18 What then? Only that in every way, whether in pretense or in truth, Christ is proclaimed; and in this I rejoice, yes, and I will rejoice.**

In reading these verses carefully, we can see that some people were preaching Christ out of envy, strife, and selfish motives (to make money or to obtain prestige); some were preaching Christ, not even believing in Him (in pretense). What was Paul's reaction to these people who were preaching Christ with all of these ungodly motives? He rejoiced! He was delighted that the name of Jesus Christ was being spoken and that Christ was being made the topic of conversation.

I emphasized to the brothers at the luncheon that our fellowship was not around water baptism, the baptism of the Holy Spirit, church organization, our belief on the Tribulation or Rapture, or any other such thing. I reminded them that our fellowship was only around the person of Jesus Christ.

As long as someone is preaching Jesus Christ as the Son of God and as the only way to heaven, he is my brother and in that I will rejoice. I may disagree with him on many theological subjects, but I will absolutely rejoice that he is preaching Christ, and I will do anything I can to encourage him.

I have heard various Christians say that they do not "buy" Billy Graham, Oral Roberts, Bill Bright or Kenneth Hagin, for example the list could go on and on. I may not agree with Hal Lindsay or Chuck Smith on the timing of the Rapture, but so what? Our fellowship is around Jesus Christ. Every one of these men is preaching Jesus Christ as the Son of God and the only way to heaven, and I rejoice in their ministries. I may not agree with everything that each of them teaches, but I praise God for them, from the bottom of my heart, because they are proclaiming Christ. They are my brothers and I am thrilled that God is using them, and I hope that their ministries grow. When times get rough, as I believe they will in the not-too-distant future, we are all going to need to stand together, shoulder to shoulder in unity, and not to cast stones at one another.

There is a good chance that you are not going to agree with everything that I will share in this book. One of the reasons is that I am still learning, as I said earlier; God is still teaching me things. I rejoice that we *can* continue to grow in the Lord. If we do not agree on who Israel is, for example, or on positive confession for healing, or on many other theological subjects, should this affect our fellowship and our oneness in Christ? Not as far as I am concerned, and I hope you feel the same way. I am proclaiming Christ and if you are proclaiming Christ we can each rejoice in what the other is doing and praise the Lord for one another.

I believe that the Lord is calling us to renewed unity in the body of Christ. I believe that the divisions and segments that have been created, which separate the body of Christ, are not of God but are a work of Satan. Just as the Lord is going to re-new a unified church of true believers, there is also going to be a world church of those who really don't know and follow Jesus Christ. If we are to effectively combat Satan and this false world church that is coming, we must be united in our love for one another, we must rejoice over the ministries of our brothers in Christ and we must praise God when any brother lifts up Christ. The adage used by our early American forefathers I believe will be true for us in the days ahead: "United we stand; divided we fall." Christ said of us: "By this will all men know that you are my disciples, if you have love for one another" (John 13:35).

With all my heart I want to lift up Jesus Christ as God's only Son and the only way to the Father and to eternal life. I want to glorify Him and the Father in all that I do. So even though you may not agree with everything that you read in this book, my prayer is that it will draw you closer to God.

## TWO MAJOR GROUPS OF CHRISTIANS

We will now look further at the subject we introduced at the beginning of this chapter, concerning differing rewards to Christians. You may view all Christians as in a continuous spec-trum, ranging from those who live totally devoted to Jesus Christ to those who, after receiving Christ, choose to live basically for themselves. However, in His letters to the seven churches in the book of Revelation, Christ Himself divides the spectrum into two major groups, as we will soon see.

I would like to review something that I discussed in my book, *Now You Can Understand the Book of Revelation.* In it I mentioned that many Christians have read and studied through the book of Ephesians many times. The book of Ephesians is Paul's letter to the church at Ephesus.

If you were to ask the same Christians how many had read and studied through Christ's letter to the church at Ephesus (found in Revelation 2:1-7), the answer would be very few. Even though it is all the word of God, one would wonder why

Christians tend to emphasize Paul's letter to the church at Ephesus more than Christ's letter to the same church. That doesn't make any sense at all to me.

The general format of Christ's letters to seven different churches is discussed on pages 41 and 42 of my book, *Now You Can Understand the Book of Revelation:*

> In Chapters 2 and 3 of the book of Revelation, we find the letters that Jesus Christ is writing to the seven churches. All of the letters follow a general form, although there are some exceptions. There are basically four parts to each of the letters.
>
> In the first part of each letter, Christ identifies Himself with a portion of the vision that John has just had. The portion of the vision is usually uniquely geared for the needs of the partiuclar church.
>
> In the second part of each letter, Christ praises the members of that church for the good things that they are doing. This is included in all of the letters except the last one—the letter to Laodicea. Evidently, He could not find anything there worthy of praise.
>
> In the third part of each letter, Christ criticizes the church for what they are doing wrong, or what they could do better. The exception here is the church at Philadelphia. Evidently, they were moving in the Lord's will, and He saw no need for criticism.
>
> The fourth part of each of these letters contains the promises that Christ makes to the overcomers within that church. We should point out that all of the Christians in these churches were not overcomers, and special blessings were promised by Christ to those Christians who were to become, or who already were, overcomers. We will not be dealing with the overcomers and the promises made to them in this book, since it is such a vast subject. In fact, it is the subject of a new book that Lord has laid on my heart.
>
> —Omega Publications

That book that the Lord had laid on my heart back when I wrote the book on Revelation is the one you are reading now.

## CHRIST'S LETTER TO THE CHURCH AT EPHESUS

In looking at the two groups of Christians that Christ defines in His letters, let's begin with the first letter in Revelation 2, which is written to the church at Ephesus:

1  "To the angel of the church in Ephesus write:
The One who holds the seven stars in His right hand, the One who walks among the seven golden lampstands, says this:

2  'I know your deeds and your toil and perseverance, and that you cannot endure evil men, and you put to the test those who call themselves apostles, and they are not, and you found them *to be* false;

3  and you have perseverance and have endured for My name's sake, and have not grown weary.

4  'But I have *this* against you, that you have left your first love.

5  'Remember therefore from where you have fallen, and repent and do the deeds you did at first; or else I am coming to you, and will remove your lampstand out of its place—unless you repent.

6  'Yet this you do have, that you hate the deeds of the Nicolaitans, which I also hate.

7  'He who has an ear, let him hear what the Spirit says to the churches. To him who overcomes, I will grant to eat of the tree of life, which is in the Paradise of God.' . . ."

I would love to discuss in detail the entirety of Christ's letter to the church (all believers) in Ephesus, but I will simply refer you to my earlier book on Revelation for that discussion. The significant thing, germane to this book, is found in verse 7. The first 6 verses are written to all Christians in Ephesus, whereas the last half of verse 7 deals with a subset of all the believers in Ephesus, just the overcomers. To the overcomers are promised things that are not promised to all of the other Christians. In this particular case, the promise is to eat of the tree of life which is in the paradise of God.

## CHRIST'S LETTERS TO THE OTHER SIX CHURCHES

In His letters to each of the other six churches, Christ also promises unique things to the overcomers.

The letter to the church at Smyrna is found in Revelation 2:8–11. Verse 11 is addressed to the overcomers:

11  'He who has an ear, let him hear what the Spirit says to the churches. He who overcomes shall not be hurt by the second death.'
—Revelation 2

Christ's letter to the church at Pergamum is found in Revelation 2:12–17. The promises to the overcomers are found in verse 17:

> 17 'He who has an ear, let him hear what the Spirit says to the churches. To him who overcomes, to him I will give some of the hidden manna, and I will give him a white stone, and a new name written on the stone which no one knows but he who receives it.'
>
> —Revelation 2

Christ's letter to the church at Thyatira is found in Revelation 2:18–29. This letter has some significant points, so we will include the entire letter:

> 18 "And to the angel of the church in Thyatira write:
> The Son of God, who has eyes like a flame of fire, and His feet are like burnished bronze, says this:
> 19 'I know your deeds, and your love and faith and service and perseverance, and that your deeds of late are greater than at first.
> 20 'But I have *this* against you, that you tolerate the woman Jezebel, who calls herself a prophetess, and she teaches and leads My bond-servants astray, so that they commit *acts* of immorality and eat things sacrificed to idols.
> 21 'And I gave her time to repent; and she does not want to repent of her immorality.
> 22 'Behold, I will cast her upon a bed *of sickness,* and those who commit adultery with her into great tribulation, unless they repent of her deeds.
> 23 'And I will kill her children with pestilence; and all the churches will know that I am He who searches the minds and hearts; and I will give to each one of you according to your deeds.
> 24 'But I say to you, the rest who are in Thyatira, who do not hold this teaching, who have not known the deep things of Satan, as they call them—I place no other burden on you.
> 25 'Nevertheless what you have, hold fast until I come.
> 26 'And he who overcomes, and he who keeps My deeds until the end, TO HIM I WILL GIVE AUTHORITY OVER THE NATIONS;
> 27 AND HE SHALL RULE THEM WITH A ROD OF IRON, AS THE VESSELS OF THE POTTER ARE BROKEN TO PIECES, as I also have received *authority* from My Father;
> 28 and I will give him the morning star.

**29** 'He who has an ear, let him hear what the Spirit says to the churches.' . . ."

—Revelation 2

In verse 23 Christ says, "I will give to each one of you according to your deeds." Of course, the "each one" means each Christian because He is writing to the Christians at Thyatira.

In verse 24 we see that not all of the Christians in Thyatira are tolerating an immoral prophetess and that some of them did not hold to her teachings. Thus, a subset of all of the Christians in Thyatira is discussed in verse 24. I believe that this same subset are the overcomers and the promises to them are contained in verses 26 through 28.

The letter to the church at Sardis is in Revelation 3:1–6. The things that are promised to the overcomers that Christ doesn't promise to the rest of the Christians in Sardis are found in verse 5:

**5** 'He who overcomes shall thus be clothed in white garments; and I will not erase his name from the book of life, and I will confess his name before My Father, and before His angels. . . .'

—Revelation 3

Christ's letter to all of the Christians in Philadelphia comprises Revelation 3:7–13. The things that He uniquely promises to the overcomers are found in verse 12:

**12** 'He who overcomes, I will make him a pillar in the temple of My God, and he will not go out from it anymore; and I will write upon him the name of My God, and the name of the city of My God, the new Jerusalem, which comes down out of heaven from My God, and My new name. . . .'

—Revelation 3

Christ's letter to all of the believers in Laodicea is in Revelation 3:14–22. The promises that He makes just to the overcomers are found in verse 21:

**21** 'He who overcomes, I will grant to him to sit down with Me on My throne, as I also overcame and sat down with My Father on His throne. . . .'

—Revelation 3

## PROMISES TO THE OVERCOMERS

As we have just read, Christ makes some startling and unique promises to him who overcomes that He does not make to the rest of the Christians. These promises are summarized in the following table:

| Revelation | Promise |
|---|---|
| 2:7 | He will eat of the tree of life |
| 2:11 | He will not be hurt by the second death |
| 2:17 | He will be given hidden manna |
| 2:17 | He will be given a white stone with a new name written on it |
| 2:26 | He will be given authority over the nations |
| 2:27 | He shall rule the nations with a rod of iron |
| 2:28 | He will be given the morning star |
| 3:5 | He shall be clothed in white garments |
| 3:5 | Christ will not erase his name from the book of life |
| 3:5 | Christ will confess his name before His Father and the angels |
| 3:12 | He will be made a pillar in the temple of God |
| 3:12 | He will not go out of the temple |
| 3:12 | Christ will write on him: |
| | a. the name of His God |
| | b. the name of the city of His God (the new Jerusalem) |
| | c. His (Christ's) new name |
| 3:21 | He will be granted to sit down with Christ on His throne |

It may be that some of these promises—such as not erasing the names of the overcomers out of the book of life, being able to eat of the tree of life and not being hurt by the second death —may, by God's grace, be given to all Christians. However, we know that these are definitely promised to the overcomers.

Beyond these, there are certain things promised to overcomers, in other places in the Scriptures, that we know the rest of the Christians will not receive. We will be examining some of these later in this chapter.

This thought of the overcomers having rewards that the rest of the Christians do not have and that there will be various classes of Christians that will exist throughout eternity may be hard for you to grasp. You should be aware that I am not trying to teach you anything. Only the Holy Spirit can take the word of God and make it real and alive to your heart. I would encourage you to pray and ask God to let His Holy Spirit teach you what in this book is of Him and to shield your heart from anything that might not be of Him.

As this age draws to a close, I think God is revealing many things that have been hidden in His word because we are going to need to know them in these end days. So I would encourage you to be open to the Lord and to let Him speak to you.

In order to help you begin to assimilate in your spirit the overcomers being a unique group among Christians, I would like to approach the subject from a very different perspective.

## WHO IS THE BRIDE OF CHRIST?

I have been taught all of my Christian life that the church is the bride of Christ and I had never questioned it because it was taught to me by Bible teachers whom I respected. On the other hand, I had never really investigated it in the Scriptures for myself.

When I was writing the book *Close Encounters of the Highest Kind,* the climax of the book was going to be union with Christ, when we (the church) will become the bride of Christ. When I got to that point in writing the book, I decided that I should find the scriptural basis for believing that the church is the bride of Christ. When I began to look, I was surprised that I could find only two verses that even *might* imply that the church is the bride of Christ (those verses could also imply other things). However, I found a number of Scriptures that would indicate that the church is not the bride of Christ.

This then set me on a two-year search. If the church was not the bride of Christ, who was? I first began to look at the wedding feast. In the Old Testament, the bride was never at the wedding feast. There was usually a two- or three-day feast and the bride was brought in at the very end of the feast to go off with the groom. The marriage of Jacob is an example of this (Genesis 29:20-15). Jacob did not know that the bride was Leah until the next morning! If Leah had been there during the entire wedding feast, he surely would have known that she was not Rachel. Yet Christ encourages us to be at the wedding feast (Matthew 22:1-14) and the book of Revelation says, "Blessed are those who are invited to the marriage supper of the Lamb." (Revelation 19:9). If the bride isn't at the wedding feast, and yet we are encouraged to be at the wedding feast, this strongly suggests that we are not the bride.

Then I began to wonder if, as the body of Christ, we might not be part of the groom, rather than part of the bride. Without belaboring all of the blind alleys that I wandered down in my search for the truth concerning the bride of Christ, suffice it to say that for two years every time I came in contact with a man or woman of God that I really respected, I would ask that individual whom he or she felt the bride was. Almost everyone would say "the church." Then when I asked them their scriptural basis for believing that, I came to find out that they didn't have any. They had simply believed what they had been taught on the subject.

There was one particular case when I asked a lady this question. She didn't have an answer (a scriptural basis) but said she would go dig it out and call me. After a few days she had not called, so I called her and asked her if she had found a biblical basis yet for believing the church is the bride of Christ. Her response was, "I know what I believe; I just can't find any Scriptures to back it up!" That's incredible! I thought we were supposed to start with the Scriptures and let them tell us what to believe.

Finally, a brother in Austin, Minnesota shared something with me that the Lord used to show me who the bride of Christ is. . . .

## THE BRIDE OF CHRIST

We are going to be dealing primarily with Revelation 21 and 22 in this section. I believe that the Holy Spirit wants to reveal many new things to us here, so I trust that your heart is open to whatever He might have to teach you.

> 7 "He who overcomes shall inherit these things, and I will be his God and he will be My son. . . ."
>
> —Revelation 21

Here God promises that "he who overcomes" (the overcomers) shall inherit "these things." What are "these things"? "These things" are the things that God outlines in the first six verses of Revelation 21. Let's now examine that entire passage:

> 1 And I saw a new heaven and a new earth; for the first heaven and the first earth passed away, and there is no longer *any* sea.
>
> 2 And I saw the holy city, new Jerusalem, coming down out of heaven from God, made ready as a bride adorned for her husband.
>
> 3 And I heard a loud voice from the throne, saying, "Behold, the tabernacle of God is among men, and He shall dwell among them, and they shall be His people, and God Himself shall be among them,
>
> 4 and He shall wipe away every tear from their eyes; and there shall no longer be *any* death; there shall no longer be *any* mourning, or crying, or pain; the first things have passed away."
>
> 5 And He who sits on the throne said, "Behold, I am making all things new." And He said, "Write, for these words are faithful and true."
>
> 6 And He said to me, "It is done. I am the Alpha and the Omega, the beginning and the end. I will give to the one who thirsts from the spring of the water of life without cost.
>
> 7 "He who overcomes shall inherit these things, and I will be his God and he will be My son. . . ."

There is so much in these verses that I could write a small book on them. Before we look at them, we need to place this passage in its proper setting. The Tribulation has ended, climaxed by the battle of Armageddon in Revelation 19.

Then in Revelation 20 we see Christ ruling and reigning for a thousand years (the millennium) here on the earth, while Satan is bound. At the end of the thousand years, Satan is released and deceives some of the nations on the earth (the current earth). He and his army are then destroyed by fire that comes down from heaven. Then we have the Great White Throne Judgment before God the Father.

Evidently, somewhere between Revelation 20 and Revelation 21 the current earth and heaven are destroyed. We know from 2 Peter that the earth will be destroyed by fire and intense heat (2 Peter 3:10). However, I should hasten to add that this is at least a thousand years away, so the end of this earth is not an imminent thing.

In verse 1 of Revelation 21, we see that God has created a new heaven and a new earth. Incidentally, I should point out something here that I mentioned in one of our earlier books. Many preachers through the centuries have said something like this: "Everyone will spend eternity in heaven or hell." That is not true; no one will spend eternity in either heaven or hell. The non-Christians will spend eternity in the lake of fire (Revelation 20:14–15) and the Christians will spend eternity on the new earth (Revelation 21: 1, 2, 27).

In verse 2 of Revelation 21, the new Jerusalem is descending out of heaven onto the new earth. But remember, we saw in verse 7 that "these things" mentioned in the first six verses are promised just to the overcomers. Thus, the new Jerusalem is promised to the overcomers and not to Christians who are not overcomers.

Verse 3 says that the tabernacle (dwelling place) of God will be among men. However, remember that this too is a promise to the overcomers.

Verse 4 is interesting: God says that He will wipe away every tear from "their eyes" (the overcomers' eyes). There will no longer be any death, mourning, or pain for the overcomers. (It is noteworthy that He did not promise this for the rest of

the Christians). In verse 6, He further promises to give to the
overcomers "the water of life without cost."

Now let's turn specifically to the bride of Christ. As we do
this, keep in mind that when the Bible talks about Sodom and
Gomorrah being wicked, this does not mean that the streets and
houses were wicked, but the inhabitants. Also, when Christ
lamented over Jerusalem, He was not crying over the walls, the
buildings and the gates; He was lamenting over the inhabitants
(Matthew 23:37-39). When the Bible refers to a city, often it is
actually referring to the inhabitants of that city.

With this in mind, let's read about the city, the new
Jerusalem:

> 9 And one of the seven angels who had the seven bowls full of
> the seven last plagues, came and spoke with me, saying, "Come
> here, I shall show you the bride, the wife of the Lamb."
> 10 And he carried me away in the Spirit to a great and high
> mountain, and showed me the holy city, Jerusalem, coming down
> out of heaven from God, . . .
>
> —Revelation 21

In verse 9, the angel tells John that he is going to show
him "the bride, the wife of the Lamb." Then he carries him
away and shows him the holy city, the new Jerusalem. Thus,
we see that the new Jerusalem is the bride, and we know that
this is not talking about the walls and dwelling places in the new
Jerusalem, but about the inhabitants of the new Jerusalem.
Right?

Thinking back to Revelation 21:1-7, to whom was the
new Jerusalem promised? . . . To the overcomers. So we begin
to see that the overcomers are the inhabitants of the new Jerusalem and therefore are the bride of Christ. There will be more
evidence concerning this in just a moment, so let's hasten on.

The description of the new Jerusalem covered in verses 11-
21 of Revelation 21 is not germane to our discussion, so we will
start reading about the new Jerusalem again in verse 22:

> 22 And I saw no temple in it, for the Lord God, the Almighty,
> and the Lamb, are its temple.
> 23 And the city has no need of the sun or of the moon to shine

upon it, for the glory of God has illumined it, and its lamp *is* the Lamb.

24  And the nations shall walk by its light, and the kings of the earth shall bring their glory into it.

25  And in the daytime (for there shall be no night there) its gates shall never be closed;

26  and they shall bring the glory and the honor of the nations into it;

27  and nothing unclean and no one who practices abomination and lying, shall ever come into it, but only those whose names are written in the Lamb's book of life.

—Revelation 21

God the Father and the Lamb will be the temple in the new Jerusalem and the glory of God will illumine the city, according to verses 22 and 23.

However, when we get to verse 24, we find that there are "nations" on the new earth that evidently do not dwell in the new Jerusalem. They can bring their glory into it (visit it), but they do not dwell in it. Also in verse 24, we see that these nations on the new earth have kings over them.

Who are these nations that dwell on the new earth that can visit the new Jerusalem but cannot dwell in it? Verse 27 tells us. These are nations of Christians—people "whose names are written in the Lamb's book of life." Thus, we see that there will be nations dwelling on the earth, who will walk in the light of the new Jerusalem and will visit it, but who will not be able to dwell there. (I do not think these will be racially-oriented nations but more likely nations of people with the same level of spiritual maturity.)

This is further amplified in the next chapter of Revelation:

1  And he showed me a river of the water of life, clear as crystal, coming from the throne of God and of the Lamb,

2  in the middle of its street. And on either side of the river was the tree of life, bearing twelve *kinds of* fruit, yielding its fruit every month; and the leaves of the tree were for the healing of the nations.

3  And there shall no longer be any curse; and the throne of God and of the Lamb shall be in it, and His bond-servants shall serve Him;

4 and they shall see His face, and His name *shall be* on their foreheads.

5 And there shall no longer be *any* night; and they shall not have need of the light of a lamp nor the light of the sun, because the Lord God shall illumine them; and they shall reign forever and ever.

—Revelation 22

The tree of life, spoken of in verse 2, yields twelve kinds of fruit, possibly a different fruit each month. This indicates that one does not eat of the tree of life just once in order to live forever, but evidently one must eat of it periodically (perhaps once a month). (It is interesting to note the reappearance, here in the book of Revelation, of the tree of life, mentioned in Genesis 2. We will have more to say on this in Chapter 3. Also, remember that in Revelation 2:7, it was promised to the overcomers that they would be granted to eat of the tree of life.)

Also in verse 2 the leaves of the tree of life are said to be for the healing of the nations. Evidently the nations will still need healing, but the overcomers have been promised that they would never again need healing (Revelation 21:4).

Verse 3 of Revelation 22 brings us to something that we will deal with in depth in a later chapter and that is God's bondservants. A more accurate term is "bondslaves," and we will see why later. I believe that the term "bondslaves" is an equivalent term to "overcomers." One of the reasons for this is that two things promised to the bondslaves in verses 4 and 5 (of Revelation 22) are also promised to the overcomers. Remember the promises made to the overcomers in Christ's letters to the seven churches? The overcomers were promised that God's name would be on their foreheads and that they would reign with Christ. Since the same promises are made to the bondslaves and to the overcomers, it is reasonable to assume that they are the same group of people. Speaking of reigning, Revelation 22:5 says that the overcomers (bondslaves) will reign forever and ever. Over whom will they reign? Over the Christian nations on the new earth, of course.

Another thing promised to the overcomers, in one of the letters to the seven churches, is that they will never leave the temple of God (Revelation 3:12). Where is the temple of God? It is in the new Jerusalem. We saw earlier (Revelation 21:22) that God the Father and the Lamb will be the temple. Thus, the overcomers will never leave the new Jerusalem. It will be their permanent dwelling place.

## WHEN GOD FORMS A BRIDE

Let's consider one other aspect in looking at the overcomers as the bride of Christ. When God decided to make a bride for Adam, He could have made Eve out of some more dust. However, God instead decided to take part of Adam's body to form a bride for him. When Adam saw his bride, he commented that she was made out of the same substance of which he was made. We read about this in Genesis 2:

> 21  So the LORD God caused a deep sleep to fall upon the man, and he slept; then He took one of his ribs, and closed up the flesh at that place.
> 22  And the LORD God fashioned into a woman the rib which He had taken from the man, and brought her to the man.
> 23  And the man said,
>      "This is now bone of my bones,
>      And flesh of my flesh;
>      She shall be called Woman,
>      Because she was taken out of Man."

Christ is referred to, in the Scriptures, as the second Adam. Therefore, it would follow God's pattern if He were to take part of Christ's body for the bride of Christ. I think this is a beautiful picture of what is going to happen. Since the overcomers are just part of the body of Christ, it would be consistent if God used them to form the bride.

## WHY BE AN OVERCOMER?

With my whole heart I want to be an overcomer, not so I can rule and reign over the nations—I could care less about that. I want to be an overcomer because I love the Father and I love Jesus Christ with all of my heart, and I want to spend eternity near them, living in the new Jerusalem with them. It would break my heart to live out in one of the Christian nations and only be able to visit the new Jerusalem occasionally. I want to be right there where Jesus and the Father are, just as close as possible. We all want to be as close as possible to those we love the most, right?

If I were to ask you right now if you want to be an over-comer, you would probably answer with an enthusiastic "yes." I praise God for that and would encourage you in that desire. You probably are beginning to wonder just what an overcomer is.

Shortly we will be looking at what an overcomer is, what we overcome, how we overcome it, what a bondslave is, and some things that hopefully the Holy Spirit can use to help transform you into an overcomer.

However, first there are some fundamental things that you need to understand before some of that will make sense. Therefore, I would strongly encourage you not to skip over to the chapter on the overcomers, but to read this entire book in the sequence that the Holy Spirit has had me to write it. Okay?

What we will be doing in the next few chapters is laying a foundation for becoming an overcomer. The first foundational truth that we need to think through and pray through together starts at the very beginning and deals with why we were created.

# 2

# WHY WERE YOU CREATED?

Everything in nature does what it was created to do. The birds fly south in the winter and back north in the spring. The plants and trees drop their leaves in the fall and put out new leaves in the spring. The planets rotate about the sun and the sun, as part of this galaxy, rotates in a giant pinwheel fashion. Everything that was created, no matter how small or how large, does what it was created to do, except one—*man*. Man is the only one that does not do what he was created to do.

I have asked individuals in many Christian groups as I have spoken around the country, why they thought they were created. What purpose did God have for them when He created them? I have received an amazing variety of answers. If I were to ask you that question—"Why were you created?"—what would you answer? Why don't you pause before continuing to read and write your answer in the space below:

Please take the time to write in your answer before going on.

From mature Christians I receive answers to that question such as this:

1.  to have fellowship with God

2.  to tell others about Christ

3.  to know God

I could go on with these answers, all of which are *good,* but they are not why the Bible says we were created. How could we possibly be doing what we were created to do, unless we know *why* we were created? This is one of the most critical questions that a Christian can ask himself. We need to know why we were created in order to please God. The Bible gives us the answer:

> 7  *Even* every one that is called by my name: for I have created him for my glory, I have formed him; yea, I have made him.
> —Isaiah 43, *KJV*

This verse says that we were created to glorify God. Pause and think about that for a moment. That is why *you* were created. You were created to glorify God in all of your actions and in all of your thoughts.

## THE DEFINITION OF SIN

The definition of sin then becomes very simple. It is simply not doing what you were created to do. This is pointed out very distinctly in Romans:

> 23  For all have sinned, and come short of the glory of God; . . .
> —Romans 3, *KJV*

Do you see? All of us have sinned by coming short of what we were created to do, which is to glorify God. I do not think that anyone would claim that he has glorified God all of his life in everything that he has thought and done. Thus, we are *all* sinners.

This definition of sin can have a real impact on the life of a dedicated Christian. When considering whether to do something or not, we do *not* need to ask ourselves little questions like "Would my mother approve?" or "Could I take Jesus with me?" and so forth. If you really stop and consider, there are many instances in which we could answer "yes" to those kinds of questions, but if we ask ourselves if it glorifies God, the answer would have to be "no," if we were truthful. All things are lawful for us (1 Corinthians 10:23), but not all things glorify God.

We could take a simple thing like going to a football or baseball game. There is nothing intrinsically wrong with it, but does it glorify God? At times at a sporting event like that I have seen Christians who get angry and are about ready to go out and choke one of the officials or slug one of the opposing players who were responsible for crippling one of their own players. Do these kinds of emotions glorify God? However, it could be, for example, that if the Lord led you to take a non-Christian to a ball game and share Christ with him and show love to him, this could indeed glorify God.

Do you see what I am trying to say? We cannot use the criteria of "is it good or bad?" We must use the criteria of "does it glorify God?" This is a far higher standard, but it is the one that I think God wants us to apply as He is calling Christians to righteousness and holiness in these end times.

## JESUS GLORIFIED THE FATHER

Christ was without sin. Right? Therefore, He must have glorified the Father during His entire life. The Bible frequently talks about Christ glorifying the Father. We will just look at two examples:

31  When therefore he had gone out, Jesus said, "Now is the Son of Man glorified, and God is glorified in Him;
32  if God is glorified in Him, God will also glorify Him in Himself, and will glorify Him immediately. . . ."

—John 13

13  "And whatever you ask in My name, that will I do, that the Father may be glorified in the Son. . . ."

—John 14

As we can see from these verses, Christ's purpose was to glorify the Father. So if you want to see a life that totally glorified God in every way, reread Christ's life as portrayed in the Gospels.

Christ also taught His disciples what to do so that they too could glorify God. If you and I are to glorify God, don't you think it would behoove us to look in the Bible and find out what it says we can do that will glorify God? I would recommend that you take your concordance and look up words such as "glorify," "glorified," and "glory" to see what it has to say about how you can glorify God.

We will examine just a few of the things that the Bible says we can do that will explicitly glorify God.

## DOING GOOD WORKS

Hopefully we all know that doing good works can never gain our salvation. However, many churches almost avoid talking about good works. This is unfortunate because this is one major way that Christians should be glorifying God:

> 12 Having your conversation honest among the Gentiles: that, whereas, they speak against you as evildoers, they may by *your* good works, which they shall behold, glorify God in the day of visitation.
>
> —1 Peter 2, *KJV*

> 16 "Let your light shine before men in such a way that they may see your good works, and glorify your Father who is in heaven. . . ."
>
> —Matthew 5

We can see from these verses that we should let our light shine before men in such a way that they will see our good works and glorify God. There is a way that they can see our good works and glorify us. For example, if we make cookies for a sick neighbor, help a neighbor haul trash or weed someone's garden, that person could tell us: "Oh, I really appreciate that. You are such a thoughtful and wonderful person." We could then say:"Thank you. It was nothing." But if we do this, who is getting the glory?

In that case, we would be getting the glory. However, in response we could say: "I am under the marching orders of my heavenly Father and He told me to come over and help you. He was simply expressing His love to you through me." Now who gets the glory? Right . . . God does.

I think it is a shame that many evangelical and charismatic Christians neglect good works. I can give you a couple of examples of this from when I lived in Dallas. There was an evangelical pastor of a church north of Dallas who had always looked down his spiritual nose at a Methodist pastor down the street. There was a tornado alert in Dallas and the evangelical pastor rushed home to take care of his family. As it turned out, at the same time, the Methodist pastor was phoning his parishioners telling them where to bring food and clothes to give to those who would be left homeless by the tornado. He was organizing this effort so that as soon as the tornado stopped, they could rush in and help those who had been left destitute. Later the evangelical pastor admitted how much God had convicted him over his lack of concern for others and for good works.

We can become so concerned about preaching the Gospel that we neglect this important area of simply helping people and loving people, which often speaks louder than words. Look at Christ's life. How many times did He stop and heal someone or feed someone? Often . . . and he did this to glorify the Father.

Another example involved a very poor family from Oklahoma who had all their earthly possessions tied to the top of their car. They stopped at a big Baptist church in Dallas, needing a place to stay and some food. They were told that the church didn't do that sort of thing, but if they would go down a few blocks, they would come to the Salvation Army and those people would help them. I think of the parable of the Good Samaritan and wonder if those members of that Baptist church were being "good neighbors" and if they were glorifying God by their good works. We often criticize liberal Christians for their emphasis on good works. Oh, that we could glorify God *more* by doing good works, and by doing them in such a way that would glorify God!

## BEARING FRUIT

There is some confusion about bearing fruit and gathering fruit. Let me first address that question by looking at what it means to gather fruit:

35  "Do you not say, 'There are yet four months, and *then* comes the harvest'? Behold, I say to you, lift up your eyes, and look on the fields, that they are white for harvest.

36  "Already he who reaps is receiving wages, and is gathering fruit for life eternal; that he who sows and he who reaps may rejoice together. . . ."

—John 4

In these verses, we see that the harvest is not ours and the fruit is not ours; we simply *"gather"* fruit. We are gathering fruit when we lead someone to the saving knowledge of Jesus Christ. The fruit is not ours; it is the Lord's. New Christians are birthed by the Holy Spirit, not by us.

When we "bear" fruit, something is birthed in us. We are encouraged to bear much fruit in order to glorify God. This is found in John 15:

8  "By this is My Father glorified, that you bear much fruit, and so prove to be My disciples. . . ."

I believe that the fruit we bear is the fruit of the Spirit spoken of in Galatians 5:

22  But the fruit of the Spirit is love, joy, peace, patience, kindness, goodness, faithfulness,

23  gentleness, self-control: against such things there is no law.

These are characteristic of someone walking in such a way that he is continuously filled with the Holy Spirit. If you want to know the characteristics of a Spirit-filled Christian, here they are. If you will notice, there are no words like "power," "authority," or "dynamics." You get the picture of a tender, gentle, loving individual, as you read of the fruit of the Spirit.

But returning to the main thought, if we bear much fruit (the fruit of the Spirit), this glorifies God. Jesus is the vine (tree trunk); we are branches. If we were branches on an apple tree, we would bear apples. If we are branches on a Jesus tree, we bear "Jesus fruit": love, joy, peace, gentleness . . . we become like Him!

## FINISHING GOD'S WORK

It is one thing to *start* a task for the Lord, with vigor and enthusiasm, that He has commanded you to do. Unfortunately, that by itself does not glorify God. Let's read a statement that Christ made concerning this:

> **4 I have glorified thee on the earth: I have finished the work which thou gavest me to do.**
>
> —John 17, *KJV*

Here we see that Christ glorified God while He was on earth and one of the ways that He did this was by *finishing* the work which God gave Him to do here.

When God gives us a task to do, there may be a time of baptism when the Holy Spirit descends on us like a dove; there may be preaching to the multitudes. However, our work may not be finished at this point. There may follow a time of persecution and suffering or even death. There could come a point of agony when we beg God not to make us finish the task. Yet it will glorify God if we do finish the work that He has called us to do, regardless of the difficulties that may arise, and regardless of our desire sometimes to run away.

## HAVING A STRONG FAITH

Paul, in talking about Abraham, had this to say about Abraham's faith:

> **20 He staggered not at the promise of God through unbelief; but was strong in faith, giving glory to God; . . .**
>
> —Romans 4, *KJV*

Isn't it great that having a strong faith gives glory to God! We are going to need to have faith during the time of persecution that is coming. We can read about faith in Hebrews 11. Let's look specifically at a few verses:

> **32 And what more shall I say? For time will fail me if I tell of Gideon, Barak, Samson, Jephthah, of David and Samuel and the prophets,**

33 who by faith conquered kingdoms, performed *acts of* righteousness, obtained promises, shut the mouths of lions,

34 quenched the power of fire, escaped the edge of the sword, from weakness were made strong, became mighty in war, put foreign armies to flight.

35 Women received *back* their dead by resurrection;

36 and others experienced mockings and scourgings, yes, also chains and imprisonment.

37 They were stoned, they were sawn in two, they were tempted, they were put to death with the sword; they went about in sheepskins, in goatskins, being destitute, afflicted, ill-treated

38 *(men* of whom the world was not worthy), wandering in deserts and mountains and caves and holes in the ground.

39 And all these, having gained approval through their faith, did not receive what was promised,

40 because God had provided something better for us, so that apart from us they should not be made perfect.

—Hebrews 11

We can see here that through faith, dead were raised, others accepted torture and imprisonment, some were even stoned and sawn in half, while others lived in mountains and in dens and caves. It was by their faith that they glorified God.

## ONENESS OF HEART AND MIND

In the body of Christ there can be contention and strife, factions, and even splits; this does not glorify the Lord. What does glorify the Lord is when each individual member has the mind of Christ and, thus, as a body the members have a singleness of mind. This is described in Romans:

5 Now the God of patience and consolation grant you to be likeminded one toward another according to Christ Jesus:

6 That ye may with one mind *and* one mouth glorify God, even the Father of our Lord Jesus Christ.

7 Wherefore receive ye one another as Christ also received us to the glory of God.

—Romans 15, *KJV*

If the local body of Christ that you are part of does not have a oneness of mind and if they are not praising God with one mouth, they may not be glorifying God the way they should. Pray for oneness, work for oneness (blessed are the peacemakers), but do it in a way such that *you* do not receive the glory, but all the glory goes to God.

## CONFESSING JESUS AS LORD

There is an interesting use that we are to make of our tongue which implies that it cannot be silent:

> 11 And *that* every tongue should confess that Jesus Christ *is* Lord, to the glory of God the Father.
>
> —Philippians 2, *KJV*

As we say out loud that Jesus is God and that Jesus is the Lord of our life, we bring glory to God the Father. You may be proclaiming this as you witness to someone who doesn't know Christ, or it may be simply a greeting to another Christian, such as this: "Good morning, my brother. Jesus is Lord of my life!" Isn't that beautiful?

## LOVE, EXCELLENCE, BEING SINCERE, BEING FILLED

This next pertinent Scripture is so full that one could write an entire chapter just on this alone:

> 9 And this I pray, that your love may abound yet more and more in knowledge and *in* all judgment;
>
> 10 That ye may approve things that are excellent; that ye may be sincere and without offence till the day of Christ;
>
> 11 Being filled with the fruits of righteousness, which are by Jesus Christ, unto the glory and praise of God.
>
> —Philippians 1, *KJV*

As we can see from this passage, we need to have love and our love needs to abound. Remember, love is the key to the Christian life, but it should be in knowledge and in judgment. We don't just wholeheartedly accept any minister that comes through, but we discern the spirits and we exercise love tempered with knowledge. We are also to approve things that are excellent (things that will bring glory to God).

Paul also prayed that the Philippians would be "sincere." In the Bible the word "sincere" means "sun tested." In those days, unscrupulous potters might have a pot crack on them. If this occurred, they would fill in the crack with wax and then paint the outside. All was well until one took the pot home and put hot water into it: the wax would melt and the pot would be no good. In order to avoid this fraud, people would hold the jug or pot up to the sun and the sun would shine through the wax-filled crack, if there was one. What this is saying is that if we have a secret sin that we think is hidden from the rest of the world, we need to be "Son" tested. We need to be held up to the light of Christ so that any hidden flaws can be recognized and removed.

Lastly, we should be filled with the fruits of righteousness, and I believe this is the fruit of the Holy Spirit. In this passage, we see four things that we can do that will all bring glory to the Lord:

1.  Love in knowledge and in judgment.

2.  Approve excellent things.

3.  Be without hidden sin.

4.  Be filled with the fruits of righteousness.

Conversely, the lack of any of these doesn't bring glory to the Lord and, therefore, must be sin.

## OUR BODIES

We should glorify God in our bodies. This would entail both having a healthy body and using our bodies to do things that please God.

**20  For you have been bought with a price: therefore glorify God in your body.**

−1 Corinthians 6

How do we glorify God in our bodies? This is amplified in Chapter 12 of Romans:

> 1 I urge you therefore, brethren, by the mercies of God, to present your bodies a living and holy sacrifice, acceptable to God, *which is* your spiritual service of worship.
>
> 2 And do not be conformed to this world, but be transformed by the renewing of your mind, that you may prove what the will of God is, that which is good and acceptable and perfect.
>
> —Romans 12

This is another passage on which we could spend an entire chapter. But looking at it briefly, I would like to encourage you, rather than trying to present your body as a whole to God, to take each member and dedicate it to God. If we dedicate our *mouth* to the Lord, this involves what we eat, what we drink, what we say, who and how we kiss, what we smoke, witnessing, preaching, and much more.

If we dedicate our *eyes* to the Lord, this determines what we read, how much we read the Bible, how we look at other people, what television programs we watch, what movies we go to see, what magazines we read and the needs we might see around us.

If we dedicate our *hands* to the Lord, this would involve who we hug, who we pat on the back, and what we do (working, cleaning, helping others). If we dedicate our *knees* to the Lord, this determines a lot about our prayer life, our humility, how we scrub floors, and so forth. If we dedicate our *feet* to the Lord, this involves dancing, where we go, and how we drive our car. Our *ears* determine what we listen to, whether it be jokes, stories, conversation or music.

You might want to take some time to get alone with the Lord and dedicate each part of your body as a living sacrifice to Him, yearning not to be conformed to this world, but to be transformed by the renewing of your mind.

## SUFFERING

Strangely enough, the Bible says that in our suffering we can glorify God and Christ. We can be glorified together with Him.

16 The Spirit itself beareth witness with our spirit, that we are the children of God:

17 And if children, then heirs; heirs of God, and joint-heirs with Christ; if so be that we suffer with *Him,* that we may be also glorified together.

—Romans 8, *KJV*

Interestingly, this says that we are joint-heirs with Christ *if* we suffer with Him. This is spelled out even more clearly in the following verses:

14 If ye be reproached for the name of Christ, happy *are ye;* for the spirit of glory and of God resteth upon you: on their part he is evil spoken of, but on your part he is glorified.

15 But let none of you suffer as a murderer, or *as* a thief, or *as* an evildoer, or as a busybody in other men's matters.

16 Yet if *any man suffer* as a Christian, let him not be ashamed; but let him glorify God on this behalf.

—1 Peter 4, *KJV*

It says here that if we suffer as a Christian for the sake of Christ, we glorify God. To most Christians in America, suffering is very foreign. Yet many Christians in other parts of the world are suffering even today. When suffering comes to us, let us with one voice glorify God.

## THE MANNER OF DEATH

There are all sorts of ways to die. One can die as a coward or as a brave man. One way is an honor and the other is a shame. We can die in the service of Christ, as some missionaries have done. I yearn, as I am sure most of you do, that God would not only be glorified in my life, but also in my death.

19 Now this He said, signifying by what kind of death he would glorify God. And when He had spoken thus, He said to him, "Follow Me!"

—John 21

Christ, in speaking of Peter's death, stated the kind of death that God wanted him to die, and in this way he would glorify

God. Then He tells us to "follow Him" by having the attitude also of wanting to glorify God in our death.

## EVERYTHING YOU DO

The first and greatest key to the Christian life, I believe, is to love God with all of your heart, soul, mind and strength, and to love your neighbor as yourself. I believe another great key is found in 1 Corinthians 10:31 (you might want to memorize this):

> 31 Whether, then, you eat or drink or whatever you do, do all to the glory of God.
>
> —1 Corinthians 10

This says that whatever we do—whether it be sitting down to eat or drink, or anything else that we might do—we should do to the glory of God. You might pray about some of your recreational hobbies, which may be fine and good within themselves, to be sure that you are able to do them to the glory of God; if not, you may need give them up. Other things that you do, you may not be doing in a way that glorifies God; perhaps all you need to do is to learn to do them in a way that does glorify God.

I yearn for you and for myself that everything we do might give glory to God—every decision we make, every song we sing, every conversation we have, every recreational activity, and every good work. Thus we will fulfill the purpose for which we were created.

# 3

# KNOWLEDGE OF GOOD AND EVIL

Now that we have seen that we were created to glorify God and that not glorifying God is sin, the question comes, why don't we glorify God? The answer to that question might be slightly different for those who know Jesus Christ and those who do not, but in many ways the answers for both groups come back to a common denominator.

The reason that we often don't glorify God—the reason that we don't do what we were created to do—is involved with this second bedrock foundational truth that I have rarely seen taught. It deals with the first commandment given to man; therefore, God must have thought it was very important. It was the prohibition against gaining knowledge of good and evil. It has far more implications than one might realize, so stay with us as we go back and review the two special trees in the garden of Eden.

4 This is the account of the heavens and the earth when they were created, in the day that the LORD God made earth and heaven.

5 Now no shrub of the field was yet in the earth, and no plant of the field had yet sprouted, for the LORD God had not sent rain upon the earth; and there was no man to cultivate the ground.

6 But a mist used to rise from the earth and water the whole surface of the ground.

7 Then the LORD God formed man of dust from the ground, and breathed into his nostrils the breath of life; and man became a living being.

8 And the LORD God planted a garden toward the east, in Eden; and there He placed the man whom He had formed.

9 And out of the ground the LORD God caused to grow every

tree that is pleasing to the sight and good for food, the tree of life also in the midst of the garden, and the tree of the knowledge of good and evil.

—Genesis 2

As we can see in this passage, there were many trees of all kinds in the garden of Eden. But there were two special trees:

1. The tree of life

2. The tree of the knowledge of good and evil

As we all know, God forbade Adam and Eve to eat of the tree of the knowledge of good and evil, as is recorded further in Genesis 2:

15  Then the LORD God took the man and put him into the garden of Eden to cultivate it and keep it.

16  And the LORD God commanded the man, saying, "From any tree of the garden you may eat freely;

17  but from the tree of the knowledge of good and evil you shall not eat, for in the day that you eat from it you shall surely die."

It is interesting that they were not forbidden to eat of the tree of life. It is possible that they ate regularly from the tree of life. Perhaps that is one of the reasons they lived to be almost one thousand years old.

In Genesis 3 we find God casting Adam and Eve out of the garden so that they could no longer eat of the tree of life.

22  Then the LORD God said, "Behold, the man has become like one of Us, knowing good and evil; and now lest he stretch out his hand, and take also from the tree of life, and eat, and live forever"—

23  therefore the LORD God sent him out from the garden of Eden, to cultivate the ground from which he was taken.

24  So He drove the man out; and at the east of the garden of Eden He stationed the cherubim, and the flaming sword which turned every direction, to guard the way to the tree of life.

—Genesis 3

The reason God no longer wanted them to eat of the tree of life is because they had gained something God never wanted them to have—the knowledge of good and evil.

The fall of Adam and Eve involved much more than the sin of disobeying God. Because of that sin, they gained the knowledge of good and evil. If gaining the knowledge of good and evil was such a terrible thing that God cast them out of the garden, we need to understand why it was so bad and find out if it is also bad for you and me.

## YOU CAN KNOW GOD *OR* GOOD AND EVIL, BUT NOT BOTH

I have first stated the conclusion—"you can know God *or* good and evil, but not both"—and would now like to present the evidence for it. This is a fairly bold statement that requires a close examination.

Before they ate of the forbidden fruit of the tree of the knowledge of good and evil, Adam and Eve could make decisions such as naming the animals, but for any moral decision, they had to go ask God. Evidently He walked frequently in the garden of Eden, and any questions they had concerning what was right or wrong, good or bad, they simply asked God and He told them.

He did not want them making their own moral judgments as to what was good and evil based on their own knowledge. This is the reason that He prohibited them from eating of that particular tree. Satan in the worst way wanted to break this relationship of dependence upon God, as we see recorded in Chapter 3 of Genesis:

> 1 Now the serpent was more crafty than any beast of the field which the LORD God had made. And he said to the woman, "Indeed, has God said, 'You shall not eat from any tree of the garden'?"
>
> 2 And the woman said to the serpent, "From the fruit of the trees of the garden we may eat;
>
> 3 but from the fruit of the tree which is in the middle of the garden, God has said, 'You shall not eat from it or touch it, lest you die.'"
>
> 4 And the serpent said to the woman, "You surely shall not die!
>
> 5 "For God knows that in the day you eat from it your eyes will be opened, and you will be like God, knowing good and evil."

6 When the woman saw that the tree was good for food, and that it was a delight to the eyes, and that the tree was desirable to make one wise, she took from its fruit and ate; and she gave also to her husband with her, and he ate.

7 Then the eyes of both of them were opened, and they knew that they were naked; and they sewed fig leaves together and made themselves loin coverings.

8 And they heard the sound of the LORD God walking in the garden in the cool of the day, and the man and his wife hid themselves from the presence of the LORD God among the trees of the garden.

9 Then the LORD God called to the man, and said to him, "Where are you?"

10 And he said, "I heard the sound of Thee in the garden, and I was afraid because I was naked; so I hid myself."

11 And He said, "Who told you that you were naked? Have you eaten from the tree of which I commanded you not to eat?"

—Genesis 3

Adam and Eve had been naked from the beginning, and evidently neither they nor God had seen anything wrong with it. However, once they ate of the tree of the knowledge of good and evil, Adam and Eve realized they were naked and concluded that it was wrong. They then made themselves aprons of leaves to cover their nakedness. When God came into the garden, He called them out from their hiding place.

I can just imagine Him asking them where they got those silly clothes and Adam and Eve responding that they had made them. God might have asked, "Why did you make them? Why did you hide yourself?" and Adam would have replied, "Because I was naked." I imagine that God might have responded, "So what?" Then Adam must have said, "But that is wrong."

God must have wept inside as He asked them who told them they were naked and what made them think it was wrong. He already must have known the answer, but then He asked them if they had eaten of the tree of the knowledge of good and evil.

Before Adam and Eve ate the fruit of the tree of the knowledge of good and evil, when they had to make a moral decision they went to God, and they did whatever He said. After they ate of it, they could use their own knowledge, reasoning and feelings about what was right and wrong to make all of these decisions, independent of God. Either Adam and Eve could make their decisions based on knowing God and what He told them to do in each specific situation, or they could make decisions based on their knowledge of good and evil, but they couldn't do both. They had chosen to rely on their own knowledge and therefore were cast out of the garden, away from the presence of God and basically away from the guidance of God. Actually, it was because of His mercy that God cast them out of the garden, away from the tree of life, because He didn't want them to live forever in their sinful state, relying on their own knowledge instead of on Him.

You could state the principle in this way:

*Knowing God and knowing good and evil are mutually exclusive.*

Certainly the Pharisees knew what was right and wrong and what was good and evil, but they didn't know God.

13 "But woe to you, scribes and Pharisees, hypocrites, because you shut off the kingdom of heaven from men; for you do not enter in yourselves, nor do you allow those who are entering to go in.

14 "Woe to you, scribes and Pharisees, hypocrites, because you devour widows' houses, even while for a pretense you make long prayers; therefore you shall receive greater condemnation.

15 "Woe to you scribes and Pharisees, hypocrites, because you travel about on sea and land to make one proselyte, and when he becomes one, you make him twice as much a son of hell as yourselves. . . .

23 "Woe to you, scribes and Pharisees, hypocrites! For you tithe mint and dill and cummin, and have neglected the weightier provisions of the law; justice and mercy and faithfulness; but these are the things you should have done without neglecting the other. . . .

25 "Woe to you, scribes and Pharisees, hypocrites! For you clean the outside of the cup and of the dish, but inside they are full of robbery and self-indulgence.

26 "You blind Pharisee, first clean the inside of the cup and of the dish, so that the outside of it may become clean also.

27 "Woe to you, scribes and Pharisees, hypocrites! For you are like whitewashed tombs which on the outside appear beautiful, but inside they are full of dead men's bones and all uncleanness. . . .

37 "O Jerusalem, Jerusalem, who kills the prophets and stones those who are sent to her! How often I wanted to gather your children together, the way a hen gathers her chicks under her wings, and you were unwilling. . . ."

—Matthew 23

As we can see, Christ condemned the Pharisees who did everything according to their knowledge of good and evil. They were not close to God, did not hear God, and even rejected God's very own Son.

In verse 37 of Matthew 23, Christ cries out to the inhabitants of Jerusalem, yearning to gather them in a loving way as a hen gathers her chicks, yearning to reestablish this personal relationship. But they were so enslaved to their knowledge of good and evil that they could not have a personal relationship with God through His Son, Jesus Christ.

A strong teaching on this subject is found in Proverbs:

5 Trust in the LORD with all thine heart; and lean not unto thine own understanding.

6 In all thy ways acknowledge him, and he shall direct thy paths.

—Proverbs 3, *KJV*

In these verses it says that if we do three things, *then* God will guide us (direct our paths). It says we are to:

1. Trust in the Lord with all our heart.

2. Lean not to our own understanding.

3. In all our ways acknowledge Him.

If we do those three things, *then* He promises that He will direct our paths. The second of these requirements is by far the hardest. It is that we do not lean to our understanding, and I believe this means our understanding of what is good and evil, or right and wrong. The smarter an individual is, the more difficult this is for him. But the strong implication is that you can either have God guide your paths *or* you can lean to your own understanding, but you cannot do both. On what do you base your decisions? On your knowledge of good and evil or on what God tells you to do?

A lot of churches teach things like "Do not handle this," "Do not taste that," "Do not touch the other." This kind of instruction is based on their knowledge of good and evil, which they try to impose upon their members. These people mean well, but they forget what Colossians 2 says on this:

> **20 If you have died with Christ to the elementary principles of the world, why, as if you were living in the world, do you submit yourself to decrees, such as**
> **21 "Do not handle, do not taste, do not touch!"**
> **22 (which all refer to things destined to perish with the using)— in accordance with the commandments and teachings of men?**
> **23 These are matters which have, to be sure, the appearance of wisdom in self-made religion and self-abasement and severe treatment of the body, but are of no value against fleshly indulgence.**
> **—Colossians 2**

As we can see from these verses, having these lists of "do's" and "don'ts" gives an appearance of wisdom, but the Bible says they are of *no value* against fleshly indulgence. In other words, the knowledge of good and evil will never keep us from sinning and indulging in things in the flesh. Knowing God and having a close personal relationship with Him will keep us from indulging in these fleshly things. So once again we see that knowing God and knowing good and evil are mutually exclusive.

### THE DIFFERENCE BETWEEN "KNOWING" AND "DISCERNING"

If we "know" something this means that we have studied and learned it, and it is in our memory and our thinking patterns.

On the other hand, "discerning" is something that we sense rather than learn. For example, the Bible admonishes us to test or discern the spirits (1 John 4:1) and the discerning of spirits is one of the gifts of the Spirit listed in 1 Corinthians 12. This means that while a person is speaking, the Holy Spirit can enable us to sense whether or not that person is speaking with the anointing of God or whether a different spirit is speaking. Parents can discern when their children are telling the truth or when they are lying. Discernment is not something that is learned, but it is something that comes from God and is perfected through practice.

In Hebrews we see this concept of discerning applied to good and evil (as it also is in numerous other places in the Bible):

**14 But solid food is for the mature, who because of practice have their senses trained to discern good and evil.**

—Hebrews 5

I believe that "discerning" good and evil means that in each situation you discern what God's will is for you to do. Of course, doing God's will is good and not doing His will is evil. I also believe that the discerning of good and evil is similar to discerning spirits, that is, discerning good spirits and evil spirits. This discernment is something supernatural that comes directly from God. On the other hand, knowledge of good and evil is something that we gain ourselves and we learn, and we can make our decisions on our learned knowledge of good and evil. Unfortunately those decisions might be totally apart from God and God's will.

## KNOWLEDGE OF GOOD AND EVIL CAN PREVENT US FROM OBEYING GOD

It is interesting to note that our own knowledge of good and evil can cause us to sin (sin being disobedience to God and not glorifying Him). This sounds like an incredible statement, but put yourself in the place of Abraham. What if God told you to go out and kill or sacrifice your only or your favorite child? Most of us would argue with God and say, "But God, that is wrong." Our knowledge of good and evil would prevent us from obeying God.

It is not only our knowledge of good and evil that can

keep us from obeying God; it is also our logical mind (which perhaps is just another facet of the knowledge of good and evil). For example, Abraham was living in the Ur of the Chaldees in a very luxurious home. This home has been excavated and it was a two-story brick home, which one can visit today if one can get into Iraq. He had a very comfortable life and was evidently very content when God told him to pack up everything and to "Go West, young man" to a land that He would show him. Abraham didn't even know where he was going, nor how he would get there, nor how he would recognize it when he arrived.

To many of Abraham's friends, I'm sure this was a stupid, illogical and insane thing to do. God frequently asks us to do things that don't seem logical or that seem to violate our sense of what is right and wrong. Many people, had they been in Abraham's situation, would have allowed their knowledge of good and evil to prevent them from leaving their plush homes, businesses and surroundings to become nomads living in tents. You might even ask yourself the question, if God asked you right now to leave everything you own, taking a minimum of possessions, to start moving north or south, and to live in a tent, what would you do?

Baptism is an interesting example of what we are discussing. If someone stands up in front of a church and publicly declares that he has received Jesus Christ as his Savior, there is absolutely no logical reason to be baptized. I believe that at the very beginning of our Christian life God asks us to do something that is illogical and to do it simply because He asks us to. This is to prepare us so that when He later asks us to do very difficult things that are illogical, we will be used to obeying.

God has asked me to do a number of highly illogical things. As I was zooming up the IBM management ladder, He said: "Take a year's leave of absence and go live on Catalina Island in a cove, where there is no electricity or telephones, and no roads into the place, and be a caretaker at a camp." I did this, and God tremendously blessed it. Later, I was living in Los Angeles and God told me to move to Canada. There was no logical reason to move to Canada but I did, and there I found my wife, Jeani. I am absolutely convinced that He took me to Canada just to find her. Many Christians would have allowed their logical reasoning and their knowledge of good and evil to prevent them from obeying God in these and many similar situations.

You might say: "But Abraham was before the Ten Commandments. God asked him to sacrifice his son before the commandment 'thou shalt not kill' was given." Alright, let's take a look at what happened after the Ten Commandments were given in Exodus 20. We find this recorded in Exodus 32, after Moses came back down from the mountain:

> 22  And Aaron said, "Do not let the anger of my lord burn; you know the people yourself, that they are prone to evil.
>
> 23  "For they said to me, 'Make a god for us who will go before us; for this Moses, the man who brought us up from the land of Egypt, we do not know what has become of him.'
>
> 24  "And I said to them, 'Whoever has any gold, let them tear it off.' So they gave it to me, and I threw it into the fire, and out came this calf."
>
> 25  Now when Moses saw that the people were out of control— for Aaron had let them get out of control to be a derision among their enemies—
>
> 26  then Moses stood in the gate of the camp, and said, "Whoever is for the Lord, come to me!" And all the sons of Levi gathered together to him.
>
> 27  And he said to them, "Thus says the Lord, the God of Israel, 'Every man of you put his sword upon his thigh, and go back and forth from gate to gate in the camp, and kill every man his brother, and every man his friend, and every man his neighbor.'"
>
> 28  So the sons of Levi did as Moses instructed, and about three thousand men of the people fell that day.
>
> 29  Then Moses said, "Dedicate yourselves today to the Lord— for every man has been against his son and against his brother—in order that He may bestow a blessing upon you today."
>
> —Exodus 32

Had you been there and had you been a son of Levi (part of the priesthood), would you have strapped on your sword and gone out, under God's command, to kill all those who were sinning by worshiping the calf, whether they be your brother, your friend, or your neighbor? That is what the sons of Levi did. Many Christians living in the United States today would have refused to obey God because their "knowledge of good and evil" would have told them that it was *wrong*.

## LESSONS FROM ELIJAH

We might excuse Moses and the sons of Levi from these types of acts. Perhaps even Joshua. God told him to go into a town and kill everyone, including the old women and babies even one day old. Our knowledge of good and evil would have caused most of us to refuse to be a part of it. The same would be true of the victorious time at Jericho, when God caused the walls to fall down. Every one of God's children there went forward into the city over the crumbled walls and, at God's command, killed all of those in the city; Rehab the harlot and those who were with her in her house were the only ones left alive. You might discount this because Joshua was the military leader of his people. That's true, but he was under marching orders from God.

So let's go to a man we would all consider a true prophet and a man of God, Elijah. No doubt we have all studied and rejoiced in the fact that Elijah had the contest with 450 of Baal's prophets, and that God honored him by bringing fire down from heaven and consuming the sacrifice, the wood, and even the water in the trench. All rejoiced in God's power and victory. But we tend to stop before the end of the story:

22 Then Elijah said to the people, "I alone am left a prophet of the LORD, but Baal's prophets are 450 men. . . ."

36 Then it came about at the time of the offering of the *evening* sacrifice, that Elijah the prophet came near and said, "O, LORD, the God of Abraham, Isaac and Israel, today let it be known that Thou art God in Israel, and that I am Thy servant, and that I have done all these things at Thy word.

37 "Answer me, O LORD, answer me, that this people may know that Thou, O LORD, art God, and *that* Thou hast turned their heart back again."

38 Then the fire of the Lord fell, and consumed the burnt offer-

ing and the wood and the stones and the dust, and licked up the
water that was in the trench. . . .

40  Then Elijah said to them, "Seize the prophets of Baal; do not
let one of them escape." So they seized them; and Elijah brought
them down to the brook Kishon, and slew them there.

—1 Kings 18

At the end of the story Elijah had to kill the false prophets
of Baal. It is all part of the story. Many of us would love to have
been there and prayed and seen the fire come down from heav-
en, but likely, because of our knowledge of good and evil, we
would have refused to have killed the 450 false prophets of
Baal. Perhaps that is why we do not have the power of God like
Elijah did, because we want to selectively obey God based on
our knowledge of good and evil.

Let's track further and see another very significant event
in the life of Elijah:

9  Then the *king* sent to him a captain of fifty with his fifty. And
he went up to him, and behold, he was sitting on the top of the hill.
And he said to him, "O man of God, the king says, 'Come down.'"

10  And Elijah answered and said to the captain of fifty, "If I am
a man of God, let fire come down from heaven and consume you
and your fifty." Then fire came down from heaven and consumed
him and his fifty.

11  So he again sent to him another captain of fifty with his fifty.
And he answered and said to him, "O man of God, thus says the
king, 'Come down quickly.'"

12  And Elijah answered and said to them, "If I am a man of God,
let fire come down from heaven and consume you and your fifty."
Then the fire of God came down from heaven and consumed him
and his fifty.

13  So he again sent the captain of a third fifty with his fifty.
When the third captain of fifty went up, he came and bowed down
on his knees before Elijah, and begged him and said to him, "O man
of God, please let my life and the lives of these fifty servants of
yours be precious in your sight.

14  "Behold fire came down from heaven, and consumed the first
two captains of fifty with their fifties; but now let my life be precious in your sight."

15  And the angel of the Lord said to Elijah, "Go down with him;

do not be afraid of him." So he arose and went down with him to the king.

—2 Kings 1

Here, on two occasions, we see Elijah calling down fire from heaven and destroying a captain and his 50 men. So in this passage, Elijah killed, under the orders of God and by the power of God, 102 men, in addition to the 450 he had killed earlier. We normally do not think of a man of God, a prophet, in this kind of a role.

If God had led us twice to bring down fire and destroy opposing armies, most of us would have "assumed" that God wanted us to do the same thing again when we saw the third group of 50 coming toward us. So we would have called down fire and destroyed them. But Elijah, a real man of God, was listening to God on every occasion, and the third time God said to do exactly the opposite; He said to go with them. Again, perhaps this is why we do not have the power that Elijah had. God will only give that kind of power to people who, on every occasion, will walk sensitive to the leading of the Holy Spirit.

You may think: "Well this was all in the Old Testament. Nothing like this would ever occur in the New Testament." I would like to take two examples from the New Testament. The first one fits right in with what we have been discussing about Elijah. It is found in Revelation 11:

> 3 "And I will grant *authority* to my two witnesses, and they will prophesy for twelve hundred and sixty days, clothed in sackcloth."
> 4 These are the two olive trees and the two lampstands that stand before the Lord of the earth.
> 5 And if anyone desire to harm them, fire proceeds out of their mouth and devours their enemies; and if anyone would desire to harm them, in this manner he must be killed.
> 6 These have the power to shut up the sky; in order that rain may not fall during the days of their prophesying; and they have power over the waters to turn them into blood, and to smite the earth with every plague, as often as they desire.

Here we see that God is again going to give the kind of power that Elijah had; the two witnesses (and I believe that is two witness companies, not two individuals) will have power to call fire down from heaven to destroy their enemies. Unfortunately, most Christians could miss becoming part of the two witness companies because their knowledge of good and evil would prevent them from calling fire down from heaven to destroy their enemies, if God were to ask them to do such a thing.

Let me hasten to reaffirm that in no way am I for killing. I hate it. I would hate to be forced to do it. What I am saying is that I want to be *willing* to obey my God *whatever* He tells me to do in the turbulent times ahead.

I have taken many of these examples involving killing as an *extreme* illustration of the principle to help you realize the significance of what we are talking about. Now let's turn to an example that might be more likely for many people to experience:

1 "Then the kingdom of heaven will be comparable to ten virgins, who took their lamps, and went out to meet the bridegroom.

2 "And five of them were foolish, and five were prudent.

3 "For when the foolish took their lamps, they took no oil with them,

4 but the prudent took oil in flasks along with their lamps.

5 "Now while the bridegroom was delaying, they all got drowsy and *began* to sleep.

6 "But at midnight there was a shout, 'Behold, the bridegroom! Come out to meet *him.*"

7 "Then all those virgins rose, and trimmed their lamps.

8 "And the foolish said to the prudent, 'Give us some of your oil, for our lamps are going out.'

9 "But the prudent answered, saying, 'No, there will not be enough for us and you *too;* go instead to the dealers and buy *some* for yourselves.'

10 "And while they were going away to make the purchase, the bridegroom came, and those who were ready went in with him to the wedding feast; and the door was shut.

11 "And later the other virgins also came, saying, Lord, Lord, open up for us.'

12 "But He answered and said, 'Truly I say to you, I do not know you.'

13 "Be on the alert then, for you do not know the day nor the hour. . . ."

—Matthew 25

If most Christians today were one of the five virgins who had surplus oil, and the other five virgins who had run out of oil came to us, we would think that the "Christian thing to do" would be to *share* our surplus oil with them. This concept is based on our knowledge of good and evil. However, as Christ teaches, in this instance, it would have been sin for the five wise virgins, who had prepared ahead and brought extra oil, to have shared their oil with the foolish ones, who had made no preparation. Here once more we can see that our knowledge of good and evil would have caused us to sin. It is difficult to think of sharing as a sin, but anything we do can be sin if it isn't what God is telling us to do.

In times of crisis ahead, God may have led you to prepare by storing extra food, water or oil. If He tells you to share, *praise God!* Give some or all of it away, as He directs. If He tells you not to share, then don't do it. We must take our orders directly from Him and not make our decisions based on our knowledge of good and evil.

We could take many other examples from both the Old and New Testaments. It would have been sin for Noah to let additional people into the ark, even though they were dying and pounding on the door. On the other hand, it would have been sin for the widow lady (and her son) *not* to share the flour and oil with God's prophet (1 Kings 17:11–16).

We like to make little rules for ourselves, such as "it is always good to share" or "it is never good to kill." Do you see what we are doing? Once we say that we will *always* do this or we will *never* do that, God can no longer lead us in that area of our lives. Our well-meaning rules take precedence over God's leading.

In the Bible, there are times when it glorifies God to share and times when it is sin. There are times when God has asked one of His servants to call down fire to destroy enemies and other times when it would have been sin to do that. We can not depend on our rules or our knowledge of good and evil. We *must* listen to God's voice on each occasion and do what *He* tells us to do.

## CAN YOU USE THE BIBLE TO MAKE
## DECISIONS INDEPENDENT OF GOD?

You and I can actually use the Bible to make decisions independent of God. We can say, "The Bible says this here; therefore I will do such and such," without ever asking God what He wants. This assumes that God *always* wants us to do the same thing in the same set of circumstances. That may not be so. You remember the example of Elijah who twice called down fire to destroy the captains and the 50's, but the third time he did not. Instead he went with them because God told him to.

What we are saying is that some people try to make the New Testament a new law. We are no longer under the law, but we are under the Spirit and under grace (Romans 6:14, 8:2, 14).

I like to think of it this way: If I were in a car and there were speed limit signs of 55 mph all along the freeway but I were guaranteed that there were no policemen within 300 miles, I would probably go faster than 55 mph.

But if you took down all the 55 mph speed limit signs and put a policeman in the car with me and he said "Go 55," I would probably do a maximum of 54 mph.

A law is of little effect (except to show us our sin—Romans 7:7), but an indwelling Spirit can and does control us. We are no longer under the law, we are under the Spirit. This means that we live a holier and more righteous life than we would if we were under the law, so it is not an excuse for sinning. But in being under the Spirit, having a personal relationship with God, and in doing what He says, there is *life!* Following a bunch of do's and don'ts, *even* those collected from the New Testament, is *death.*

Christ did not come to keep the law, even the Ten Commandments. In fact, you can make a pretty good case that Christ broke the Ten Commandments, specifically the one about keeping the Sabbath (Exodus 16:29; Luke 6:1-5) and the one about honoring your father and mother (Matthew 12:46-50; John 2:1-4; Matthew 10:34-37). Christ *did* come to do His Father's will:

38  "For I have come down from heaven, not to do My own will, but the will of Him who sent Me. . . ."

—John 6

Christ came not to do His own will, based on His knowledge of good and evil, but the will of the Father. Christ devoted His life to doing whatever God told Him to do.

If you are questioning the thought that we are not under the Ten Commandments, let me share with you what Paul says in Romans 6:

14  For sin shall not be master over you, for you are not under law, but under grace.

As you can see here, the Bible says that we are no longer under the law. And to be sure that we understood which law he was talking about, in Chapter 7 of Romans, Paul then quotes one of the Ten Commandments. He wanted to be certain that we did not erroneously think that we were released from the ceremonial law of the Old Testament but were still under the Ten Commandments. Thus, he made it very clear that we are not under the law, including the Ten Commandments:

6  But now we have been released from the Law, having died to that by which we were bound, so that we serve in newness of the Spirit and not in oldness of the letter.
7  What shall we say then? Is the Law sin? May it never be! On the contrary, I would not have come to know sin except through the Law; for I would not have known about coveting if the Law had not said, "You shall not covet."

—Romans 7

What I am saying is that we can use the Bible, even the Ten Commandments, to make decisions that are independent of God. Our desire, like Christ's should be to do our Father's will. Thus, in everything and in every situation, we should ask God what His will is and then be careful to do it, even if it seems to contradict our knowledge of good and evil.

There are many other examples that we could give of Christ telling others not to do what we would consider to be "right," based on our knowledge of good and evil. If someone were going to follow Christ, but his father had just died, we would think that the "right" thing to do would be to go bury his father first, and then follow Jesus. But Jesus commanded the opposite and refused to let a man go to his father's funeral:

> 59  And He said to another, "Follow Me." But he said, "Permit me first to go and bury my father."
> 60  But He said to him, "Allow the dead to bury their own dead; but as for you, go and proclaim everywhere the kingdom of God."
> 61  And another also said, "I will follow You, Lord; but first permit me to say goodbye to those at home."
> 62  But Jesus said to him, "No one, after putting his hand to the plow and looking back, is fit for the kingdom of God."
>
> —Luke 9

Our thinking is not His thinking, our ways are not His ways (Isaiah 55:8, 9)! If I felt we were still under the Ten Commandments, I would "worship" on Saturday (the Sabbath or the seventh day) and not on Sunday (the first day).

> 8  "Remember the sabbath day, to keep it holy.
> 9  "Six days you shall labor and do all your work,
> 10  but the seventh day is a sabbath of the LORD your God; in it you shall not do any work, you or your son or your daughter, your male or your female servant or your cattle or your sojourner who stays with you.
> 11  "For in six days the LORD made the heavens and the earth, the sea and all that is in them, and rested on the seventh day; therefore the LORD blessed the sabbath day and made it holy. . . ."
>
> —Exodus 20

When a person treats Sunday, instead of Saturday, as the holy day, he is breaking the Ten Commandments. This is a fact, no matter how one might try to justify worshiping on Sunday. However, keeping Sunday holy might be God's will and what would glorify Christ.

## RENEWING YOUR MIND

The first two verses of Romans 12 are two of my very favorite verses:

1 I urge you therefore, brethern, by the mercies of God, to present your bodies a living and holy sacrifice, acceptable to God, *which* is your spiritual service of worship.

2 And do not be conformed to this world, but be transformed by the renewing of your mind, that you may prove what the will of God is, that which is good and acceptable and perfect.

—Romans 12

Verse 2 tells us that the way we are able to present our bodies as a living sacrifice and not to be conformed to the world is *by the renewing of our minds.* It doesn't say to make our minds new. It says to *renew* our minds. Like other words that start with "re," it means to "make it like it used to be." For example, *revive* means to restore life, and *replenish* means to bring the supply back to what it was. *Renew* means to make it new like it used to be.

So we are to renew our minds, or to make them like they used to be. Make them like they used to be *when?* Like when we were babies? Like before we were Christians? Like when we were young Christians? No, no! I certainly don't want my mind renewed to one of those states! Then what is the time period to which we are to have our minds renewed? I believe that Romans 12:2 is telling us to have our minds renewed to the way they were before the fall. In what way were Adam and Eve's minds, before the fall, different from our minds?

The only difference that I can isolate is that Adam and Eve, before they sinned, did not know good and evil, and we do. If we are going to renew our minds to be like theirs were, we are going to have to put aside our knowledge of good and evil and just *know God.* Lord, whatever it takes, help us to renew our minds to a state like the minds of Adam and Eve, before they sinned and gained the knowledge of good and evil, and stopped depending solely on You.

## DEFINITION OF SALVATION

What is your definition of salvation and eternal life? The Bible gives us a good definition in John 17:

3 "And this is eternal life, that they may know Thee, the only true God, and Jesus Christ whom Thou has sent. . . ."

We can see here that the definition of eternal life is knowing God and knowing Jesus Christ, *period*. It is not a result of knowing right from wrong, good from evil; it does not come from keeping a set of rules and regulations; it is not a result of abiding by all of the do's and don'ts of your church or fellowship. It is in knowing God and doing His will. We study the Bible to know God better. Yet we must be careful not to use the Bible to make decisions independent of God. Every decision should be brought before the Father in prayer and then we should do whatever He tells us to do.

## KNOWING GOD'S WILL

To many people, what we have shared in this chapter is scary. We are much more comfortable and secure having a set of do's and don'ts that we can follow. Realizing that in every situation we need to pray and do what God tells us to do, and that He might tell us to do different things in identical situations, leaves us with nothing to hang onto and depend on, except God.

Many people would be concerned about hearing God's voice or about how to know His will. If God cannot and does not reveal His will directly to each individual believer, then you can throw out almost the entire New Testament, because it is talking about our being under the guidance of the Holy Spirit and not under the law.

Ask yourself this question: "Is God more eager to reveal His will to you than you are to know it?" I believe that He is infinitely more eager to show you His will than you are to know it. Thus, if you look up and say, "God, show me Your will," He is not going to look down and say, "Beg me," or, "Grovel a little bit and maybe I will reveal My will to you, if you beg me enough." Once He sees a Christian who is willing to do His will, whatever it is, God has absolutely no reason to withhold revealing His will and His guidance from you. He will eagerly reveal it to you in one way or another.

There are a number of ways in which God can guide you and show you His will. Of these, one is overwhelmingly the most important. We will list this most important one last, since we will deal with it last:

1. A multitude of counselors

2. Circumstances

3. The Bible

4. Direct revelation (visions, dreams or God's voice)

5. Peace in your heart

*1. A multitude of counselors:* Let us look at these one at a time. In this first one we are simply restating what it says in Proverbs:

> 14  Where there is no guidance, the people fall,
>     But in abundance of counselors there is victory.
>
> —Proverbs 11

The *King James Version* says that "in the multitude of counselors there is safety." God can guide us through the counsel of others (and I would include words of personal prophecy in this category), but it should never be the counsel of just one person or even two. I would say that if this is the way that God is going to guide you, there should be counsel of a minimum of three godly, righteous men, ideally independent of each other, and not necessarily part of the same body of believers. I want to underscore that they must be *godly, righteous* men. Psalms 1 admonishes righteous men not to "walk in the counsel of the ungodly." If you are taking advice in any area of your life from a non-Christian, you are walking in the counsel of the ungodly and violating what God tells you to do. I would include the financial area in this admonition. If you are taking financial advice from a non-Christian, you are violating God's commands. I would encourage you to switch and take the advice of Christians only. I think the same thing is true concerning your lawyer and CPA. These men should be Christians. If the matter is big enough, whether it be financial or legal, you should let them know that you are going to seek a "multitude of counselors."

God can certainly use three or more Christian counselors to give you guidance.

*2. Circumstances:* God can use circumstances to guide us. If we are praying about going to college "A" or college "B" and college "A" rejects us and college "B" accepts us, God can use those closed doors to guide us. I emphasize *closed doors* and not open doors. I do not look at open doors as a way of God directing us, because each of us have thousands of doors open to us every day. *The need does not constitute the call.* If we were to look at needs around the world, and even in our own community or church, where we have the ability to meet the need, we could quickly become committed to ninety-five hours a day. So I do not believe that open doors are a means that God uses to guide us. However, when God closes a door, we can rejoice in the fact that He has prevented us from doing something that wouldn't be best for us and give us the maximum happiness. Even though the door that He closes might be one that we very much wanted to walk through, we still need to praise Him for His loving care and guidance.

*3. The Bible:* When I say the Bible, I mean principles in the Bible and not a specific isolated verse. People have opened the Bible and read something about islands in a verse, and they took this as God calling them to be missionaries on an island. In such cases, it usually turns out to be a disaster. But even in using principles of the Bible, we have to be careful. One can use the Bible to make decisions that are independent of God. We can say to ourselves, "Well, the Bible says this; therefore, I will do it," without ever asking God what He wants us to do.

*4. Direct Revelation (visions, dreams or God's voice):* God can guide us directly through a vision or a dream, through a visit from an angel, or He can speak to us directly. This in some ways is the most dangerous of all of the ways of guidance because all of these things are also counterfeited by Satan. Therefore, we must have a confirmation from another source to know that it is from God. We know that God spoke to Joseph (Mary's husband) through a dream. He spoke to many people in both the Old and New Testaments through angels, and frequently God has spoken directly to an individual, such as Moses or Paul. This type of guidance directly from God is usually much more rare than the previously mentioned types.

5. *Peace in your heart:* The final umpire, the final decider, the final ruler as to whether a particular plan of action that God seems to be indicating is really His will is whether or not you have peace in your heart. This is pointed out in Colossians 3:

> 15 And let the peace of Christ rule in your hearts, to which indeed you were called in one body; and be thankful.

No matter if a multitude of counselors are giving you direction in some area and the Bible seems to confirm it, if you do not have the perfect peace of God, do not proceed. We can use this in many ways.

I was speaking recently in Sioux Falls, South Dakota. A young lady came up to me, all in a dither, now knowing whether she and her husband should rent or buy a house. I told her that I sensed a total lack of peace in her, and I encouraged her to go pray and not to do anything until she had perfect peace from God.

In one of my books, I mentioned the example of Barney Coombs, who is now a pastor in Vancouver, B.C. At the time of this incident he was a pastor in England. He was driving home one night. The road to his house forked and later the two roads joined back together. Thus, he could take either the left fork or the right fork, with the time and the distance being the same. He felt a strong urging to take the right fork. Most of us would have just done it without thinking. However, Barney prayed and said, "God, if I am to take the right fork and this is of You, give me a real peace inside, and if not, give me a real disquiet." In answer to that prayer, God gave him a real disquiet, so he took the left fork instead. A little way down that road he picked up a hitchhiker who he had the privilege of leading to Christ. Satan, in the worst way, did not want him to take the left fork, and thus was giving him a strong urge to take the right fork.

We can use this technique in our daily lives. When we have a decision to make that may seem inconsequential, such as who to have lunch with, we can ask God, "God, if you want me to have lunch with Joe, then give me a real peace inside and, if not, give me an unrest." God delights in this kind of prayer and delights in answering us.

Up until now we have just talked about guidance for an isolated individual. The same thing applies to more than one person. For example, if a husband and wife are both Christians, both seeking God's will, and are contemplating a particular action, I think God will give them both peace if it is His will for them to act in a certain manner. Similarly with a group of elders trying to arrive at a decision: if it is God's will, He will give them all perfect peace. What happens in a group of elders if four of them feel peace and the fifth one doesn't? In that situation one of two things is true:

1.  It is not God's will that they take that particular action and He is using the fifth elder as a check to prevent them from making a mistake . . . or

2.  The fifth elder has a spiritual problem that needs to be dealt with and is not hearing from God.

In either case I do not believe the action should be taken until there is perfect unity in the Spirit. It may be that the group needs to pause, deal with any spiritual problems among the elders and then reconsider the question. If everyone (or both people in a couple) does not feel perfect peace, either it is something that they should not do, or at least one party is not truly seeking to do God's will. Thus, God can use peace, not only to direct individuals, but to direct groups of people as well. Thank you, Lord, for this beautiful and simple way that you let us know if we are walking in your will.

## SUMMARY AND CONCLUSION

The one thing that God did not want us to have was the knowledge of good and evil. He knew that once we had it we would attempt to live independently of Him, making our own decisions based on our knowledge of good and evil, and we would no longer rely on Him, looking to Him for guidance on decisions. Once Adam and Eve gained this knowledge of good and evil, we can see that that is exactly what happened.

Through the ages, we have seen that knowing God and knowing good and evil are mutually exclusive. Our decisions are based either on our knowledge of good and evil or on what God says (God's will). Frequently, God's will or God's guidance is illogical and contrary to our knowledge of good and evil. We also discussed how we can know God's will.

If we are not careful, we can even use the Bible to make decisions independent of God. We can overemphasize the Ten Commandments and even make the New Testament a brand new law all in itself. Trying to be under the law and a set of rules and regulations is deadly, where having a personal, vital relationship with God the Father through Jesus Christ is alive and exciting.

We realize that there is another side to this question. We have only presented one side. But it seems that this is a basic, foundational truth in the Bible from beginning to end. We yearn that we and all of our readers would look to God for guidance and direction, and not to our own knowledge of good and evil.

This has been a difficult chapter to write. Many will misunderstand and others will think I might be trying to rationalize something. With my whole heart I want to see people live righteous, holy lives and to obey and glorify our loving heavenly Father and His Son, Jesus Christ. I do not want to confuse, but only to help you draw closer to God. I believe that learning to look to God and to trust in Him, rather than relying on your knowledge of good and evil, will help you to do this.

As we draw closer to God and desire to know Him and His Son, Jesus Christ, and to become like them, we need to check our images of the Father and of the Son. Our images of them may be quite different from what they are really like.

76

# 4

# YOUR IMAGE OF JESUS

Have you ever met a person who had a sugar-coated facade and felt in your heart, "If I could only get through that wall and get to the real person, I believe I would really like him"? I believe there is a sugar-coated facade around Christ, but He did not put it there. It is one that Christian teachers through the centuries have developed and we have accepted it without question.

With God's help I would like to try to pierce through that facade that has been artificially erected and help you to see the real Jesus. I believe that when you see Him as He is, you will love Him, worship Him and adore Him even more than you do now.

Probably you have mental images of what the birth of Christ was like. I know we all would like to be realistic, because *realism* and *truth* are two sides of the same coin. But unfortunately, most of our images of the Christmas scene are idealized and frequently quite different from what the Bible actually has to say.

## THE REALISTIC BIRTH OF CHRIST

As I share with you what God has shown me, with all of my heart I want to glorify God and to lift up His Son and my precious Savior, Jesus Christ. That is my only desire in sharing the things that I will share in this chapter.

As we begin to look at the birth of Christ, the first thing that we have to realize is that it is highly unlikely that He was born on December 25th, or even in any of the winter months.

His birth probably took place in the late spring, the summer, or the early fall. There are two biblical reasons for believing this, both found in Luke 2.

1  Now it came about in those days that a decree went out from Caesar Augustus, that a census be taken of all the inhabited earth.

2  This was the first census taken while Quirinius was governor of Syria.

3  And all were proceeding to register for the census, everyone to his own city.

4  And Joseph also went up from Galilee, from the city of Nazareth, to Judea, to the city of David, which is called Bethlehem, because he was of the house and family of David,

5  in order to register, along with Mary, who was engaged to him, and was with child.

6  And it came about that while they were there, the days were completed for her to give birth.

7  And she gave birth to her first-born son; and she wrapped Him in cloths, and laid Him in a manger, because there was no room for them in the inn.

8  And in the same region there were *some* shepherds staying out in the fields, and keeping watch over their flock by night.

9  And an angel of the LORD suddenly stood before them, and the glory of the LORD shone around them; and they were terribly frightened.

10  And the angel said to them, "Do not be afraid; for behold, I bring you good news of a great joy which shall be for all the people;

11  for today in the city of David there has been born for you a Savior, who is Christ the LORD.

12  "And this *will be* a sign for you: you will find a baby wrapped in cloths, and lying in a manger."

13  And suddenly there appeared with the angel a multitude of the heavenly host praising God, and saying,

14  "Glory to God in the highest,
And on earth peace among men with whom He is pleased."

15  And it came about when the angels had gone away from them into heaven, that the shepherds *began* saying to one another, "Let us go straight to Bethlehem then, and see this thing that has happened which the LORD has made known to us."

16  And they came in haste and found their way to Mary and Joseph, and the baby as He lay in the manger.

17  And when they had seen this, they made known the statement which had been told them about this Child.

18  And all who heard it wondered at the things which were told them by the shepherds.

19  But Mary treasured up all these things, pondering them in her heart.

20  And the shepherds went back, glorifying and praising God for all that they had heard and seen, just as had been told them.

—Luke 2

In these verses, we first see that the census that Caesar commanded to be taken was in all the inhabited earth, not just in the Palestinian area. This would include areas such as the Alps, where the winters are very harsh. He certainly would not have required that this be done in the middle of winter. The most likely time would have been the middle of summer, after the planting of the crops but before the harvest time, when people could travel more easily, the animals, which were used for transportation, could graze along the roads and the people could sleep along the roadside, without worrying about the harsh cold of winter.

This is further substantiated by the fact that there were shepherds staying out at night in the fields with their flocks. Bethlehem is about a ten-minute drive from Jerusalem and they are both located in the mountains of Judea. Jerusalem gets some snow in the winter and so does Bethlehem. During the winter when the weather is harsh and cold, shepherds would not be out in the fields with their sheep at night. This is further indication that the birth of Christ likely took place during the warmer months.

Also in this passage in Luke 2, we see that because there was no room in the inn, Mary gave birth to Jesus in a place where animals evidently stayed; it says that she laid Him in a feeding trough (manger). The birth likely occurred in some sort of a shelter or shack on the edge of a barnyard.

When they could not find anyplace else to sleep, Joseph probably made them a bed out of hay and possibly threw the blankets from their donkeys over the hay; he and Mary then might have laid down to sleep for the night. When Mary began to go into labor she would have had the agony and the labor pains that any woman has when giving birth. Joseph was probably struggling there in the dark, possibly with no clean water, the stench of the animal manure suffocating him in the heat of summer, wishing that they were in a clean bed with nicer conditions.

Mary and Joseph were hard-working, honest, common folks. Like most carpenters of that day, Joseph likely had strong arms and heavy calluses on his hands. Here he was trying to comfort Mary, hold her hand, and help the baby Jesus come out the birth canal. He was doing things unaccustomed and awkward to him, perhaps worrying about the umbilical cord, the afterbirth and keeping the baby away from all of the manure and mess of the barnyard.

About that time, in came some huffing, puffing shepherds, and shepherds usually don't smell so sweet themselves. They came because of the command of God. Other people evidently came by, possibly attracted by the screams of Mary in labor and the cry of the newborn baby.

Then the excited shepherds began to relate about the angelic host that they had seen, who told them about the birth of the Savior, Christ the Lord, and the fact that the host of angels proclaimed glory to God because of Christ, who was going to bring peace to the hearts of individuals who would trust Him. So it was most certainly the glory of God that made the birth of Christ a glorious thing, and not the place or conditions of His birth.

Incidentally, there is no evidence that the magi from the east were there at this time, and I can't find any evidence that there were three of them. The best information indicates that they arrived probably a year and a half later (because Herod commanded that all children two years and younger be killed— Matthew 2:1-8; 16). After the magi initially saw the star, they had to pack up, prepare for the journey and travel by camel a long distance. So there is no reason to believe that Christ would still be in the manger by the time they arrived. They stopped to ask the people in Jerusalem where He had been born and they were told to go on to Bethlehem. So they went there and the

star they had seen in the east went on before them and led them
to where Christ was.

> 11 And they came into the house and saw the Child with Mary
> His mother; and they fell down and worshiped Him; and opening
> their treasures they presented to Him gifts of gold and frankincense
> and myrrh.
>
> —Matthew 2

This verse says that they came into the "house" (not the
"stable") and saw the "child" with Mary. It doesn't say they
saw Mary and the "baby." So evidently Mary and Jesus remained
in Bethlehem, but even when He was a child, these wise men
from the east recognized that the anointing of God was upon
Christ, and they fell down and worshiped Him and gave Him
their treasures.

This picture is quite different from the little manger scenes
that we set up. I believe we should strip away the facade and
recognize that Christ went through a very real and a not-so-
glamorous birth. The smells around were those of animal manure, sweaty people and dusty straw, and yet God was glorified
in it. God used average, everyday folks to proclaim His message.
All of this causes the birth of Christ to be so magnificent to
me. Had He been born in a clean, nice situation in a palace, or
in the home of a wealthy man, it would have been easy for
Christ to get respect. But the way it happened, He was respected,
even as a child, because of God's power and God's anointing
upon Him. Praise the Lord!

Do you see that once you pierce the sugar-coated facade
built up around the birth of Christ and are able to accept the
crude, human part of His birth, you love Him even more because of what He went through to be born as a human. How
much He loves you and me to be willing to come into this
world in this lowly way. To me this makes Him even more glorious! I believe the same thing will be true when we look at
other facets of Jesus's life in a realistic way.

## YOUR IMAGE OF JESUS

About two years ago, right before I went to Hawaii to speak at a monetary conference, a brother in Medford and I had a real conflict. During my week in Hawaii I had a lot of time to do some thinking and I kept asking the Lord what the cause of it was. I knew that I was sincerely seeking to be like Jesus and I knew that this brother also sincerely desired to be like Jesus, so what could be causing the conflict?

After praying about it a great deal during that week, finally the Lord showed me that the reason we were having problems was because my image of what Jesus was like was very different from this brother's image of what Jesus was like. We were both trying to become like our image of Jesus, but those images were very different.

To help you understand how different two brothers' images of Jesus can be, let's take this one example.

I have heard Dave Wilkerson say that Christ did not create wine at the wedding feast of Cana; it was a "heavenly nectar," but definitely not fermented wine. He would probably say that Christ never created nor drank wine with any alcoholic content.

Other Christian leaders have a very different view of the same facts and feel that Christ created and drank real wine. They would point out that the same word was used when the good Samaritan poured the "wine" into the stranger's wounds as when Christ turned water into "wine" and that the good Samaritan certainly would not pour grape juice into wounds; all grape juice would do would be to attract flies, whereas wine would at least have some medicinal and sterilizing value. If two such brothers were both trying to be like their images of Jesus, one might totally reject wine (and unfortunately usually also reject Christians who drink wine), while the other would feel at liberty to drink wine.

Paul deals with this extensively in Romans 14. He points out that one man eats meat to the glory of the Lord and another abstains from eating meat, also to the glory of the Lord. We do not all have to agree on precise behavioral patterns. Applying the principle of Romans 14 to the case we have been looking at here, if one man drinks wine and feels that it glorifies the Lord, praise God! If another man abstains for the glory of the Lord, praise God! They are both trying to become like their image of what Jesus was like. They are both God's servants and have to give account to Him. I will not judge them; I will only encourage them to continually seek to be like Christ and to have their image of Christ revised by the Holy Spirit so that it comes ever closer to what Christ was really like.

This brings us to the purpose of this chapter: to try to cut through some of the sugar-coated facade that people have about what Christ was like and to get back to what the Scriptures actually say and find out more realistically and biblically what He was really like.

Because of our knowledge of good and evil, we tend to emphasize the characteristics of Christ that fit in with our knowledge of what is "good" and ignore or skip over the aspects of Christ that we would consider less desirable or, if we were honest, that do not fit our image of what is "good." God, help us to have a well-rounded, realistic picture of what your Son was like when He was here on the earth, help us to love Him more, and cause us to desire to be like Him who was victorious over sin.

## JESUS CHRIST WAS REALLY HUMAN

Jesus was really human, yet let me hasten to add that He was also divine. Most Christians readily accept Christ's divinity, but they have a much harder time accepting His humanity.

Some people have an idealized picture of Christ. They may not realize it, but they actually feel that if He ever did cut His finger or skin His knees while working in His father's carpenter shop, for example, He would pray and be instantly healed. These people would probably feel that if a germ or a virus of measles, mumps, chickenpox or any other childhood disease entered the body of Christ, because of Christ's internal power, it would immediately be sterilized. Thus, they would conclude that Christ never had a minute of illness, physical pain from sickness, or anything of that nature. These people, with their sanitized view of Christ, could never imagine Him coming in from the carpenter shop all dirty, sweaty, and smelly, with aching muscles, so tired that He was ready to drop.

But is this image of "always in perfect health, instantly healed in all cases" really a fair picture of Christ, who came to live as one of us so that He could understand us and be able to sympathize with us when we are sick or in pain? My personal opinion, and I believe there is a scriptural basis for this belief, is that Christ experienced normal childhood diseases, and that when He cut His finger or scraped His knee, it healed in the same way that any other boy's scrapes, cuts and bruises would heal.

Those who preach that every Christian should have perfect health at all times and instant healing from all wounds may have forgotten that when Christ was beaten with the whip and had His skin ripped open, His head pierced by the crown of thorns and nails driven through His hands and feet, there was not any instant healing. He could have instantly healed Himself in all of these cases, but this would have invalidated one of the purposes for which He came. He wanted to experience what we experience so that He could truly empathize with us and be able to comfort us in all things.

I believe that Christ got hungry and thirsty. When His stomach growled, He was eager to be fed. He indeed lived as we live and experienced what we experience. There were possibly times when He was really tempted to turn rocks into bread to satisfy His hunger. However, this was not the Father's will and to do so would have been sin. There were other occasions when the Father told Him to multiply the fish and bread and it would have been sin for Him not to do so. He came to do His Father's will, even if at times it "seemed" to contradict what His Father's will had been on other occasions.

## THE MANY TEMPTATIONS OF JESUS CHRIST

Frequently when we talk about the temptations of Christ, we think of the forty days He spent in the wilderness, right after His baptism by John. However, I believe that the temptations of Christ occurred throughout His lifetime, from His child-hood to the end of His ministry. That forty-day period was simply a time of intense temptation by Satan.

First we need to recognize the difference between tempta-tion and sin (even mental sin). Billy Graham once said that when a man looks at a woman once it is a temptation. When he takes a second look it is sin. None of us can help the thoughts that come through our minds, such as "I would like to have that guy's new car," "I would like to choke that person," or "I would like to get that person of the opposite sex alone for a couple of hours." However, when we begin to enjoy such a thought in our minds or to dwell on it, and even begin to day-dream about how it could come about, we have committed that sin in our heart. So *temptation* is a thought about committing a specific sin that comes to our mind, whereas committing that *sin* in our heart is when we begin to lust after the act of carry-ing out that tempting thought.

I feel the Lord wants me to say a word about lust before we proceed. *Lust* is anything I want that I want *now* and I don't care about the consequences. It is sin whether the act is actually committed or not. We can lust after food, sex, a better job or house or car. We can lust after anything. For example, Esau lusted after the stew that Jacob had and was willing to give away his birthright for it. He wanted that stew "right now" and either didn't think or didn't care about the consequences. His lust was sin even if Jacob had not given him the stew. Most of us do not "lust" after things most of the time, but Satan, as he keeps tempting us, tries to convince us we are lusting. If he can convince a Christian that temptation is lust, that Christian will live a defeated life. Every time a temptation passes through his mind he will condemn himself for sinning.

This ties in clearly with some of the things that the Lord has shown us thus far. If I am lusting after something, I am con-cerned with what *I want* and not with what will glorify God. In fact, if I am lusting after something, I'm not concerned if it is "good or evil," I just want it. So once a temptation leads to mental lust, there is no concern on the individual's part either about knowing God's will or knowing good and evil. His selfish desires take preeminence and, hence, it is sin because he is no longer glorifying God.

But let us return to considering the temptations of Christ. Hebrews 4 sheds some light on this:

14  Since then we have a great high priest who has passed through the heavens, Jesus the Son of God, let us hold fast our confession.

15  For we do not have a high priest who cannot sympathize with our weaknesses, but one who has been tempted in all things as *we are, yet* without sin.

16  Let us therefore draw near with confidence to the throne of grace, that we may receive mercy and may find grace to help in time of need.

—Hebrews 4

Here it says that Jesus Christ sympathizes with our weaknesses because He was tempted in *all things* as we are (or the *King James Version* says in *all points*). This means that there is not a single temptation that anyone has that was not experienced by Jesus Christ. This means that the thoughts (temptations) went through His head, but He did not dwell on them nor yield to them and He was therefore without sin. This means that He was tempted to cheat, to gossip, to bust someone in the mouth, to kill someone, to have immoral sex, to steal, to cheat on paying taxes and every other temptation that you or I or any human being has ever had. But because He was tempted in all of these areas, He sympathizes with us and understands us totally. For this reason we can come to Him in confidence, knowing that He has experienced the very temptation that we are struggling with. He found a way to get through the temptation without sinning and is eager to show you and me that way to escape also.

## WHAT JESUS DID WAS NOT SIN

Because of our knowledge of good and evil, discussed in the previous chapter, many things that Christ did or didn't do some of us would almost classify as wrong. Let's take just a couple of examples. The first one is found in John 2:

14  And He found in the temple those who were selling oxen and sheep and doves, and the moneychangers seated.

15  And He made a scourge of cords, and drove *them* all out of the temple, with the sheep and the oxen; and He poured out the coins of the moneychangers, and overturned their tables;

16  and to those who were selling the doves He said, "Take these things away; stop making My Father's house a house of merchandise."

Here we see that Christ made a whip out of cords and He used that whip to drive the sheep, oxen and other animals out of the temple. He also turned over the tables of the money-changers. This would have caused the coins to roll all over and probably many people grabbed the coins. Thus, in a very violent way, He ruined the businesses of the money changers and the people who sold the animals in the temple. Some people think of Christ as so gentle and mild that He wouldn't make a whip, He wouldn't use one on animals, and He certainly wouldn't ruin any man's business, *but He did.*

If we are to be like Jesus, what should the counterpart be in our lives? Jesus was strongly, even physically and violently, opposed to the enemies of God. Should we also be like that? I can't answer that for you, but, as God directs, I believe we need to be willing to very strongly oppose God's enemies.

Continuing on the same thought, Christ also called the enemies of God some very ugly names:

27  "Woe to you, scribes and Pharisees, hypocrites! For you are like whitewashed tombs which on the outside appear beautiful, but inside they are full of dead men's bones and all uncleanness.

28  "Even so you too outwardly appear righteous to men, but inwardly you are full of hypocrisy and lawlessness.

29  "Woe to you, scribes and Pharisees, hypocrites! For you build the tombs of the prophets and adorn the monuments of the righteous,

30  and say, 'If we had been *living* in the days of our fathers, we would not have been partners with them in *shedding* the blood of the prophets.'

31  "Consequently you bear witness against yourselves, that you are sons of those who murdered the prophets.

32  "Fill up then the measure *of the guilt* of your fathers.

33  "You serpents, you brood of vipers, how shall you escape the sentence of hell? . . ."

—Matthew 23

Christ called these religious leaders "whitewashed tombs," which look pretty on the outside but on the inside they stink and are unclean. He also called them serpents and vipers (poisonous snakes). (My concept of "good" is to respect one's elders . . . maybe I should repray about this. . . .)

We are to love our enemies (Matthew 5:44). Does this apply to the enemies of God? Christ was never angry with His own enemies but He did show anger toward the enemies of His Father. Who are God's enemies today? Should we be angry with them? Can we love them and still be angry with them? Is this what Jesus did?

## CHRIST AND HIS PARENTS

Another area in which Christ's behavior does not follow the average Christian's concept of what is "good" and "right" was His relationship to His "parents." What would you think of a 12-year-old child who went with his parents on a trip and when they decided to leave, the child decided he wasn't going to go with them and wandered off to do something else? You would likely think that that child was disobedient, discourteous and should be spanked severely. Let's read about Christ in a similar situation:

41  And His parents used to go to Jerusalem every year at the Feast of the Passover.

42  And when He became twelve, they went up *there* according to the custom of the Feast;

43  and as they were returning, after spending the full number of days, the boy Jesus stayed behind in Jerusalem. And His parents were unaware of it,

44  but supposed Him to be in the caravan, and went a day's journey; and they began looking for Him among their relatives and acquaintances.

45  And when they did not find Him, they returned to Jerusalem, looking for Him.

46 And it came about that after three days they found Him in the temple, sitting in the midst of the teachers, both listening to them, and asking them questions.

47 And all who heard Him were amazed at His understanding and His answers.

48 And when they saw Him, they were astonished; and His mother said to Him, "Son, why have You treated us this way? Behold, Your father and I have been anxiously looking for You."

49 And He said to them, "Why is it that you were looking for Me? Did you not know that I had to be in My Father's *house?*"

—Luke 2

There are other examples in the New Testament where Christ did not seem to honor His parents, at least based on our "knowledge of good and evil" definition of what it means to honor one's father and mother. In fact, in the case just quoted, when they finally found Him, He didn't even seem sorry or apologize.

Jesus came to know His heavenly Father and to do His heavenly Father's will, regardless of whether it cut across all of the customs, standards and laws of His day, and even if it meant displeasing or defying those in authority over Him, such as Jewish religious leaders or His mother and Joseph. He seemed to be concerned only about doing the Father's will. This is a very heavy word, so be careful if you say you want to be like Jesus. Also be careful how you apply "submission" and "honor." One could unknowingly teach others the opposite of what Christ actually did.

We also ought to take a look at Christ's view of His relationship to His physical family and His view of His relationship to His spiritual family.

46 While He was still speaking to the multitudes, behold, His mother and brothers were standing outside, seeking to speak to Him.

47 And someone said to Him, "Behold, Your mother and Your brothers are standing outside seeking to speak to You."

48 But He answered the one who was telling Him and said, "Who is My mother and who are My brothers?"

49 And stretching out His hand toward His disciples, He said, "Behold, My mother and My brothers!

50 "For whoever does the will of My Father who is in heaven, he is My brother and sister and mother."

—Matthew 12

Who did Christ consider more important, His spiritual family or His physical family? From this passage in Matthew, it is clear, at least to me, that He considered His spiritual family more important. He even taught this principle explicitly, as is recorded in Luke 14:

26 "If anyone comes to Me and does not hate his own father and mother and wife and children and brothers and sisters, yes, and even his own life, he cannot be My disciple.

27 "Whoever does not carry his own cross and come after Me cannot be My disciple. . . ."

As we can see here, Christ taught us to hate (or love less) our father, mother, wife, husband, children, brothers and sisters if we are going to be His disciples. We saw this exemplified in Christ's life. He put the Father's will and His spiritual family ahead of His physical family. Is this your image of Jesus? Do you want to be like Jesus? Are you willing to do God's will even if it means ignoring or going against the wishes of your physical family? This does not mean that we should not love and care for our physical family; we simply must not put them ahead of doing God's will.

## CHRIST AND WINE

There are just two more aspects of Christ's human nature that I would like to deal with before turning to some significant parts of His spiritual life. The first one is in Luke 7:

33 "For John the Baptist has come eating no bread and drinking no wine; and you say, 'He has a demon!'

34 "The Son of Man has come eating and drinking; and you say, 'Behold, a gluttonous man, and a drunkard, a friend to tax-gatherers and sinners!'. . . ."

We see that Christ was a popular dinner guest and friend of tax gatherers and sinners. He is contrasted with John the Baptist who ate no bread and drank no wine. But Jesus Christ freely ate and evidently freely drank wine. In Luke 7:34 in the *King James*

*Version,* Christ refers to himself as a winebibber. Each Christian is going to have to wrestle with this one for himself, but however you come out, I have a word of counsel for you. If the Lord shows you that you should not drink fermented wine, then don't let any other Christian try to squeeze you in the mold of drinking it. If you come out convinced that Jesus Christ drank wine and have peace that you can, don't let any other Christian try to squeeze you into the mold of thinking that it is wrong. We each should yearn to be like Jesus, however we see Him. Of course we need to ask God daily to correct, clarify and purify our image of Jesus Christ, and we need to spend much time in the Bible so that God *can* show us what Jesus was like.

## CHRIST'S SEXUALITY

The last part of the humanity of Christ that I would like to discuss, in an attempt to help us get a realistic, well-rounded picture of Jesus, is the area of sexuality and physical affection. Let's look further in Luke 7:

> 36  Now one of the Pharisees was requesting Him to dine with him. And He entered the Pharisee's house, and reclined *at the table.*
>
> 37  And behold, there was a woman in the city who was a sinner; and when she learned that He was reclining *at the table* in the Pharisee's house, she brought an alabaster vial of perfume,
>
> 38  and standing behind *Him* at His feet, weeping, she began to wet His feet with her tears, and kept wiping them with the hair of her head, and kissing His feet, and anointing them with the perfume.
>
> 39  Now when the Pharisee who had invited Him saw this, he said to himself, "If this man were a prophet He would know who and what sort of person this woman is who is touching Him, that she is a sinner."
>
> 40  And Jesus answered and said to him, "Simon, I have something to say to you." And he replied, "Say it, Teacher."
>
> 41  "A certain moneylender had two debtors: one owed five hundred denarii, and the other fifty.
>
> 42  "When they were unable to repay, he graciously forgave them both. Which of them therefore will love him more?"
>
> 43  Simon answered and said, "I suppose the one whom he forgave more." And He said to him, "You have judged correctly."

44 And turning toward the woman, He said to Simon, "Do you see this woman? I entered your house; you gave Me no water for My feet, but she has wet My feet with her tears, and wiped them with her hair.

45 "You gave Me no kiss, but she, since the time I came in, has not ceased to kiss My feet.

46 "You did not anoint My head with oil, but she anointed My feet with her perfume.

47 "For this reason I say to you, her sins, which are many, have been forgiven, for she loved much; but he who is forgiven little, loves little."

48 And He said to her, "Your sins have been forgiven."

49 And those who were reclining *at the table* with Him began to say to themselves, "Who is this *man* who even forgives sins?"

—Luke 7

Most people think of Jesus as being somehow sexually sterile or of having no sexuality at all. To think of Him being tempted to have sex with a young woman or to have a homosexual affair is absolutely unthinkable.

However, on two recorded occasions Christ received a perfumed-oil foot rub, the first one (quoted above from Luke 7) by a woman referred to by most translations as a sinner or an immoral woman. She not only gave Him a foot rub with scented oil, but she also kept kissing His feet and rubbing them with her hair. A second such occurrence is recorded in John 12:1–3 where Mary, the sister of Martha, anointed the feet of Jesus with a pound of very costly perfume and wiped His feet with her hair. Jesus was reclining at the table in the home of Lazarus in Bethany on that occasion. Matthew 26:6–13 records that, while Jesus was reclining at the table in the home of Simon the leper in Bethany, a woman came to Him and poured a vial of costly perfume on His head.

Jesus must have been pleased with this affection because in none of these instances did He ask the woman to stop what she was doing. And yet, praise God, He did not lust after the woman but was instead able to minister to her spiritually. Praise the Lord that Jesus experienced so much of what we experience and yet He knew how to overcome sin and to live a holy and righteous life.

I'm so glad that Jesus exhibited anger, called the enemies of God harsh names, enjoyed a foot rub by a sinful woman, so that I can come to Him knowing that He has been where I am and He understands me. Whatever my problem may be or whatever my temptation is, Jesus experienced it as a red-blooded man. He therefore can help me like no one else can. We don't have to pussyfoot with Jesus; we can openly tell Him exactly what we feel.

## JESUS *LEARNED* OBEDIENCE

As we think of Christ finding out what the Father's will was and then obeying it, in our idealized view of Christ, we assume that He just *naturally* obeyed. We assume that, from the time He could talk and understand, obeying was easy for Him, whereas sometimes it is such a struggle for us. The Scriptures present a different and more realistic picture of Christ's struggle to be obedient.

> 41 And He withdrew from them about a stone's throw, and He knelt down and *began* to pray,
> 42 saying, "Father, if Thou are willing, remove this cup from Me; yet not My will, but Thine be done."
> 43 Now an angel from heaven appeared to Him, strengthening Him.
> 44 And being in agony He was praying very fervently; and His sweat became like drops of blood, falling down upon the ground.
> —Luke 22

> 7 In the days of His flesh, He offered up both prayers and supplications with loud crying and tears to the One able to save Him from death, and He was heard because of His piety.
> 8 Although He was a Son, He learned obedience from the things which He suffered.
>
> —Hebrews 5

In verse 8 of Hebrews 5, we see that obedience didn't come either automatically nor easily for Jesus. He had to *learn* obedience just as we do, and He had to keep on learning it right up to the time of His death. His will must have conflicted with the will of God the Father at times (otherwise He would not have had to *learn* to be obedient). We know this was the case in the garden of Gethsemane. He sweated over having to die to submit to the Father's will, but after the struggle was over, He wanted to do the will of the Father more than He wanted to live.

It was not easy for Christ to learn to be obedient. It was painful. He learned obedience by suffering and dying to self (the same way we learn it). There were times when in the worst way Christ did not want to do what the Father was asking. When you are struggling and trying to yield to God's will, remember that Jesus had that problem and He had it all of His life. To be like Jesus is to die to our own will.

## DID JESUS USE POWER NOT AVAILABLE TO US?

The answer to this question—did Jesus use power not available to us?—can prove to be one that can revolutionize your Christian life. Christ had no human father and thus has broken the *imputed* sin from Adam and the *inherited* sin from one's physical forefathers. Discussion of these types of sin is not relevant to the matter at hand, so we will not take this space to explain it.

We know that Jesus Christ committed no *personal* sin and He perfectly did His Father's will. The question comes, did He use power to meet temptations, to live without sin, and to do His Father's will that we do not have available to us? If He did use power that is not available to us, then He lived as a man with an unfair advantage and we could rightfully claim that the reason He did not yield to temptation was because He had power that we do not have.

I believe that Jesus Christ, while He was here on the earth, *could* have used divine power that is not available to us but that He limited Himself to only use power that is also available to you and me. I believe this is pointed out in Philippians 2:

> 5  Have this attitude in yourselves which was also in Christ Jesus,
> 6  who, although He existed in the form of God, did not regard equality with God a thing to be grasped,

**7 but emptied Himself, taking the form of a bond-servant, and being made in the likeness of men.**

**8 And being found in appearance as a man, He humbled Himself by becoming obedient to the point of death, even death on a cross.**

Verse 7 says that Jesus Christ "emptied Himself." In the original language this means that He "laid aside His privileges and powers." He voluntarily limited Himself to using only the power that we human beings also have available to us. In fact, every miracle of Christ has been duplicated by the early disciples, by Old Testament individuals or even by Christians today in some part of the world. The Bible records Peter performing the miracle of healing (in the name of Jesus and by the power of God), Paul raising someone from the dead, and Elijah multiplying food in the incident with the widow and her son (1 Kings 17:9–16). We see the gift of knowledge exhibited in the United States and many other places today.

Two of the temptations of Christ by Satan in the wilderness were to turn stones into bread and to jump off of the pinnacle of the temple (Matthew 4:1–7). Basically these were temptations for Christ to step across the line and use His divine power that we do not have access to.

If we have the same power available to us that Christ had available to Him, then we should be able to do the works that He did. To me doing the "works" that Christ did implies doing miracles that He did, doing the Father's will as He did, and living a life where temptation is victoriously dealt with as He did. Christ states this truth in John 14:

**12 "Truly, truly, I say to you, he who believes in Me, the works that I do shall he do also; and greater *works* than these shall he do; because I go to the Father. . . ."**

If you begin to let that soak in, it can have incredible implications in your life. Jesus was primarily our Savior. Some look down their spiritual noses at those who think of Christ as "an example." The reason is because those people who emphasize Christ as an example frequently deny His role as the divine Son of God and Savior of mankind. Yet our Savior had real feelings and real desires. His temptations were earthly and real, and yet He overcame them.

I believe Jesus was *both* our Savior and our example. Jesus is our divine Savior, for which I am very grateful. But I believe He was also our example of what a Christian *can* be. His life is an example of what *our* lives can be! Wow!

## EXAMINE YOUR IMAGE OF JESUS

When the Lord showed me that many of the conflicts that arise between brothers and sisters in Christ result because they have different images of what Jesus was like when He walked on the earth, He led me to write down some questions about Christ that could help a person determine what his image of Jesus really is. I have since expanded this to the following questionnaire with this in mind: if two brothers or sisters are having difficulty over a particular issue, it might be helpful if each of them filled out this questionnaire so that they could at least see what the differences were in their images of Jesus. Both of them are likely trying to be like their image of Jesus, but those images could be very different.

I pray that this questionnaire will not be misinterpreted, but that it might serve as a tool to help you come to know Christ in a fuller and better way. Scripture references have been included for those questions where there is a Scripture that might shed some light on the answer. I suggest that you first fill out the questionnaire without looking up the references given and later look up the Scriptures to see if your answer matches what the Bible teaches about Christ.

The questionnaire appears on pages 97 and 98.

## YOUR IMAGE OF JESUS QUESTIONNAIRE

Most Christians easily accept Christ's divinity, but have a harder time accepting His humanity. To define your view, in the space after the question number place a "Y" if you feel the answer is "Yes" and an "N" if you think the answer is "No."

1. ____ Did Jesus ever have measles, mumps or any childhood disease?

2. ____ Did Jesus ever cause His parents to worry? *(Luke 2:41-49)*

3. ____ Did Jesus ever need His mother's care and comfort?

4. ____ Did Jesus ever cut His finger working in the carpenter shop?

5. ____ Did Jesus ever sweat or smell bad?

6. ____ When Jesus was with the 12 disciples and had to perform a bodily elimination function (bowel movement or urination) did He use the everyday term for it?

7. ____ Was Jesus ever angry?

8. ____ Was Jesus ever sad? *(John 11:35)*

9. ____ Was Jesus ever tired? *(John 4:5-6)*

10. ____ Did Jesus break the rules of the religious leaders who were over Him? *(Matt. 15:2; Luke 11:38)*

11. ____ Would Jesus make a whip? *(John 2:14-16)*

12. ____ Would Jesus use a whip to drive animals? *(John 2:14-16)*

13. ____ Would Jesus damage a man's business for any reason? *(John 2: 14-16)*

14. ____ Would Jesus call someone an ugly name? *(Matt. 23:27-33)*

15. ____ Would Jesus call someone a rattlesnake or "trash." *(Matt. 23: 27-33)*

16. ____ Did Jesus always do the socially proper thing, such as saying "thanks" and "goodbye" to His host before moving on? *Mark 1: 32-39)*

17. ____ Would Jesus tell someone not to attend his father's funeral? *(Luke 9:59-62)*

18. ____ Did Jesus have hard, tough requirements for those who chose to follow Him? *(Mark 8:34-35)*

19. ____ Was Jesus persecuted? *(John 15:20)*

20. ____ Did Jesus drink wine? *(Luke 7:33-34; John 2:1-10)*

21. ____ Did Jesus spend time with really bad sinners (those that "good people" would shun)? *(Luke 7:33-34)*

22. ____ Did Jesus show forgiveness, mercy and compassion? *(John 8:3-11)*

23. ____ Would Jesus have liked a scented oil foot rub by an ex-prostitute? *(Luke 7:36-50)*

24. ____ Did Jesus consider His spiritual family more important than His physical family? *(Matt. 12:46-50; Luke 14:26-27)*

25. ____ Did Jesus pray for hours at a time? *(Mark 1:35)*

26. ____ Did Jesus spend time studying and digging into the Scriptures? *(Luke 24:27)*

27. ____ Did Jesus pay His full taxes? *(Matt. 17:24-27)*

Questions 28–37 deal with temptation. Temptation is when we think a thought once. Sin is when we dwell on that thought.

28. ____ Was Jesus ever tempted to cheat?

29. ____ Was Jesus ever tempted to gossip?

30. ____ Was Jesus ever tempted to bust someone in the mouth?

31. ____ Was Jesus ever tempted to kill someone?

32. ____ Was Jesus ever tempted to have sex with a young lady?

33. ____ Was Jesus ever tempted to have a homosexual affair?

34. ____ Did Jesus experience every temptation that any human has experienced? *(Heb. 4:14-16)*

35. ____ Did Jesus successfully resist yielding to all of these temptations? *(Heb. 4:14-16)*

36. ____ Was Jesus tempted to not die on the cross? *(Luke 22:41-42)*

37. ____ Was there ever a struggle within Jesus whether to do His own will or the Father's will? *(Heb. 5:8)*

38. ____ Did Jesus speak in a language that the people couldn't understand? *(Matt. 27:46)*

39. ____ Did Jesus baptize with the Holy Spirit? *(Acts 1:5)*

40. ____ Did Jesus exhibit the fruit of the Spirit?

Christ had divine power which He laid aside and He voluntarily limited Himself to the status of a human.

41. ____ Was Jesus ever tempted to use His divine power? *(Matt. 4:3)*

42. ____ Did Jesus only use the power that is available to us? *(Phil. 2:5-8)*

43. ____ Jesus is primarily our Savior. Was He also an example of what a Christian can be?

44. ____ Can a Christian do even greater things than Jesus did? *(John 14: 12)*

## SUMMARY AND CONCLUSION

We have covered a great deal of ground in this chapter. We have tried to punch through the sugar-coated facade that Christian teachers through the centuries have built up around Christ and to look realistically at Christ's birth, childhood, manhood and how He met the multitude of temptations that He faced daily.

Our aim has not been to detract from who Christ is, but rather to try to see Him as He really was when He lived on the earth. I believe that as we see Him more realistically, He will become more approachable in our eyes and it will enhance our love for Him and our adoration of Him.

Christ was a carpenter and probably had the strong hands and biceps of a carpenter, rather than being a frail, almost sissy-type of an individual, as many paintings of Him depict. He was willing to go against His parents' wishes and the religious establishment in order to call people back to a personal relationship with God.

He was angry with the enemies of God and was willing to destroy their businesses, drive their animals out with a whip and to call them names that were not nice at all, but names that, in the case of the religious leaders, described what they were really like.

I hope this chapter won't be an end in itself but a beginning. I would encourage you this year to take a chapter a day and read through the four gospels. As you read, *daily* ask God this:

"SHOW ME THE REALISTIC VIEW OF WHAT CHRIST WAS LIKE AND GIVE ME A BURNING DESIRE TO LIVE LIKE HIM AND TO BE IN A CONDITION TO DO THE WORKS THAT HE DID."

The most exciting thing to me, and my main reason for writing this chapter, is to help you realize that Christ did not use power that is not also available to us. If we have available to us *all* of the power that Jesus used (He had divine power that He voluntarily did not use), then we too can do miracles like those that He did, we too can live holy lives as He did, we too can have a heart of compassion for sinners and reach out as He did, and we too can show love, mercy and compassion as He did. I also believe that we can resist temptation as He did. Praise the Lord for our beautiful Savior! I am so glad that Jesus is also an example of what God wants our lives to be like today. He was an overcomer and He wants to show us how to be overcomers too! He overcame sin only using power that is available to us today. Praise be to God!

May your determination be like Paul's, as stated in the second verse of 1 Corinthians 2:

> 2 **For I determined to know nothing among you except Jesus Christ, and Him crucified.**

If this is your determination, I am absolutely convinced that it will be the source of incredible growth for you, to the glory of God and His Son, Jesus Christ.

# 5

# KNOWING GOD

As we go through life we have the opportunity to meet a number of people. Of those people that we meet, some we choose to get to know and others we do not. A great deal of our life is determined by those that we choose to get to know.

Before we talk about getting to know God, I would like to share with you about an individual whom I was reading about the other day. He had some characteristics that most people would consider highly undesirable. He had given some people poisoned water to drink and it killed a number of them. He had a couple of guys working for him and one of them he forced to kill a bunch of his neighbors. Another one he forced to murder a high government official. (This is not very well known.)

He was evidently involved with evil spirits and had the power to order them about. There is evidence that he sent an evil spirit to a particular guy and caused him to go crazy.

Some people say that the reason he did all of these "terrible things" was because he took revenge. If someone did something against him that offended him, he would punish that person severely in return.

Would you like to get to know such a person? What would say if your children wanted to become friends with an individual like him? Would you discourage them from getting to know him? What would you say to them?

You might just pause here for a moment and think through what your answers would be to these questions.

## GETTING TO KNOW GOD

Many Christians would say that we should get to know God and certainly not an individual such as the one described above. Yet what many Christians do not realize is that the individual just described, who did all these things, *was God,* as we will see in just a moment.

God is loving and merciful; these are characteristics of God that we like to emphasize. Yet if that is all we believe about Him, we have a very slanted and unrealistic picture of God. Most people mainly read about God in the New Testament and ignore the picture of God that we find in the Old Testament. Yet all of the characteristics of God from the Old Testament are still true of Him, because God never changes (Malachi 3:6). I would like to help you develop a more rounded and complete picture of our God and Father.

Let's first look at some Scriptures that talk about some of the things that God did in Old Testament times. The first passage we will discuss is found in Jeremiah 9:

13 And the LORD said, "Because they have forsaken My law which I set before them and have not obeyed My voice nor walked according to it,

14 but have walked after the stubbornness of their heart and after the Baals, as their fathers taught them,"

15 therefore thus says the LORD of hosts, the God of Israel, "behold, I will feed them, this people, with wormwood and give them poisoned water to drink. . . ."

We see in this passage that the Lord God gave some people poisoned water to drink.

Some Christians think that one should not kill under any circumstances, even war. Other Christians feel that it is okay to kill during a time of war in self-defense, but it would never be okay to commit a murder. We are going to read about what happened when the children of Israel did evil in the sight of God. God raised up someone to come in and conquer their land, as is recorded in Judges:

12 Now the sons of Israel again did evil in the sight of the LORD. So the LORD strengthened Eglon the king of Moab against Israel, because they had done evil in the sight of the LORD.

13   And he gathered to himself the sons of Ammon and Amalek; and he went and defeated Israel, and they possessed the city of the palm trees.

14   And the sons of Israel served Eglon the king of Moab eighteen years.

15   But when the sons of Israel cried to the LORD, the LORD raised up a deliverer for them, Ehud the son of Gera, the Benjamite, a left-handed man. And the sons of Israel sent a tribute by him to Eglon the king of Moab.

16   And Ehud made himself a sword which had two edges, a cubit in length; and he bound it on his right thigh under his cloak.

17   And he presented the tribute to Eglon king of Moab. Now Eglon was a very fat man.

18   And it came about when he had finished presenting the tribute, that he sent away the people who had carried the tribute.

19   But he himself turned back from the idols which were at Gilgal, and said, "I have a secret message for you, O king." And he said, "Keep silence." And all who attended him left him.

20   And Ehud came to him while he was sitting alone in his cool roof chamber. And Ehud said, "I have a message from God for you." And he rose from his seat.

21   And Ehud stretched out his left hand, took the sword from his right thigh and thrust it into his belly.

22   The handle also went in after the blade, and the fat closed over the blade, for he did not draw the sword out of his belly; and the refuse came out.

23   Then Ehud went out into the vestibule and shut the doors of the roof chamber behind him, and locked *them*.

—Judges 3

After they were captured and were being punished by God, the children of Israel cried to the Lord for a deliverer. God raised up a left-handed man named Ehud. The reason that his being left-handed is significant is because he could hide a dagger on the side opposite to that where a dagger would be carried by a right-handed man. Thus, he could sneak a dagger into the king's chamber.

When Ehud—the deliverer that God raised up, who was under God's marching orders—was alone with the king, he murdered (assassinated) him. Thus, we see not only a lack of honor for those placed in authority, but also a premeditated murder committed by God's deliverer.

After the children of Israel had come out of Egypt, as we all know, they had Aaron make them a golden calf. When Moses came down off the mountain and saw this, here is what transpired:

> 25  Now when Moses saw that the people were out of control—for Aaron had let them get out of control to be a derision among their enemies—
> 26  then Moses stood in the gate of the camp, and said, "Whoever is for the LORD, *come* to me!" And all the sons of Levi gathered together to him.
> 27  And he said to them, "Thus says the LORD, the God of Israel, 'Every man *of you* put his sword upon his thigh and go back and forth from gate to gate in the camp, and kill every man his brother, and every man his friend, and every man his neighbor.'"
> 28  So the sons of Levi did as Moses instructed, and about three thousand men of the people fell that day.
> 29  Then Moses said, "Dedicate yourselves today to the LORD—for every man has been against his son and against his brother—in order that He may bestow a blessing upon you today."
>
> —Exodus 32

God, through Moses, commanded that the sons of Levi kill everyone who was worshiping the golden calf, whether it be his neighbor or even his brother. Verse 29 says that everyone who did that would receive a blessing from God.

The bloody scene of the sons of Levi taking their swords and either running them through the stomach of one of the idol worshipers or cutting off someone's head, even if it were someone that the sword bearer loved, is hard for us to even stomach as a scene, much less to attribute it to being something that God Himself ordered to occur. And yet this is the same God that we know and love and serve. He has not changed.

Christians have heard and read about demons and evil spirits. After King Saul had sinned and Samuel had anointed David as the replacement king for Saul, God took his revenge on Saul. We normally think of evil spirits as being directed and controlled by Satan, so what we find in 1 Samuel 16 may be surprising to many people:

14  Now the Spirit of the LORD departed from Saul, and an evil spirit from the LORD terrorized him.

15  Saul's servants then said to him, "Behold now, an evil spirit from God is terrorizing you.

16  "Let our lord now command your servants who are before you. Let them seek a man who is a skillful player on the harp; and it shall come about when the evil spirit from God is on you, that he shall play *the harp* with his hand, and you will be well."

—1 Samuel 16

Here we see that God Himself sent an evil spirit to torment and to terrorize Saul. In fact, the spirit drove him to do crazy things, as we read in 1 Samuel 18:

10  Now it came about on the next day that an evil spirit from God came mightily upon Saul, and he raved in the midst of the house, while David was playing *the harp* with his hand, as usual; and a spear *was* in Saul's hand.

11  And Saul hurled the spear for he thought, "I will pin David to the wall." But David escaped from his presence twice.

## GOD TAKES REVENGE

In most of the situations that we have just discussed, the people disobeyed or displeased God and He took revenge on them and punished them severely, in many cases actually causing their physical death.

Many of us have often read verse 19 of Romans 12:

19  Never take your own revenge, beloved, but leave room for the wrath *of God,* for it is written, "VENGEANCE IS MINE, I WILL REPAY," says the LORD.

However, when we see the wrath of God and the vengeance of God described in graphic detail in the Old Testament, we have a hard time handling it.

## THE FEAR OF THE LORD IS THE BEGINNING OF WISDOM

Would you like to be wise? Of course you would, and so would I. The Bible says that the place to begin in acquiring wisdom is to "fear the Lord." People had tried to whitewash or soften the word "fear" and to change it to words like "respect" and so forth. I believe that if the writers of the Bible had meant "respect," they would have said "respect." I think "fear" here is plain old vanilla *fear*. Children "fear" their parents because they know there is a spanking that comes if they do not obey them. If we want wisdom, we should have that same sort of fear of God, knowing that He has and does punish disobedience.

This is in no way an attempt to take away from the loving, forgiving, merciful side of God. What we are trying to do is bring out the neglected side of God's character that we don't particularly like to look at. God has many facets. He is tender, loving, and forgiving, and yet He is also a God of wrath, punishment, revenge and violence against those who disobey Him. Many times the Scriptures tell us that He is a jealous God (Exodus 34:14, for example).

Looking further at this neglected side, we find that, among other things, God:

1.   Ordered a man (Abraham) to kill his favorite son (Genesis 22:1, 2).

2.   Said He would visit His wrath unto the fourth generation, so that even unborn babies would be punished for their grandfather's sins (Deuteronomy 5:9).

3.   Killed the oldest child of all the Egyptians, whether or not they were against the Israelites leaving their country (Exodus 13:15).

4.   Sent a flood that killed everyone, except a small handful of people and animals. This means that little babies just a day or two old and the elderly were all drowned in the flood. (Genesis 7:5–22).

5.   Destroyed Sodom and Gomorrah by fire. Here again, even little babies one or two days old were killed, along with everyone else. (Genesis 19:24, 25).

## SPOILED CHILDREN

If parents are *only* gentle and forgiving and never punish and spank their children, the children wind up spoiled rotten and are a pain to be around. "Spare the rod and spoil the child." According to Proverbs 13:24, a parent who "spares the rod" hates his children, while those who really love their children discipline them diligently.

If God the Father is all sweetness and tenderness, and the fear of the paddle is removed, Christians with that view of God will become like spoiled children. Unfortunately, I think that is probably a description of the majority of the Christian churches in America today. They are spiritually soft and flabby; all they feel they have to do is "positively confess" and they can get what they want.

What they don't realize is that the disciplining hand of God is being raised and it is about to fall. Unfortunately, many spoiled children, when they get a rare spanking, tell their human father, "You don't love me anymore." (Do we do the same with God?)

Obviously it is not true, but the child feels this very strongly. When I was a small boy I remember my mother spanking me and telling me it hurt her worse than it did me. I used to think that was a bunch of baloney, but now I understand what she meant.

Whether the Father is dealing with us gently or spanking us, in either case, He is showing us how much He loves us. Also, in either role, He is holy, righteous and abhors that which is evil. He would never lead anyone to do anything that is evil, *according to HIS standards.* But His ways are not our ways, and His thoughts are not our thoughts (Isaiah 55:8, 9). Thus, some of the things that He may tell us to do can be confusing to us, as they possibly were to Abraham, Joshua, Elijah, Ehud and others that God asked to be instruments of His vengeance.

In no way is looking at this more realistic view of God a license to sin, to do wrong or evil. What we are seeking to do is to get to know God as He really is.

## GET TO KNOW THE REAL GOD

I would encourage you to read through the following books of the Old Testament and to ask God to show you afresh what He is really like:

| | |
|---|---|
| Genesis | 1 Kings |
| Exodus | 2 Kings |
| Joshua | Job |
| Judges | Psalms |
| 1 Samuel | Jeremiah |
| 2 Samuel | Ezekiel |

We tend to emphasize the loving, forgiving, merciful God and to ignore all of the other aspects of His character. We emphasize the characteristics of God that we think are "good" and skip over those that we would consider "less good" or, if we were really honest with ourselves, we would almost consider them "evil."

In Chapter 3, we said that we can either know God or we can know good and evil but we can't do both because they are mutually exclusive. As for me and my house, we will seek after the knowledge of God, rather than the knowledge of good and evil.

Bob Mumford has many excellent things to say. (I do not agree with everything he teaches but some of his teachings I consider outstanding.) In the November-December, 1980 issue of his bi-monthly newsletter, *Life Changers* (P.O. Box 22948, Fort Lauderdale, FL 33335), he had an article entitled "The Necessity of Knowing God." He has given us his permission to quote extensively from that article wherein he emphasizes the positive benefits of the knowledge of God. He has expressed it so beautifully that I see no reason to try to improve on it. In that issue he said the following:

> Satan is not concerned with the number of people who are saved in evangelistic campaigns or with believers who beat tambourines and shout, 'Praise the Lord!' He starts to tremble, however, when a Christian sets his heart to really know and fellowship with the Lord because the believer who really *knows* the Lord is a threat to Satan and his kingdom. . . .

### What Is The Knowledge Of God?

Knowledge, in the Scriptural sense, is a Hebrew concept that goes far beyond our Western understanding of knowledge as an intellectual comprehension or ascent to a set of facts. William Manchester wrote his best selling biography, *American Caesar,* covering the most minute and intimate details of General Douglas MacArthur's life. Manchester probably knew as much, if not more, about Douglas MacArthur than any man who actually was acquainted with the General himself. In spite of his great volumes of facts, Manchester never really *knew* MacArthur in a personal or intimate way. His knowledge and understanding of the man was gained through research and the testimony of those who did know him.

Do you believe that it is possible to be a Christian only from the eyebrows up? It is very easy for us to carry around a wealth of knowledge about the Lord that we have gained from research and listening to others who know Him; yet, we can be barren when it comes to really interacting and relating personally to the Lord. It is by interacting and being acquainted with the Lord that we gain the Scriptural knowledge of the Lord. Knowing God is more than the understanding gained by study and research, it is the knowledge that comes only from years of personal interaction and relationship with another Being.

How does a person begin to really *know* the Lord? Knowing God is, first of all, a *product of God's grace.* Unless God chooses to reveal Himself to us, He will never be known—it is a gift. Throughout the Scriptures we find God taking the initiative in unfolding His character and person to His people. Rarely do we find that a man sought the Lord. Always it is God looking, seeking, searching, and taking the initiative in love toward a people who have turned their back on Him. It doesn't make any difference how much a man searches for God, unless He wants to be found, the search is in vain. It has always been amusing that God can chase a man for years, sovereignly arrange people and circumstances in his life, run him down, get him broken and vulnerable in a corner, put His foot on his neck, and, at death's door, the man finally says, "Lord, I surrender!" The next night the man walks into a meeting and says, "Last night I *found* the Lord." Someone has said, "God is great, and therefore, He will be sought; He is good, and therefore, He will be found!"

Part of receiving God's revelation of Himself is learning to understand the package in which God sends it. In Psalm 73 we find an interesting scenario of a man who was enjoying God's goodness and lost his ability to understand how God was manifesting and revealing Himself to him. The Psalm begins, "The Lord is good to Israel!" Then, speaking of himself he says, ". . . as for me, my feet came close to stumbling. . . ." The Psalmist began to see all the problems in the world—he saw the prosperity of the wicked, their fat bodies, and the seeming lack of dealings and troubles of those who were not even trying to follow their God. He ends up saying, "In vain, I have kept my heart pure. . . ." He became senseless and ignorant; . . . like a beast before thee." (Cf vs. 22)

The Psalmist grumbled at God and said, "You've got it all messed up. You're not handling this thing right; the wrong people are being blessed and our people are getting the raw end of the deal!" He grumbled, complained, and questioned God's goodness because he didn't have the insight or understanding to see what God was doing —*until* he says, "I came into the sanctuary (presence and knowledge) of God." Once he came into the presence of God he received new insight and understanding on the situation and he "perceived their (the wicked) end."

We can beg and pray and say, "Oh, God, please speak to me. Reveal Yourself to me." All the time we are praying we don't realize that God *is revealing* Himself to us in a multitude of circumstances and situations that go on around us every day. The problem is our insensitivity and lack of insight into what God is doing. God desires to reveal Himself to his people *through* the circumstances and happenings of their everyday lives. It is too much of a habit, however, to brush daily occurrences aside and callously run on to "more important things" and not really see that all the while, God is working to bring us to a knowledge of Himself.

Our ability to interpret and understand what is happening will be largely based on two things: First, our knowledge and use of God's revelation of Himself in the Scriptures. I do not believe it is possible to really walk with the Lord apart from an active life in God's word. It is our primary source of spiritual food, comfort, knowledge, wisdom, direction, and insight.

Second, in our willingness to take the time and effort to become sensitive to the small voice within us and the working of God in our daily lives, much of our personal knowledge of God must come to us through our dealings with God. Just as we only know our husbands and wives through years of interaction and personal involvement with them, likewise, it is not possible to know the Lord without dealing with Him and getting to know Him on a personal basis. Many people are afraid, unwilling or do not understand how to really deal with the Lord God. All too often, we neglect to carry situations and circumstances to a final resolution and just let things slide along in our lives without ever inquiring of the Lord or seeking understanding on what is happening to us. It is a lot easier to let a difficult situation slide by and say benignly, "It was God's will," and never really take the time to pray, seek God and fast until we have the necessary insight and understanding to say, "God did thus and so and His purpose was this." Thomas Hood's powerful line describes the response perfectly, "Spontaneously to God should turn the soul, like the magnetic needle to the pole."

### The Knowledge Of God Brings . . .

How do you know that you *really* know the Lord? Apart from that personal and internal witness of the Holy Spirit that each of us must have, that we really *know* God, there are certain objective evidences in the life of the believer which we can see and measure.

• *The Knowledge of God brings life.* Jesus prayed in John 17:3, "This is eternal life, that they may *know* Thee the only true God. . . ." Eternal life is knowing God. I used to think that eternal life meant an unbroken duration of existence. We should realize that we would never want an unbroken existence if God was not there! Eternal life is not so much a length of time as it is a *quality* of existence in the presence of God. When a person knows the Lord in such a way as to actually *experience* the quality of life that God possesses, it shines out all over them. Some Christians mope around under a gloom cloud, overwhelmed by the circumstances, devoid of joy and peace, and generally defeated and miserable. They have no real knowledge of God because there is no *life* coming out of them. A person who is knowing and experiencing God's life can find joy and radiance even in the midst of the most difficult dealings and trials.

• *The Knowledge of God Transforms our life.* 2 Peter 2:20 says that we "have escaped the defilements of the world by the knowledge of the Lord Jesus Christ." Once we come to know God in a real way, we *cannot* remain the same. God said to me one time, "Bob, you and I are incompatible." As I pondered that for a few moments He added, "And I don't change!" Walking with God demands change. It is more, however, than a "bootstrap" change whereby we take on a new set of rules and regulations in order to reform our life. Knowing God motivates and energizes us deep in our being to bring about transformation we never thought possible.

• *The Knowledge of God changes our value system.* Heroes are not made by bravery, they are made by value systems. Shadrach, Meshach and Abednego were not anxious to go into the fiery furnace, but they had a value system that made death preferable to the transgression of their conscience and relationship with the Lord. A value system is impossible without the knowledge of Someone higher and absolute to Whom we have to answer for our actions. It means we will no longer be ruled by crowd pressure, the opinion polls, or what the situation dictates for the moment. This is why Daniel said, "those who knew their God would display strength and take action."

The answer for America today is not only a Christian president— it is for the Christians to change and get to know their God in some manner we have been missing until now. The hope of this nation is for a renewed and revived Body of Christ to rise up in the land and become a prophetic voice dropping the plumbline of God's Word in the name of the Scriptures and the law of God. But until the knowledge of God is burned across the tablets of our own hearts, we will not find the prophetic courage to speak out and be to our world what we need to be.

• *The Knowledge of God produces hope.* Hope means that we believe that at any time God could show up on the scene and change everything. He could save your son who is on drugs, miraculously heal your broken leg, or get rid of the Ayatollah Khomeni. We might say, "God doesn't always do those things!" No, He doesn't, that is why it is called hope! Hope is the ability, through the knowledge of God, to reach past the circumstances to an unseen security that God is in control and in the end will have the victory. The Scripture says hope is an "anchor of the soul." Anyone who has ever been on a boat during a storm knows that an anchor, locked securely onto a rock at the bottom of the sea, can be your only hope against being washed ashore and shipwrecked. Like an anchor, hope is able to reach beneath the stormy waves of life and lock securely onto the rock of Christ Jesus and hold us steady when everything around is awash and floundering in the midst of a storm.

• *The Knowledge of God is God taking us into His confidence.* There is no greater privilege than having God share with us what is on His mind. When God came down to destroy the cities of Sodom and Gomorrah, He said, "Shall I hide from Abraham what I am about to do?" (Gen. 18:17). When God begins to share with us what is on His mind, it means He is asking us to carry some of the burden of the things that weigh on Him. Many times, if we begin to carry a deep burden for another person or a particular project in the Kingdom of God that is the Lord's way of sharing His burdens and His mind with us as His people. Too often we look at those as *personal* burdens rather than understanding that the Lord is laying something on us to carry as one of His children.

Part of being in God's confidence is understanding that we must be involved in certain projects of His. God never places an ad in the morning paper saying, "Wanted. Preachers of the Gospel. Fifteen dollars an hour. Apply at the nearest church." God keeps His work within the family. As His kids, He is going to be calling on us from time to time to be involved in His work in the earth for the ongoing of the Gospel and the Kingdom of God.

• *The Knowledge of God means that we have influence with God.* Probably the surest way to know whether or not a man knows God and has influence with Him is by whether or not the Lord answers his prayers. A man who knows God and has His ear gets his prayers answered. The Lord said to Moses, "I am going to destroy Israel."

Moses protested, "Lord, You can't do that!" What about Your name?!"

God said, "Get out of My way, I am going to get rid of these people."

Moses argued, "God You can't do that, what about Your enemies?!"

Finally God agreed, "Okay, Moses, for your sake, I will let them alone." That is influence with God! For a man to stand and intercede with God, when He is angry, and turn His face back from judgment, requires a secure knowledge of God and one's position with Him.

That kind of influence, however, comes only on the basis of knowing God, being in His confidence, and walking with Him in a kind of intimate relationship that is only produced through the refinement, purging, and interactions with God.

As believers, we cannot afford to be sold short of the knowledge of God. It is all too easy to take the second best and settle for some religious or emotional side trip. There are a multitude of teachings, doctrines, and spiritual emphases today proclaiming secrets to maturity and all types of blessings by following their teachings or joining their groups. Usually these run dry for the individual after two to four years and he finds himself disillusioned, hungry, and longing for the simplicity of devotion to Christ which he knew when he first began to walk with Him. The knowledge of God is the only thing in his life of ultimate worth and it is also the most expensive thing we will ever seek to obtain. The prophet said that the knowledge of God would one day fill the earth "as the waters cover the sea." It is our privilege, as God's children, to begin to fill our lives with the knowledge of Him here and now.

This is the end of the quote from Bob Mumford's article. As you can see, it is incredibly important to know God and to seek the knowledge of God. We should yearn to know all about God, to know Him as He really is, and to know all of the different facets of His personality.

I believe that many people's image of God the Father is distorted and incomplete, even more so than their image of Christ. Once you break through the sugar-coated facade that people have built up around God the Father these past centuries and see Him as He really is, I believe that you will love Him more, worship Him more intensely, and yearn to please and glorify Him more than ever. This has certainly been the effect that it has had on me as I have grown to know God better.

This brings us to the major purpose for writing this chapter. If we are going to discourage people from relying on their knowledge of good and evil, we have an obligation to put something in its place. What we believe should be put in its place is knowing God and Jesus Christ better and more realistically and then doing God's will.

## GOD, OUR FATHER

Just as most Christians do not have a good picture of God's punishing, wrathful, vengeful side, they also have a very distorted image of God as a loving, heavenly Father.

Let's first examine the love of an earthly father for his son. If, as a small boy, the son attempts to build something for the first time—say a bookcase—it is likely that the saw cuts will not be very straight and it may take many bent nails to get one hammered in straight. The end result will look far from a beautiful, polished, finished piece of furniture. So what does the earthly father say to his son? He does not say:"You stupid, uncoordinated oaf. Look what a messy job you did. You should never try to do anything like that again!" Of course he would not say that, because he loves his son. Rather he tells him that it was a pretty good effort for the first try and, as he works with the tools more and more, he will get more proficient and will improve as times goes by. A loving earthly father encourages his children.

Similarly, if a boy is learning to play football and the first time he ever carries the ball, he either drops it or falls down, what does his father say? He does not say: "You clumsy ox— you fell down and dropped the ball! You should give up and never try carrying the ball again." Rather the loving earthly father picks up his son, dusts off his pants, gives him a swat on the seat and says, "Get back in there and try again; you'll do better next time."

When the son does something that is noteworthy the earthly father doesn't grumble at him, but he tells him how proud and pleased he is.

These are the kinds of expressions of love that an earthly father gives to his son. Do you not think that our heavenly Father is even more loving than any earthly father could ever be? I believe God is a far more loving Father than the most loving earthly father.

So what does God say to us when we slip and fall? He doesn't clobber us, but He picks us up, dusts us off, and encourages us. What happens when we try something for God that turns out to be quite imperfect? He doesn't tell us that we should never try again. What's more, He lets us know that we have made a good start and that next time we'll do better.

You might even ask yourself when you last heard God tell you, "I'm proud of you." Many Christians have never or rarely heard God say that to them. Yet God is a loving, heavenly Father and at various times He tells His children that He is proud of them. The problem is that we are simply not tuned in to hear it. The reason we are not tuned in is because of our distorted image of God. We can hardly bring ourselves to think of Him as a loving heavenly Father who encourages us and is proud of us when we do something good.

Dr. Robert Frost shared these and many other ideas with me about our loving heavenly Father. I would recommend his cassette album on "The Fatherhood of God," available from Ministries of Vision, Box 4636, Medford, Oregon 97501.

## AS THE END OF THE AGE APPROACHES

As the end of this age approaches and Christ's return becomes imminent, we are going to need a much more realistic image of God and His Son, Jesus Christ, so that we can understand what will be happening and know the Father's heart.

We should digress for a moment and look at the end of this age. At the end of Christ's ministry, His disciples came to Him and asked Him to tell them what things would be like at the end of the age preceding His return. This is recorded in Matthew 24:

> 3 And as He was sitting on the Mount of Olives, the disciples came to Him privately, saying, "Tell us, when will these things be, and what *will be* the sign of Your coming, and of the end of the age?"
>
> 4 And Jesus answered and said to them, "See to it that no one misleads you.
>
> 5 "For many will come in My name, saying 'I am the Christ,' and will mislead many.
>
> 6 "And you will be hearing of wars and rumors of wars; see that you are not frightened, for *those things* must take place, but *that* is not yet the end.
>
> 7 "For nation will rise against nation, and kingdom against kingdom, and in various places there will be famines and earthquakes.
>
> 8 "But all these things are *merely* the beginning of birth pangs.
>
> 9 "Then they will deliver you to tribulation, and will kill you, and you will be hated by all nations on account of My name.
>
> 10 "And at that time many will fall away and will deliver up one another and hate one another.
>
> 11 "And many false prophets will arise, and will mislead many.
>
> 12 "And because lawlessness is increased, most people's love will grow cold.

13 "But the one who endures to the end, he shall be saved.

14 "And this gospel of the kingdom shall be preached in the whole world for a witness to all the nations, and then the end shall come.

15 "Therefore when you see the ABOMINATION OF DESOLATION which was spoken of through Daniel the prophet, standing in the holy place (let the reader understand),

16 then let those who are in Judea flee to the mountains,

17 let him who is on the housetop not go down to get the things out that are in his house;

18 and let him who is in the field not turn back to get his cloak.

19 "But woe to those who are with child and to those who nurse babes in those days!

20 "But pray that your flight may not be in the winter, or on a Sabbath;

21 for then there will be a great tribulation, such as has not occurred since the beginning of the world until now, nor ever shall. . . ."

—Matthew 24

We see in this passage of Scripture that the great Tribulation starts at verse 21. However, in answering the question of what the end of the age would be like, Christ said that there would be a period of time that preceded the great Tribulation which He called "the time of birth pangs," during which there would be a world war, famine, earth upheavals, persecution of Christians and the gospel would be taken to all nations.

Regardless of what you believe about when the rapture might occur, we are all going through this time of birth pangs. If the rapture is before the great Tribulation, then it would occur between verses 20 and 21 of Matthew 24. Now let's relate our image of God to this time of birth pangs and to the great Tribulation.

## GOD IS IN CHARGE OF THE TRIBULATION

God and His Son, Jesus Christ, are in charge of the time of birth pains that precedes the great Tribulation and they are also in charge of the great Tribulation itself. Satan is definitely not in control of it.

More and more I am convinced that the time of birth pains that precedes the great Tribulation (described in Matthew 24) and the first six seals in Revelation 6 are describing the same events. We know that at God's instigation there is going to be a famine, even before the great Tribulation. We know that when God "pushes the button" (Christ breaks the seal) there is going to be another world war.

Many Christians would ask, "But how can a loving God do that?" What they are actually saying is that they don't truly know God as He really is. God has done these kinds of things in Old Testament and in New Testament times (remember that God struck Ananias and Sapphira dead for lying and stealing—Acts 5:1-10). I believe He is doing them today and through prophecy we know that He is going to do them again in the future.

Jesus Christ came the first time as a lamb; He's coming the second time as a lion. It is hard for us to imagine our sweet wonderful Jesus ruling the nations with a "rod of iron." Have you ever thought about what the rod of iron means? That means there will be harsh, firm discipline. When Christ comes back, He is going to begin His reign by killing all of the members of the army that is gathered at Armageddon (Revelation 19.11-21).

But back to the Tribulation and the time of birth pains . . . if we have a slanted image of what God is like and these terrible events do occur, at God's instigation, Christians are going to be shaken and distressed. On the other hand, if we have a realistic image of God and how He has operated through the centuries, then we will not be surprised when calamities come upon the earth.

## NOW IS THE TIME TO PREPARE

Once we begin to get to know God better, to love Him more and to have a healthy fear of Him, then we will begin to get our lives in order for what is coming. Spiritually we will allow God to purge out the corruption that remains and we will move increasingly into purity and holiness as we progress toward the holy of holies, because God is holy and pure.

We will make spiritual preparation in order to be part of the army of God rather than a civilian bystander. We will begin to learn now how to fight spiritual enemies (while loving them). We will learn to walk in the supernatural power of the Holy Spirit and to be sensitive to His guidance moment by moment. We will become overcomers, voluntary slaves of God.

As we get to know God and see what He is about to do to this earth, we will then be in a position to let Him guide us as to what financial and physical preparations to make. If a man is going to provide for his family, he needs to give much thought and prayer as to how he will provide food if there is a famine. (He could store food, or he could be in a position to raise his own or to hunt and fish for his food.)

There may be things in the financial area that God would have a Christian do to get ready for this coming time of birth pains. The deep desire of my heart is to do anything I can to help God's people see what is coming down the road and to help them prepare for it.

God has given me a real love and concern for people, especially those who belong to God through Jesus Christ, and I want to do all that I can to help them become more like our Savior and our wonderful heavenly Father. I also would hate to see them caught unprepared for what lies ahead of us, since it has been outlined in prophecy. Now is the appointed day to get your house in order and to get ready for what is coming. The first thing to do is to get to know the real God.

Remember that God dwells in the holy of holies. We can only enter the holy of holies (God's presence) through the blood of Christ. This means that if we want to come in close to God and to really know Him, we have to be willing to have all evil purged from our lives and to be washed clean by Jesus' blood. God wants holy and righteous Christians to draw closer to Him and to know Him as they have never known Him before.

This concept of Christians moving into the holy of holies deals with the symbolic significance of the tabernacle. The tabernacle is one of the major Old Testament pictures of the progression in the life of a Christian. We will develop this exciting concept in the next chapter.

# 6

# THE PROGRESSION OF A CHRISTIAN

Before we discuss what a bondslave is and what is involved in being one, we would like to take a step backward and view the life of a Christian in its totality.

In the Old Testament there are three major pictures, or types, of the life of a Christian. Each of these are divided into three parts (three being a number reminiscent of the Trinity). These types in the Old Testament are the tabernacle, the Feasts, and the movement of the children of Israel from Egypt to the promised land.

## THE TABERNACLE

As we begin to look at the tabernacle, we should first examine it as it was in the Old Testament. Here is a diagram of it:

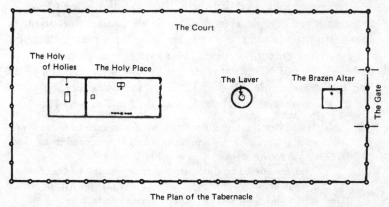

The Plan of the Tabernacle

Figure 6.1

To refresh your memory, there was the outer court where the people could come to bring their sacrifices. Then there was the holy place, where the priests could go, but not the rest of the people. At the very core was the holy of holies where God dwelt, and only the high priest could go in there and, at that, he could only go in once a year. If we correlate this to the progression of the Christian's life today, we would have to say that all those who are outside the tabernacle would represent the non-Christians. These are the people who do not know Christ as Savior. (I repeat what I said in the first chapter: if you are reading this and you are not absolutely sure that if you died tonight you would go to be with God because of your relationship with Jesus Christ, I would encourage you to pause and read Appendix A entitled "How To Become A Christian.")

One enters the tabernacle by the door or the gate. We know that Christ is the door and the way to God and that no one can come to God except by Him (John 14:6). Thus, we enter through the gate into the outer court. The "outer court" Christians are those who have received Christ as their Savior, but they have never been baptized (filled) with the Holy Spirit.

In the holy place are those Christians who are Spirit baptized (Spirit filled). Many "outer court" Christians yearn to be baptized with the Holy Spirit and to move into the holy place and a closer walk with God. Perhaps as you read this book, the Spirit can and will do this for you. For an outer court Christian to become a holy place (Spirit-baptized) Christian, it requires going first to the altar in the tabernacle. This means that you need to truly present yourself as a living sacrifice to God and be willing to lay down your life for Jesus Christ in order to be Spirit baptized and enter into the holy of holies. Placing yourself on the altar in this manner is described in Romans 12:

> 1  I urge you therefore, brethren, by the mercies of God, to present your bodies a living and holy sacrifice, acceptable to God, *which is* your spiritual service of worship.
> 2  And do not be conformed to this world, but be transformed by the renewing of your mind, that you may prove what the will of God is, that which is good and acceptable and perfect.

We have already discussed these verses twice. We discussed "renewing" our minds, which means making our minds like Adam's mind was before the fall. We also discussed presenting our bodies piece by piece to Christ as a living sacrifice. I believe this is a prerequisite to our being baptized in the Spirit and moving into the holy place.

Some of you reading this book may know that you have received Christ and that you are Christians, but perhaps you have never been baptized in the Holy Spirit. It may be that you are on a spiritual plateau. God is blessing you and everything is fine, but if you look at where you are now spiritually and where you were a year or two ago, you may be at about the same place. If you are satisfied with where you are in Christ Jesus, there is a good chance that you, like the Pharisees, have "earplugs" in and are not open to what God is trying to teach you. I would encourage you to ask God to get rid of the earplugs and to open your heart and give you a real hunger to move into the deeper things of God.

## BEING BAPTIZED (FILLED) WITH THE HOLY SPIRIT

I was raised as a Methodist and tended to discount (discard is probably a better word) anything concerning being baptized with the Holy Spirit. We thought that those who taught such a thing were trying to say that we needed a "second blessing" and, hence, we tended to look down our noses at them. However, now that I have grown in the Lord, I have discovered that the Bible states clearly that there is indeed a "second blessing." There is something beyond salvation that God wants to give to us and that is the baptism in the Holy Spirit. (Actually I prefer the expression to be "filled with the Holy Spirit," but that term is so misused that I will use "baptized in the Holy Spirit"). Let's read about this in Acts 8:

14 Now when the apostles in Jerusalem heard that Samaria had received the word of God, they sent them Peter and John,

15 who came down and prayed for them, that they might receive the Holy Spirit.

16   For He had not yet fallen upon any of them; they had simply been baptized in the name of the Lord Jesus.

17   Then they *began* laying their hands on them, and they were receiving the Holy Spirit.

These verses tell us that people in Samaria had received Jesus Christ and had been baptized in the name of the Lord Jesus. Evidently, though, there was something they still lacked. Therefore, the disciples in Jerusalem sent Peter and John all the way up to Samaria to help them get this thing that they lacked, even though they indeed believed in Christ.

From Jerusalem to Samaria is very rugged terrain. The journey by foot was long and hard, and it must have taken Peter and John at least a couple of days. Yet they were willing to walk all that distance and risk the dangers of the rugged countryside in order that the believers in Christ in Samaria might receive the baptism of the Holy Spirit. That is how important it was to Peter and John, and they should have known the importance, because they walked and talked and lived with Jesus Christ.

When Peter and John got to Samaria, they prayed for the Christians there and they received the baptism of the Holy Spirit. I believe it is as important for Christians today to be baptized in the Holy Spirit as it was in this incident when Peter and John went to Samaria. There has been much confusion on the baptism of the Holy Spirit; perhaps I can clear up some of it, as I share with you the things that God has laid on my heart concerning it.

The first question that comes is: "How does a Christian know whether or not he has been baptized in the Holy Spirit?" I believe that when a Christian is baptized in the Holy Spirit, something supernatural (unexplainable in human terms) happens to him or through him. The supernatural thing might be seeing a vision; it might be praying for someone and he is healed; it might be prophesying, singing in the Spirit, performing a miracle, speaking in tongues or something else. I do not believe that it has to be speaking in tongues, although that is the most common manifestation of the baptism of the Holy Spirit. The Holy Spirit will give each person whatever gift He wants him to have (1 Corinthians 12:1-11). But it will be something miraculous that can't be explained in human terms. If you have never had something supernatural happen to you or through you, there is a good chance that you have not yet been baptized in the Holy Spirit.

If you think you might have been baptized in the Holy Spirit but are unsure, I would encourage you to ask God to give you afresh a supernatural confirmation of your baptism in the Holy Spirit.

If you are an "outer court" Christian and you would like to be baptized in the Holy Spirit (you have accepted Jesus Christ as your Lord and Savior and would like the power of God's Spirit operating in your life), the logical question is, how do you receive this? There is much confusion on the subject, which there need not be. I would like to relate something that happened to me one time when I was ministering at a church in Minnesota.

Rarely at the end of a message do I feel impressed of the Holy Spirit to give an invitation. Even more rarely do I ask for those who want to be baptized in the Holy Spirit to come forward. But on this particular Sunday I felt the Lord wanted me to do this. So I asked any of those who would like to receive the baptism of the Holy Spirit to come forward. The pastor suggested that they go into a back room, which they did. I stayed out front and counseled and prayed with a few people and about ten minutes later I went back and joined them in this room.

What I saw there really grieved my spirit. The man trying to help these people receive the baptism of the Spirit was telling them to drop their jaws, to hold up their hands, not to say anything in English, to make sounds and so forth. I thought, "Oh my! There is no way they are going to receive the baptism of the Holy Spirit this way!" So I asked the man if I could say something. (Since I was the visiting minister, he just about had to say yes.)

I then related to these precious brothers and sisters how I had initially received the baptism of the Holy Spirit. It had occurred a number of years before when I was flying from Houston to Dallas. This particular plane had a compartment up front with eight seats that was totally isolated from the rest of the cabin. I was the only one in this front compartment and I began to pray, as I frequently do on a flight. As I talked to God, I began to tell Him how wonderful, glorious, magnificent and all-powerful He was and to thank Him that He was so holy, pure and righteous. Pretty soon my human words seemed so inadequate to express what I was feeling toward God. I then began what I call "spiritual humming." (I have only heard one other person do this since then.) As the pitch of my hum went up it seemed like it touched God and as the pitch of the humming came down it was as though it touched my heart. I sat there humming from high notes to low notes, to high notes to low notes, communing with God, praising Him, worshiping Him, and adoring Him in a way that was above and beyond what I could do in English words.

After sharing this experience, I encouraged the people who had come forward to get their minds off of the gifts of the Spirit or speaking in tongues and just to begin to worship and praise God. I told them that when English became totally inadequate to express their adoration, God would take over beyond that.

That evening several of these people came up to me stating that they had received the baptism of the Holy Spirit during the afternoon between the morning and the evening services. I particularly remember one young man who came up to me with tears in his eyes. He said that for eight years he had been seeking the baptism of the Holy Spirit and that every time an invitation was given for those who wanted to receive the baptism of the Spirit, he came forward. Evidently he had been forward literally dozens of times during this eight-year period. However, he had never received the baptism of the Holy Spirit.

With tears rolling down his cheeks, he related to me how driving home from church that morning, after I had shared what God had laid on my heart, he began to praise the Lord and, as his words became inadequate, he began to fluently speak and sing in another tongue. He said that he wanted to jump and dance all over the place and had to pull his car to the side of the road and stop, because he was afraid he would have an accident. He said that he was so grateful to me for helping him get his eyes off of the gifts of the Spirit and the baptism of the Holy Spirit and helping him to refocus on God and on Jesus Christ.

I might relate one other incident about a friend of mine who was a dedicated Christian but had recently left the church that he had been attending. His daughter started going to an Assembly of God church with a friend of hers. One Sunday morning when he picked her up after church, she had tears in her eyes and she said, "Daddy, this morning I was baptized in the Spirit and spoke in tongues." This really shook up my friend because he did not believe that those things were for today. He went home and after lunch went into his bedroom alone, knelt down beside the bed and began to talk to God. He said, "God, if this is of You, I want it. I want all that you have for me." As he was praying, a glorious light came upon him and he began to praise God in heavenly singing that was not in English.

I could write an entire book on our relationship with the Holy Spirit. We certainly receive the Holy Spirit when we receive Christ. He comes to indwell us and to seal us (2 Corinthians 1:22; Ephesians 1:13, 14). However, being baptized with the Holy Spirit is something that *can* occur when we receive Christ but frequently occurs later in our Christian life. If you wish to pursue the subject, I would recommend this book:

> *Nine O'Clock In The Morning,* by Dennis Bennett
> Logos International
> Plainfield, NJ 07060

As we are baptized in the Holy Spirit we move from the outer court into the holy place. There God's Spirit, in a new and more powerful way, begins to nurture us and to use us. He gives us gifts to build up the body of Christ, to help other Christians grow to the maturity and likeness of Jesus Christ our Savior. When we are filled with the Holy Spirit, we are controlled by Him and we are at His disposal as His tools. However, many Christians who have been baptized in the Spirit have frequent lapses, sometimes of long duration, when they are not living filled with the Holy Spirit and their lives are no better, and frequently worse, than those of Christians in the outer court. Sanctification is a process by which a larger and larger percentage of the time we are filled with, and controlled by, the Holy Spirit.

## THE HOLY OF HOLIES

Unfortunately many people who have been baptized in the Holy Spirit think that that's the end of the road and that there is nothing beyond it. I have news for them—there is a giant step beyond that. That is moving into the holy of holies. This means moving into the realm of a bondslave or an overcomer. Below we have repeated the diagram of the tabernacle, adding the groups of people that each area represents today.

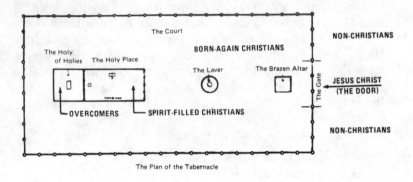

Figure 6.2

We will not discuss bondslaves and overcomers here because that is the message of the remainder of this book. Let me just say this to you: If you have already been baptized in the Holy Spirit, the remainder of this book could contain some of the most important teachings that you will ever read, other than the Bible, of course. God wants you to move deeper into Himself. He wants you to progressively live a more holy and righteous life. This book can be a road map to point the way.

## THE THREE FEASTS

Just as with the tabernacle, the Feasts of the Lord in the Old Testament reveal to us a progression or a "road map" of what God desires for our Christian lives. There were seven convocations in the Old Testament times, but these were grouped into three major feasts. This is depicted in the diagram below:

| CONVOCATION | FEAST |
|---|---|
| Passover (Leviticus 23:5) <br> Unleavened Bread (Leviticus 23:6) <br> Firstfruits (Leviticus 23:10) | Passover |
| Pentecost (Leviticus 23:15–16) | Pentecost |
| Trumpets (Leviticus 23:24) <br> Day of Atonement (Leviticus 23:27) <br> Tabernacles (Leviticus 23:34) | Tabernacles |

Figure 6.3

These feasts are described in Chapter 23 of Leviticus. You can take your time and read about them if you wish to pursue the subject. In summary, the three major feasts are:

1. The Feast of the Passover
2. The Feast of Pentecost
3. The Feast of Tabernacles (Booths)

These three feasts have New Testament counterparts. The New Testament equivalent of the Passover occurred with the sacrifice of Jesus Christ on the cross, His death, burial and resurrection. He provided the "blood of the Lamb" to protect us and save us from our sins.

The feast of Pentecost is also called "the Feast of Weeks" (Deuteronomy 16:10) and "the Feast of Harvest" (Exodus 23:16). The term "Pentecost" tells of its relation in time to the

Passover (fifty days from the day after the Sabbath of the Passover). The New Testament equivalent of the Feast of Pentecost occurred when the Holy Spirit filled or baptized the early disciples at Pentecost, as is described in Acts 2.

I do not believe that we have yet had the New Testament equivalent of the Feast of the Tabernacles (or Feast of Booths, as it is sometimes referred to), but I feel that it will occur soon. During the Feast of the Tabernacles in the Old Testament, there was the Day of Atonement and the annual day (Yom Kippur) when the high priest went into the holy of holies. But also as part of this feast the people left their homes, went out into the wilderness and built themselves a tabernacle or a "booth" (we would call it a "lean to") and lived there for seven days. They spent that time fasting, meditating and communicating with God. When they came out of their booths or tabernacles and came back together, they had a great feast—the greatest feast of the year—with rejoicing, singing, dancing and banqueting. The New Testament equivalent of this feast will probably have its culmination when Christ returns to the earth to dwell (tabernacle Himself) with us here on the earth for one thousand years. Then indeed will be the greatest feast of all, celebrated with great rejoicing.

## THE THREE FEASTS—A TYPE OF OUR CHRISTIAN LIFE

Just as the three areas of the tabernacle depicted a progression in our Christian life, so do these three major feasts from the Old Testament.

We begin our life as a Christian at the Feast of the Passover. There are things from that Feast that we need to apply to our personal lives. When we become Christians, we apply the blood of the Lamb (the blood of Jesus Christ, the only begotten Son of God) to our lives to wash away our sins and make us as white as snow. This is the salvation experience, when the "death angel"—that of eternal, spiritual death—passes over us because of the blood of Christ. We are saved from the eternal death that we deserve for our sins, because we have applied the blood of the Lamb to our lives. It is here that we have an encounter with Jesus Christ, God's Son.

It is God's desire, I believe, that we do not remain at the Feast of the Passover but move on to the Feast of Pentecost. This is where, just like the early apostles, the Holy Spirit is applied to our lives and we receive the filling with the Spirit (or baptism of the Spirit), as we discussed earlier in this chapter. God gives us supernatural power and we allow Him to control us to the extent that He can use us as tools for His eternal purpose. At this Feast we have an encounter with the Holy Spirit.

As we mentioned earlier, some people think that the Feast of Pentecost is the end of the road—that once they have arrived there, there is nothing beyond it. What they don't realize is that in reality the Feast of Pentecost is simply the "halfway" point, if you wish to think of it that way.

A Christian can choose to remain at the Feast of Pentecost or he can choose to go on to the Feast of Tabernacles. (God always gives us the choice to move on into a deeper relationship with Him or to stay where we are. He won't force you now anymore than He did when you first received Christ into your heart and life.) In the Feast of the Tabernacles, I believe that we have a major encounter with the third person of the Trinity, the Lord God Almighty (God the Father). Of course, we can only do this through His Son, Jesus Christ, but many people emphasize Christ almost to the exclusion of God the Father.

Christ's real purpose in coming was to bring us into a right relationship with our Father God. As we move through the Feast of the Passover and the Feast of Pentecost, we are dying to that which is illegal, that which is overt sin. However, as we move on to the Feast of Tabernacles and encounter God's purifying power, His holiness and His righteousness, we also learn to die to that which is legal for us to do. We begin to die to ourselves, to the desires of our flesh, and we yearn to be God's holy and pure servants or slaves.

There is an excellent book written on these three Feasts that we have been discussing. It is entitled *The Feasts of the Lord,* by Dr. Robert Thompson, who is a renowned Bible scholar and teacher. His forthcoming book, *What Comes After Pente-*

*cost?*, will deal in depth with the Feast of Tabernacles. Both of these books should be available in most Christian bookstores or can be obtained directly from the publisher: Omega Publications, Box 4130, Medford, Oregon 97501. I would encourage you to get copies of these books and to pursue this subject. There are so many beautiful concepts and insights involved with these Feasts that can enhance and enrich your Christian life.

## DELIVERANCE, TRAINING, CONQUEST

We again see this three stage progression with the children of Israel in the Old Testament when they came out of Egypt, lived for forty years in the wilderness, and then moved into the promised land. When they were being *delivered* from Egypt, God took all the initiative and did all the fighting for them. This stage is equivalent to when one first becomes a Christian: God takes the initiative in bringing us to Christ and in the early days of our Christian life He does much of the fighting for us.

The children of Israel then went through a time of *training* in the wilderness. The training was both physical and spiritual: they had to learn to trust God to provide for their physical needs and to get by on what He provided, and they also had to learn to be obedient to God. However, in the physical realm, God took them from being a group of rag-tag slaves and molded them into an incredible fighting machine. They became a powerful and efficient army. This time of training is equivalent to the stage of our being baptized (or filled) with the Holy Spirit and learning to walk under the anointing and power of the Holy Spirit. The sooner we learn to do this, the sooner we can move on to the next exciting step; remember, the children of Israel wandered in the wilderness as long as they did because of disobedience.

After the training experience, God took the children of Israel in to *conquer* the promised land. In this stage of conquest, the soldiers in the Israeli army did most of the fighting. God occasionally miraculously intervened but basically, as they obeyed God and listened to Him, He led them in such a way that they could do their own fighting and win. This is equivalent to the stage of being an overcomer in our experience. So here again you can see that there is a giant step beyond being filled with the Holy Spirit and that is in the realm of *conquest,* where God expects us to do the fighting.

The bringing of Israel out of Egypt and into the promised land is dealt with in a beautiful way in Robert Thompson's book, *The Land of Promise* (also available from Omega Publications). He points out that, just as with the children of Israel, our promised land is occupied by evil forces. He goes on to say that God wants to train us to invade, fight, and overthrow those forces that occupy our promised land. I found the book to be inspirational and helpful.

## BROTHER, WORKER, SOLDIER

In the New Testament, we see the same three-stage progression in the book of Philippians, as Paul was talking about his good friend Epaphroditus:

> 25 But I thought it necessary to send to you Epaphroditus, my brother and fellow worker and fellow soldier, who is also your messenger and minister to my need; . . .
>
> —Philippians 2

Here we see that Paul calls Epaphroditus:

1. brother
2. fellow worker
3. fellow soldier

I see here the same progression that we saw in the Old Testament examples. When a person becomes a Christian, he is our *brother.* This corresponds to the "outer court Christian" in the diagram of the tabernacle, the "Feast of the Passover Christian," and the "delivered Christian" in our last example. Someone at this stage knows Christ as his Savior, but that is as far as he has gone.

The *fellow worker* stage would correspond to the "holy place Christian," the "Feast of Pentecost Christian," and the

Christian "in training" (in the wilderness). These are Christians who have been baptized or filled with the Holy Spirit and they are doing work for God in the power of the Holy Spirit.

Yet there is a third stage—that of being a *soldier*. This would correspond with the "holy of holies Christian," the "Feast of Tabernacles Christian," and the "conquering Christian." This is the stage of being an overcomer.

God wants us to progress through these three stages and to move into the third stage. If you have just received Christ, you can know that there are two more stages ahead of you. If you have been baptized in the Holy Spirit, you are only at the midpoint. There is much more yet ahead.

## SUMMARY AND CONCLUSION

Both the Old and New Testament patterns that we examined in this chapter involved three progressive stages. The tabernacle of the Old Testament comprised the outer court, the holy place and the holy of holies. In the progression of our Christian lives, there are the following three stages. There are "outer court" Christians, who have been born again (they have received Christ as their personal Savior), but they have not progressed beyond that point. In the holy place there are Christians who have been baptized with the Holy Spirit and have received some supernatural gift from the Holy Spirit. They are moving in the realm of the Spirit. In the holy of holies there are Christians who are overcomers, or bondslaves, who are willing to die to self and to live holy, righteous lives, dedicated wholly to God.

Similarly, in the three major Feasts in the Old Testament, we saw this same progression. The Feast of the Passover represents the salvation experience, where we apply the blood of the Lamb to our lives to protect us and to save us. The Feast of Pentecost represents the baptism in the Holy Spirit, wherein He comes upon us and empowers us to live a life more glorifying to the Lord. Each Christian can choose to remain at Passover or at Pentecost or he can choose to move on to the Feast of Tabernacles. As we move on to Tabernacles and have an encounter with God the Father, we begin to die to that which is legal, to become more holy, pure and righteous in our living and to voluntarily become God's slaves.

We also looked at the three stages in God delivering the children of Israel from Egypt and taking them into the promised land. There was the phase of *deliverance,* wherein God took the initiative and *He* did the fighting. Then there was the phase of *training* in the wilderness, wherein the children of Israel learned to trust and obey God spiritually. Physically, they also learned to use weapons of war and to become an efficient army. The third was a stage of *conquest,* wherein God led them into the promised land that was occupied by evil forces. Here the children of Israel did the majority of fighting, with God only occasionally intervening miraculously.

In the New Testament example given, we saw the same three-stage progression. The first stage was that of being a *brother.* This would be anybody who has received Christ as Savior. The next step would be moving into the *fellow worker* realm, which we equate with being baptized in the Holy Spirit, or filled with the Holy Spirit, and learning to walk in His power. The third stage was that of being a *soldier.* This book is primarily about that third stage.

Even Christ's teaching reflects this progression in the life of His followers. Early in His ministry He taught His disciples to *believe in Him* for salvation. Later, when He appeared to them after His death and resurrection, He commanded them to wait for the promise of the Father—the baptism with the Holy Spirit (Acts 1:3-5). In His letters to the seven churches in Revelation 2 and 3, Christ addresses the third stage—that of being an overcomer.

We believe that there are two terms used for Christians who are at the third stage: "overcomers" and "bondslaves." We mentioned these terms briefly in Chapter 1 and, as we proceed, we will see further evidence that these are different names for the same group of people. These are names for those Christians who have moved on into the holy of holies or who have progressed to the Feast of Tabernacles. In the next chapter, we will deal with the "bondslave" aspect of this group of Christians and, in the following chapter, with the "overcomer" aspect.

# 7

# GOD'S BONDSLAVES

The title of this chapter is "God's Bondslaves." An even better title would probably be "God's Volunteer Permanent Slaves." When we think of the word "slave" we think of those people of Africa who were captured by force, taken to America and forced into slavery. We also might think of slaves in the ancient times, such as under the Roman Empire, when a country was captured and some or most of the people in the captured country were forced into slavery at the hands of the victors. Of course, children born to slave parents were born into slavery. Thus, our basic concept of slavery is that people are either forced into it or born into it.

It would be almost impossible for most people to conceive of a free person walking up to a slave master and volunteering to become a permanent slave. To us this would almost seem like an act of a psychotic, a sadist, or a lunatic. As we will see later in this chapter, that is precisely what God asks us to do. To those who don't know God and Christ in an intimate way, to do so may indeed seem like lunacy or psychotic behavior, but those who know God well realize that it is the only path to victory and an overcoming life.

## THE DIFFERENCE BETWEEN A SLAVE
## AND A SERVANT

Unfortunately, some of the newer translations of the Bible use the words *slave* and *servant* almost interchangeably. In many instances where the word would more accurately be translated "bondslave," it is unfortunately translated "bond-servant." The terms *slave* and *servant* are far from interchangeable.

A servant gets paid a wage, however small it may be. That servant then can go out and buy with that wage anything he or she wants to buy. The servant also has days off, during which he can do anything that he desires. Thus, he has control over a good portion of his life. Servants may live in virtual poverty, or have a low standard of living, but they are still in control of their spending and a portion of their time.

On the other hand, a slave never receives any money of his own whatsoever. Anything that he wants he must ask of his master. If he wants some new clothes, he must ask his master for them. His master may say "yes" or "no" and, if the answer is "yes," he might also specify what kind and what color. If the slave wants to take a wife, he goes and asks his master if he may have one. His master answers "yes" or "no." If the answer is "yes," the master can also decide who the slave must marry. The slave has no "rights" to marry whomever he pleases. He does his master's bidding. If the slave wants to live in a different house, have a piece of furniture or anything else, he cannot make the decision himself for he has no money to purchase these items; he must go to the master and ask him and then do whatever the master says or receive whatever the master gives.

Similarly, there is never any time at all when the slave is not a slave. He doesn't have any "days off." His time is 100 percent under the control of his master. He may be dead tired and need a vacation, but if his master says, "Work," he works. He may be sick, but if his master tells him to do something, the slave must do it, in spite of his sickness. *His time is not his own.*

In the time of the feudal lords where there were feudal slaves, the slaves were used as part of the army of the feudal lord in the event of any attack. Thus, if a master told a slave to go out into battle and charge up a particular hill, the slave had to do it, even if it meant his death. For a person to voluntarily become a slave, he was voluntarily making a commitment to die for his master, if his master wanted him to die, to have no possessions except what the master gave him, to have no discretionary spending money of his own, to have no time of his own and no rights at all. As you can see, being a slave is far, far different from being a servant. If one is a servant, one can quit whenever one wants to. If one is a slave, one can never quit.

Now let's take a look at bondslaves in the Old Testament, followed by bondslaves in the New Testament, and then examine what implications it has for you and me.

## A BONDSLAVE IN THE OLD TESTAMENT

The concept of a bondslave (a voluntary slave) in the Old Testament is found in many places. One of the best descriptions of it is in Deuteronomy:

> 12 "If your kinsman, a Hebrew man or woman, is sold to you, then he shall serve you six years, but in the seventh year you shall set him free.
>
> 13 "And when you set him free, you shall not send him away empty-handed.
>
> 14 "You shall furnish him liberally from your flock and from your threshing floor and from your wine vat; you shall give to him as the LORD your God has blessed you.
>
> 15 "And you shall remember that you were a slave in the land of Egypt, and the LORD your God redeemed you; therefore I command you this today.
>
> 16 "And it shall come about if he says to you, 'I will not go out from you,' because he loves you and your household, since he fares well with you;
>
> 17 then you shall take an awl and pierce it through his ear into the door, and he shall be your servant forever. And also you shall do likewise to your maidservant.
>
> 18 "It shall not seem hard to you when you set him free, for he has given you six years *with* double the service of a hired man; so the LORD your God will bless you in whatever you do. . . ."
>
> —Deuteronomy 15

As you can see in this passage, if a person has come to be your temporary slave, for whatever reason—whether because he owed you money or because he sold himself to you to raise money—at the end of the seventh year, you were to set him free. When you set him free, you were to give him some of your material possessions so that he did not go away empty-handed.

On the other hand, he could say to you that he did not want to go away and be free again, but instead he wanted to voluntarily become your permanent slave (bondslave). If he told you that, you would stand him against the doorpost and pierce his ear with an awl, a nail or something of that nature. The pierced ear was the mark of a permanent slave. Since he was not born into slavery, but he voluntarily became a permanent slave, he was called a bondslave.

I used to think of this passage only from the master's viewpoint. He had gotten a slave for life who would have to do his bidding, work for him, fight for him and even die for him. But as I reread it considering the slave's side, I realized that the master was also taking on the obligation and responsibility to care for that slave for the rest of his life, to protect him and to provide for him. It required a two-sided commitment, the master and the slave each committing themselves to the other and each assuming a certain responsibility.

What would cause an individual to voluntarily become a permanent slave? One certainly would not want to do so if the master were cruel, harsh or unjust. However, if the master were loving, kind, considerate and just, and if serving him were a joy, one might well consider being a voluntary permanent slave. Even though a slave might live in material luxury, he still had no freedoms of his own.

This concept of voluntarily becoming a permanent slave, because of love for the master, is recorded in Exodus:

1 "Now these are the ordinances which you are to set before them.

2 "If you buy a Hebrew slave, he shall serve for six years; but on the seventh he shall go out as a free man without payment.

3 "If he comes alone, he shall go out alone; if he is the husband of a wife, then his wife shall go out with him.

4 "If his master gives him a wife, and she bears him sons or daughters, the wife and her children shall belong to her master, and he shall go out alone.

5 "But if the slave plainly says, 'I love my master, my wife and my children; I will not go out as a free man,'

> 6  then his master shall bring him to God, then he shall bring him
> to the door or the doorpost. And his master shall pierce his ear with
> an awl; and he shall serve him permanently. . . ."
>
> —Exodus 21

I think this is a very beautiful passage because the temporary slave plainly says that he is staying because he loves his master.

This also clearly affirms that even a temporary slave had no rights at all. If the master had given the slave a wife and they had children, the wife and the children still belonged to the master. If the slave decided to leave, he had to leave his wife and children with the master. As you can see, when one is a slave, everything that person has, including his wife (or her husband) and children, belong to the master and not to the slave. Yet that is a temporary condition of one who is a temporary slave, but if one volunteers to become a permanent slave, that becomes a permanent condition.

## SLAVES VERSUS SERVANTS

In the Hebrew of the Old Testament, there are two distinct words for *servant* and *slave,* servant being one who hired and a slave being one who doesn't receive wages, and who is more of a possession of his master.

The Hebrew word for "servant" is SAKIYR (7916 in *Strong's Exhaustive Concordance* by James Strong, published by Word Books, Waco, Texas). *Strong's* gives the definition of this word as:

> "Sakiyr, a man *at wages* by the day or year:—hired (man, servant), hireling."

This Hebrew word SAKIYR is found in such places as Leviticus 22. In the *New American Standard Bible,* it has been translated as "hired man" in this instance:

> 10  No layman, however, is to eat the holy *gift;* a sojourner with
> the priest or a hired man shall not eat of the holy *gift.*
>
> —Leviticus 22

On the other hand, the Hebrew word for "slave" or a "person in bondage" (which implies slavery) is 'EBED (5650 in *Strong's Exhaustive Concordance*). *Strong's* gives the definition of 'EBED as:

" 'ebed, a *servant:* x bondage, bondman, [bond-] servant, (man-) servant."

Whenever the Old Testament talks about being a "bondservant," the Hebrew word 'EBED is used. This really means a servant who is not hired, but one who is indeed a slave, in permanent or semipermanent bondage to his master.

Turning to the New Testament, again we find that there are distinct words for slave and for servant (hired servant). The word for a slave or bondslave is DOULOS and the two Greek words for servant are OIKETES and THERAPON. Both of these latter words have the concept of a hired servant. OIKETES (3610 in *Strong's Exhaustive Concordance)* is defined as:

"Oiketes; a fellow *resident,* i.e., menial *domestic:* —(household) servant."

In the original language, this word is used in passages such as the following; here it has been translated "servant":

4 Who are you to judge the servant of another? To his own master he stands or falls; and he will, for the Lord is able to make him stand.

—Romans 14

13 "No servant can serve two masters; for either he will hate the one, and love the other, or else he will hold to one, and despise the other. You cannot serve God and mammon."

—Luke 16

The other word for a hired servant in New Testament Greek, THERAPON *(Strongs, 2324)*, is defined by *Strong* as:

"Therapon; a menial *attendant* (as if *cherishing):* — servant."

This is used rarely in the New Testament, as in Hebrews 3:

> 5 Now Moses was faithful in all His house as a servant, for a testimony of those things which were to be spoken later; . . .

However, the Greek word for slave or bondslave, DOULOS *(Strong's,* 1401), is defined as:

> "Doulos; a *slave* (lit. or fig., invol. or vol.; frequently therefore in a qualified sense of *subjection* or *subserviency): —* bond (-man), servant."

This is the word used whenever the New Testament talks of Paul being a bondslave of Christ or any other time slavery is mentioned. Now let's look in detail at some of the instances in the New Testament where someone was a "DOULOS, of God," or a slave of God or of Christ.

## BONDSLAVES IN THE NEW TESTAMENT

We find many examples of people who were called bondslaves of God in the New Testament. One of the first and most beautiful is found in Luke:

> 25 And behold, there was a man in Jerusalem whose name was Simeon; and this man was righteous and devout, looking for the consolation of Israel; and the Holy Spirit was upon him.
> 26 And it had been revealed to him by the Holy Spirit that he would not see death before he had seen the Lord's Christ.
> 27 And he came in the Spirit into the temple; and when the parents brought in the child Jesus, to carry out for Him the custom of the Law,
> 28 then he took Him into his arms, and blessed God, and said,
> 29 "Now Lord, Thou dost let Thy bond-servant depart
> In peace, according to Thy word;
> 30 For my eyes have seen Thy salvation,
> 31 Which Thou hast prepared in the presence of all peoples,
> 32 A LIGHT OF REVELATION TO THE GENTILES,
> And the glory of Thy people Israel."
> 33 And His father and mother were amazed at the things which were being said about Him.
> 34 And Simeon blessed them, and said to Mary His mother, "Behold, this *Child* is appointed for the fall and rise of many in Israel, and for a sign to be opposed—

> 35 and a sword will pierce even your own soul—to the end that thoughts from many hearts may be revealed."
>
> —Luke 2

As we discussed earlier, where Simeon refers to himself as a "bond-servant" in this translation, it really should be translated "bondslave." What are some of the things that we can discern about being a bondslave by looking at Simeon's life?

1. He was righteous.
2. He was devout.
3. The Holy Spirit was upon him.
4. The Holy Spirit revealed things to him.
5. He could give blessings in the name of God.
6. He could prophesy in the name of God.

Here is a picture of a pure, holy, righteous, devoted man of God, who has the gifts of the Spirit functioning through him.

## PAUL, A BONDSLAVE OF CHRIST

Another New Testament example, in this case said to be a bondslave of Christ rather than a bondslave of God, is the apostle Paul. We find this mentioned several places in the New Testament:

> 1 Paul, a bond-servant of Christ Jesus, called as an apostle, set apart for the gospel of God, . . .
>
> —Romans 1

> 10 For am I now seeking the favor of men, or of God? Or am I striving to please men? If I were still trying to please men, I would not be a bond-servant of Christ.
>
> —Galatians 1

> 1 Paul and Timothy, bond-servants of Christ Jesus, to all the saints in Christ Jesus who are in Philippi, including the overseers and deacons: . . .
>
> —Philippians 1

These verses shed some additional light on what a bond-slave of Christ is. In Romans 1:1 we see that a bondslave of Christ is set apart for the gospel of God. Or we could say "sanctified" for the gospel of God.

In Galatians 1:10 we learn that a bondslave of Christ strives only to please Christ and not to please men. His aim is to do that which will glorify Christ, even if it makes him unpopular with men.

## ONLY THE BONDSLAVES ARE SEALED

God's pattern through the ages has not been to take His people out of a time of turmoil, but to protect them as they went through it. We can think of Daniel in the lion's den, Shadrach, Meshach and Abed-nego in the fiery furnace, and many others whom God allowed to go through a time of turbulence or persecution, but whom He protected in it.

The children of Israel endured the plagues in Egypt but they were protected in them. About 80 percent of the plagues did not touch the children of Israel. For example, all the cattle in Egypt died, but not one of the cattle in the land of Goshen died, where God's people dwelt.

The Bible says that this pattern is going to repeat itself once again:

1 After this I saw four angels standing at the four corners of the earth, holding back the four winds of the earth, so that no wind should blow on the earth or on the sea or on any tree.

2 And I saw another angel ascending from the rising of the sun, having the seal of the living God; and he cried out with a loud voice to the four angels to whom it was granted to harm the earth and the sea,

3 saying, "Do not harm the earth or the sea or the trees, until we have sealed the bond-servants of our God on their foreheads."

—Revelation 7

Here we see that God stops the Tribulation and seals His bondslaves on their foreheads. It does not say that He seals all Christians on their foreheads, only the bondslaves.

We might ask what the purpose of this seal is. We find the answer to this in Revelation 9:

> 2 And he opened the bottomless pit; and smoke went up out of the pit, like the smoke of a great furnace; and the sun and the air were darkened by the smoke of the pit.
> 3 And out of the smoke came forth locusts upon the earth; and power was given them, as the scorpions of the earth have power.
> 4 And they were told that they should not hurt the grass of the earth, nor any green thing, nor any tree, but only the men who do not have the seal of God on their foreheads.

We see that the purpose of the seal of God was for *protection*. The locusts, with a sting like scorpions, could hurt all the men on earth *except* those who had the seal of God on their foreheads.

I covered this concept in detail in my book on Revelation. I also have pointed out that Christians really don't need to worry about taking on the mark of the beast. What they should be concerned about is being a bondslave and getting sealed on their foreheads. Once God seals them on their foreheads, Satan, the Antichrist or no one else can remove God's seal and replace it with the mark of the beast (the mark of the beast comes later in the book of Revelation, in Chapter 13). "Greater is He who is in you than He who is in the world" (1 John 4:4b). So our main concern should be to be a bondslave, so that we can be sure that we will be sealed and protected during the time of birth pangs preceding the great Tribulation.

## JESUS CHRIST WAS A BONDSLAVE OF GOD

If you stop to think about it, you realize that Christ was indeed a bondslave of God. He came to do the Father's will and not His own, and His basic desire in life was to please the Father. The extent to which he was a bondslave is beautifully pointed out in this passage:

> 5 Have this attitude in yourselves which was also in Christ Jesus,
> 6 who, although He existed in the form of God, did not regard equality with God a thing to be grasped,

7 but emptied Himself, taking the form of a bond-servant, *and* being made in the likeness of men.

8 And being found in appearance as a man, He humbled Himself by becoming obedient to the point of death, even death on a cross.

9 Therefore also God highly exalted Him, and bestowed on Him the name which is above every name,

10 that at the name of Jesus EVERY KNEE SHOULD BOW, of those who are in heaven, and on earth, and under the earth,

11 and that every tongue should confess that Jesus Christ is Lord, to the glory of God the Father.

—Philippians 2

This is one of my favorite passages of Scripture. Even though the word "love" is not mentioned in this passage, to me it speaks more of how much Christ loved you and me than any other passage in the Bible.

We see that Christ was equal with God and in the form of God, but He did not selfishly cling to that. Verse 7 tells us that He was willing to empty Himself of all of His divine privileges, to be made a man and to voluntarily become a bondslave of God. Then verse 8 says that as a bondslave of God He humbled Himself and was obedient (characteristics of bondslave) His obedience was to the extent that He was willing to die for His Master (God) and even endure the horrible death by torture on a cross. What an incredible sacrifice He made to come from being in heaven with God, with all the power of God, to being a bondslave of God, obedient even to the point of being willing to be tortured to death. He did all of this because He loves you and me and He knew that there was no way we could spend eternity with God other than through His precious death.

Every time I read that passage in Philippians 2, I fall on my knees and say, "Oh God, thank you that Jesus loved me enough that He was willing to die for me!"

Because Christ was willing to be a bondslave, God is going to exalt Him. The rest of the passage talks about the exaltation of Christ. He is going to be raised to the extent that every knee will bow to Him and every tongue will confess that He is Lord. This means *everyone*—Christians and non-Christians alike. Since *everyone* is going to bow their knees to Christ, I encourage people to do it during this lifetime so that they can enjoy eternity with Christ. If they neglect or decline to do so during their lifetime, at some point in the future they will be forced to their knees and they are going to acknowledge that Christ is Lord then, but it will be too late to receive Him as Savior and Master at that point; instead they will spend an eternity in the lake of fire away from the presence of God and Christ.

As Christians, we want to be like Jesus. If Christ was a bondslave of God, we too should yearn to be bondslaves of our heavenly Father. If we do, and if we are faithful to obey, in God's good time He will exalt us with Christ and we will rule and reign with Him, not because we deserve it, but simply because of His love and grace.

Incidentally, when I first became a Christian I thought that the better and finer things of God were on higher and higher shelves. Thus, I wanted to grow so that I could reach them. Now I know that the best things of God are on lower and lower shelves. Only lowly slaves of God can partake of them, both in this age and in the age to come. Look at the picture on the cover of this book. Those stairs to the overcomer realm go down, not up. As we become less and less, the power of God can flow through us more and more.

Just as Christ, a bondslave of God, fought against Satan and evil and overcame them victoriously, God wants you and me, His bondslaves, to also become soldiers and overcomers in this spiritual warfare. In the next few chapters we will be looking at the other name for a bondslave—that of an "overcomer."

# 8

# THE OVERCOMERS

In Chapter 1 of this book we saw that *bondslaves* and *overcomers* are two different names for the same group of people. In a moment we will further examine their commonality, but first we need to recognize that "overcoming" is a military term.

In the New Testament times, if two soldiers were in hand-to-hand combat and one was the victor, he was called the "overcomer." Similarly, if two gladiators were involved in combat in the arena, it was said that the winner "overcame" the other. Thus, "overcomer" is a term used in the military, in warfare, and to denote victory. Of course one had to be a soldier and fight before he could overcome.

Keeping in mind what we discussed in the last chapter regarding bondslaves, can you begin to see similarity between a bondslave and an overcomer? Both a slave and a soldier have essentially no rights of their own. They both must sleep where those in authority tell them to sleep, they must wear what those in authority tell them to wear, they must eat what those in authority give them to eat and do what those in authority tell them to do. Even more important is the fact that both are required to be willing to die at the command of those in authority over them. Thus, even life itself, for an overcomer or a bondslave, is not as precious as is pleasing the One who is his Master.

As we pointed out earlier, not all Christians are bondslaves of God and not all Christians are overcomers. I believe that God is calling Christians today to a life of righteousness, holiness, dedication, and overcoming. God wants you to be an overcomer.

Now the question arises: who or what are we overcoming?

If we are going to be overcomers, we need to know what it is that we have to overcome. I searched the Scriptures and spent a lot of time in prayer, both on your behalf and on mine. God showed me three things that we are to overcome.

## OVERCOMING EVIL

The first thing we need to overcome is evil. This is probably the easiest one to overcome, yet as I examine my life and the lives of others whom I know well, we don't really get very far in overcoming evil.

**17** Never pay back evil for evil to anyone. Respect what is right in the sight of all men.

**18** If possible, so far as it depends on you, be at peace with all men.

**19** Never take your own revenge, beloved, but leave room for the wrath *of God,* for it is written, "VENGEANCE IS MINE. I WILL REPAY," says the Lord.

**20** "BUT IF YOUR ENEMY IS HUNGRY, FEED HIM, AND IF HE IS THIRSTY, GIVE HIM A DRINK; FOR IN SO DOING YOU WILL HEAP BURNING COALS UPON HIS HEAD."

**21** Do not be overcome by evil, but overcome evil with good.

—Romans 12

I don't know if any of you are like me, but if somebody comes up behind me as I'm driving at night with his brights on, when he finally passes me, there is a real temptation to flip my lights on bright just to show him how it feels. Is that returning evil for evil? Yes. If I do that, I have not overcome evil. We are to overcome evil *with good.*

Have you ever had a brother who has shunned you and in return you have told yourself: "If he is going to be that way about it, I don't want anything to do with him"? That is repaying evil for evil. God says that if you are going to overcome evil, it is going to be with good. We are being childish when we react unlovingly because someone has not treated us right. I yearn that all of us would begin to walk in a righteous way and that we would never repay evil with evil.

One time I heard a man speak who gave me the impression that he was trying to be a "big shot" for God. I therefore rejected him and anytime he got up to speak, my ears were plugged. *I was returning evil for "evil"* (his "evil" being my perception of a wrong attitude in him). I have since asked forgiveness from this individual. There were probably things I did not hear that God wanted me to hear from this man. I now have a real love for this brother. There may be someone you have treated this way. Whoever it is, before you are ever going to get off your plateau, you need to go to that brother or sister, neighbor or person at work, and ask his or her forgiveness. Then you repay evil with good and you overcome evil!

## OVERCOMING THE WORLD

The second thing that we are to overcome is found in John 16:

> 33 "These things I have spoken to you, that in me you may have peace. In the world you have tribulation, but take courage; I have overcome the world."

If you are going to be an overcomer, the next thing on the list to overcome is the world. To see what "the world" consists of, let's look at 1 John 2:

> 15 Do not love the world, nor the things in the world. If anyone loves the world, the love of the Father is not in him.
> 16 For all that is in the world, the lust of the flesh and the lust of the eyes and the boastful pride of life, is not from the Father, but is from the world.
> 17 And the world is passing away, and *also* its lusts; but the one who does the will of God abides forever.

There are three things listed as part of the world:

1.  the lust of the flesh
2.  the lust of the eyes
3.  the pride of life

If you look at all of the major temptations in the Scriptures, each would fall into one of these three categories.

For example, Genesis 3:6 records that Eve saw that the fruit of the tree of the knowledge of good and evil-was nice to look at (lust of the eyes), was good to eat (lust of the flesh), and would make them wise like God (pride of life). When Christ was tempted to turn stones into bread, that was in the realm of the lust of the flesh (Matthew 4:3). Satan then told Christ to look at all the kingdoms of the world which he would give Him (Matthew 4:8, 9). That was a temptation in the area of the lust of the eyes. The temptation to jump from the pinnacle of the temple and call ten thousand angels to deliver Him was in the area of the pride of life (Matthew 4:5, 6). Satan tried to persuade Christ to "arrive in style."

As we look at the lust of the flesh, the lust of the eyes, and the pride of life, we need to understand, first of all, what lust is. Lust is anything that I want *right now* and I don't care about the consequences. We see an example of this in the Old Testament when Esau came back from hunting and was very hungry. Jacob was cooking some lentil stew and Esau wanted it. He wanted it right then and he didn't care about any future consequences. He was even willing to give up his birthright to get what he was lusting after (Genesis 25:29-34).

Christ further expands on this in the New Testament; He says that we can commit the sin of lust in our hearts, even if we do not commit the actual act. Applying this back to the situation with Jacob and Esau, it is true that Esau lusted after the soup. That would have been sin, even if Jacob had not given him some soup and he had not eaten it. Remember, God looks at the heart and not at the outward actions.

Lust of the flesh involves anything that our bodies crave. This could be something to drink, something to smoke, hot showers, comfortable beds, back rubs, sex, food, and the list could go on and on. If we lust after any of these, we are loving the world.

Lust of the eyes involves "things"—all of the things we see advertised in newspapers, magazines and on television, for instance, that say to us, "Buy me, buy me, buy me." This could be new cars, new homes, stereos, cameras, clothes, jewelry, electronic gadgets, household appliances, toys, and many other things. If I just "have to have" some *thing,* then I am loving the world.

The pride of life is involved when *I* take the glory and the credit rather than giving the glory and the credit to God. This too is loving the world. But remember that the passage we read in 1 John 2 said that if we love the world, the love of God is not in us. Do you love the world? We need to look closely to be sure that we don't.

Let's examine each of these three areas of loving the world in detail, because you meet each one differently. If you apply the wrong tactic to the wrong temptation, you are going to lose.

## Overcoming the Lust of the Flesh

How do we overcome the lust of the flesh (the things that our bodies crave)? Let's read what 2 Timothy 2 has to say:

> 22 Now flee from youthful lusts, and pursue righteousness, faith, love *and* peace, with those who call on the Lord from a pure heart.

When the lust of the flesh is involved, the Lord says to *flee*—haul anchor and shove off! Get out of there!

When I was a fairly new Christian and single, I would take a young lady out by the lake and we would park. Then I would say, "Lord, help me not to get in trouble!" Frequently I got into trouble because I was not fleeing lust! When lust of the body occurs, the thing to do is to *flee* from it. Get away! Run! This is not being a coward. A soldier (overcomer) must retreat when his Commander tells him to.

If you have trouble with sex, don't allow yourself to be alone with someone of the opposite sex. If you have a problem with overeating, don't go to a smorgasbord or an ice cream parlor! Don't put bowls heaped full of food on your table. If you have any drinking problem, don't go near a bar or keep liquor in your home. In all of these cases, avoid situations where you would be tempted beyond your capabilities to resist.

If you and I were honest with each other (we certainly have to be honest with God), we would admit that in one particular area we have a weakness with the lust of the flesh. It would be good if we would confess that to God and ask Him to help us flee any time we begin to get into a situation where we might be tempted in that area of weakness.

Let's also look at 1 Peter 2:

> 11 Beloved, I urge you as aliens and strangers to abstain from fleshly lusts, which wage war against the soul.

When you yield to a fleshly lust, what is happening? Satan is attacking your soul and winning. If your pastor was speaking and was scheduled to stop at 12:00 for lunch, but he continued to speak until 12:30 or 12:45, you might get impatient or fidgety. What is that? . . . Lust of the flesh. Some Christians have been called to fast but do not because of the lust of the flesh. The lust of the flesh is waging war against your soul, according to the verse we just read. If you are so caught up with eating or other things pertaining to the body that you can't take time off when you know God is telling you to do so, you are being overcome with the lust of the flesh. If you are going to overcome the world, you must overcome the lust of the flesh which wages war against your soul.

### Overcoming the Lust of the Eyes

The second thing that we must overcome in order to overcome the world is the lust of the eyes.

> 15 And he gave them their request; but sent leanness into their soul.
>
> —Psalms 106, *KJV*

As we said before, the lust of the eyes involves things: clothes, houses, automobiles, jewelry—things that you see advertised on television, in magazines and newspapers, that you *want,* whether you need them or not.

Billy Graham was in a wealthy Christian lady's home who had invited some of her society friends in for tea and to hear Billy Graham speak. After everyone left, she showed Billy Graham her home, her antiques and her objects of art that she had acquired in her travels. As she was seeing Billy Graham to the door, she said something about all of these worldly people.

Billy Graham turned to her and said, "Madam, even though you are a Christian, you are the most worldly person I have met in a long time because of all the 'things' you have collected."

Let's look at Mark 4 where Christ is talking about the parable of the sower and the seeds and the four different types of ground. I think this applies to Christians as well as to non-Christians:

> 18 "And others are the ones on whom seed was sown among the thorns; these are the ones who have heard the word,
> 19 and the worries of the world, and the deceitfulness of riches, and the desires for other things enter in and choke the word, and it becomes unfruitful. . . ."
>
> —Mark 4

Did you hear that? The worries of the world, the deceitfulness of riches, and the desire for things can choke out the word so that it becomes unfruitful. That is true for non-Christians, but it is also true for Christians. You can hear the word of God, but the cares of the world, the lure of money and things, or even just "busyness" with the things of the world can cause the word of God to be crowded out of your life. You haven't rejected it—but it is *crowded out,* and so it becomes unfruitful to you.

To see how to overcome the lust of the eyes, let's look at Matthew 19:

> 21 Jesus said to him, "If you wish to be complete, go *and* sell your possessions and give to *the* poor, and you shall have treasure in heaven; and come, follow Me."
> 22 But when the young man heard this statement, he went away grieved; for he was one who owned much property.
> 23 And Jesus said to His disciples, "Truly I say to you, it is hard for a rich man to enter the kingdom of heaven.
> 24 "And again I say to you, it is easier for a camel to go through the eye of a needle, than for a rich man to enter the kingdom of God."
> 25 And when the disciples heard *this*, they were very astonished and said, "Then who can be saved?"

I might just offer a word of explanation about the last part of this passage. When Christ says "the eye of a needle," He is not referring to the eye of a sewing needle. In Jerusalem they had big gates in the walls where all of the caravans came in and out of the city during the day. But because of bands of roving thieves, they would lock these gates at night. There was one tiny gate which resembled the eye of a needle that was built for men to go in and out. If someone came at night wanting to enter the city, he either had to spend the night outside and come in one of the big gates the next day, or he could come in through the eye of the needle gate. If he had a camel, in order to do this, he would have to get the camel down on its knees and it would then have to walk on its knees through this tiny gate. That process would take about an hour. It *could* be done, but it was very difficult.

If your eyes are on *things,* it is going to be very difficult to become an overcomer, just as it was difficult for the young, rich man to sell his possessions. Christ says that if lust of the eyes is your problem, get rid of the things that are causing that problem. If you lust after good camera equipment, sell it and get an instant camera. If it's clothes, sell some of what you have or give them away. Don't stop selling that thing or things until it is no longer a problem for you.

### Overcoming the Pride of Life

Let's look at the third thing we need to overcome in the world—pride—and then I would like to tie all of these together with a letter. Proverbs 13:10 *(KJV)* says that "only by pride cometh contention." If you have contention at work, in your home, with your spouse or with a brother or sister in the Lord, either one or both of you have got a pride problem. *Only by pride cometh contention.*

Is there contention in churches and meetings today? You'd better believe it. We haven't yet overcome the world, if this is true. The Scriptures are clear on this—only by pride cometh contention.

Proverbs 16:18 says that pride comes before "a fall" or

"destruction" *(KJV)*. Pride is one of the things that God dislikes vehemently.

Before we look at the solution for overcoming pride, I would like to share something. I was with IBM ten years. I knew quite well and worked closely with one of the vice-presidents of IBM. One morning as we were riding the elevator together, I thought to myself that he was so much more humble than I was, and yet he had so much more right to be haughty, like I was. I asked the Lord how I could become humble. Now I know. You fall flat on your face a few times. Pretty soon you realize you're not as good, wise, and smart as you thought you were. This verse sums it up well:

> 12 "And whoever exalts himself shall be humbled; and whoever humbles himself shall be exalted. . . ."
>
> —Matthew 23

In one way or the other, you are going to wind up humble. If you humble yourself, God will exalt you in His time. When He gets ready (perhaps in the next age), He will exalt you. But if you try to exalt yourself, He will have to crush you humble. The solution for pride is to tell God that you want to be humble. That's a tough prayer, because God is going to humiliate you. If you have pride in your heart, as most of us do, this prayer is the place to begin.

## LOVE NOT THE WORLD

Now I would like to tie together these three things that are involved in overcoming the world. The following is a letter given to Billy Graham by a pastor in North Carolina. It was from a young man from a fairly wealthy home. He went down to the University of Mexico. He had a fiancée back in the college where he had been. After a year or so in Mexico, he became a communist. This is the letter he wrote back breaking off his engagement with his fiancée.

> We communists have a high casualty rate. We are the ones who get shot, and hung, and lynched, and tarred and feathered, and jailed, and slandered, and ridiculed, and fired from our jobs and in

every other way made as uncomfortable as possible. A certain percentage of us get killed or imprisoned. We live in virtual poverty. We
turn back to the party every penny we make above what is absolutely necessary to keep us alive.

We communists don't have time or the money for many movies
or concerts or T-bone steaks, or decent homes or new cars. We have
been described as fanatics. We are fanatics. Our lives are dominated
by one great overshadowing factor, the struggle for world communism.

We communists have a philosophy of life which no amount of
money can buy. We have a cause to fight for, a definite purpose in
life, we subordinate our petty, personal selves into a great movement of humanity. And if our personal lives seem hard or egos appear to suffer through subordination to the party, we are adequately
compensated by the thought that each of us, in a small way, is contributing to something new and true and better for mankind.

There is one thing in which I am in dead earnest and that is the
communist cause. It is my life, my business, my religion, my hobby,
my sweetheart, my wife, my mistress, my bread and meat. I work at
it in the daytime and dream of it at night. Its hold grows, not lessens
on me as time goes on. Therefore I cannot carry on a friendship, a
love affair, or even a conversation without relating it to this force
which both guards and guides my life.

I evaluate people, books, ideas and actions according to how they
affect the communist cause and by their attitude toward it. I've already been in jail because of my ideas, and if necessary, I am ready
to go before a firing squad.

You show me in the Bible where Jesus Christ demanded
anything less of His followers. Now stack up your life against
that. This communist guy has overcome the world. He did it
for communism and not Christ, but he *has* overcome the world.
Pride doesn't mean anything to him; the lust of the flesh and
the lust of the eyes don't mean anything to him. He has a cause.

I yearn that you and I would get to that position where
the lust of the flesh, the lust of the eyes, and the pride of life
don't mean anything to us—where we are willing to give everything to God, to live in a tent if He told us to, and to sell everything and give it to the poor if He told us to, as Christ instructed
the rich man to do in Matthew 19. We need to be willing to

have our egos suffer, to be fanatics, to be spit at, and we even need to be willing to die because of Christ.

As I said earlier, I believe that Christians will go through the Tribulation. Even if I am wrong and the Christians are raptured out beforehand, the Bible says that things are not going to be lovely and beautiful and then the Tribulation will suddenly start; there is going to be a time preceding it when things are going to get really bad on the earth. Christ clearly taught this in Matthew 24. Many people, like Dave Wilkerson in his book, *The Vision*, have prophesied and projected that there is a real time of persecution coming for Christians. When that time comes, you have got to have already overcome the world.

## OVERCOMING SATAN

The third thing we are to overcome is Satan. This is found in 1 John 2:

> 13 I am writing to you, fathers, because you know Him who has been from the beginning. I am writing to you, young men, because you have overcome the evil one. I have written to you, children, because you know the Father.
> 14 I have written to you, fathers, because you know Him who has been from the beginning. I have written to you, young men, because you are strong, and the word of God abides in you, and you have overcome the evil one.

God wants us to overcome evil, the world, and Satan himself. Some time ago I had a tremor in my right arm for a little while. Finally, after I and other people had prayed about it, the Lord spoke to me and said: "How long are you going to put up with Satan messing around with you like this?" That made me mad! So I took dominion and I rejected and rebuked that ol' son-of-a-gun, the evil one. I said, "Get out of here, in Jesus name and by His blood. I'm tired of this." Then the Lord gave me a perfect victory!

God wants some people who want to overcome Satan. You are never going to unless you really want to! When many of us feel Satan's presence creep into a room or situation, our initial reaction is, "Oh, no! I feel an evil presence here." It is one of fear. That is not the attitude of an overcomer. Perhaps at that moment we should get angry, just as Christ did when He drove the money changers out of the temple. We should tell Satan he has no place in that room. In Jesus' power we need to rebuke him and tell him to get out! We need to take dominion over him. We are going to look at *how* that is done.

Before the years of this century are over, I believe we are going to come into head-to-head competition in spiritual war with Satan. God wants an army of overcomers who are not only willing, but eager, to overcome Satan. We do not take him on in our own power, but in the power of Jesus. There are people who have already overcome Satan. We just read about some of them in 1 John 2.

Now let's see how we are to overcome Satan:

> **10**  And I heard a loud voice in heaven, saying,
> "Now the salvation, and the power, and the kingdom of our God and the authority of His Christ have come, for the accuser of our brethren has been thrown down, who accuses them before our God day and night.
> **11**  "And they overcame him because of the blood of the Lamb and because of the word of their testimony, and they did not love their life even to death. . . ."
>
> —Revelation 12

Notice the three things that these believers used to overcome Satan:

1.   the blood of the Lamb

2.   the word of their testimony

3.   they did not love their life even to death

This is the equation or formula for overcoming the evil one. Let's take a look at each of these.

### The Blood of the Lamb

In Leviticus 17 it says that the life is in the blood. When Christ shed His blood for us, He shed his life for us. When He imparts His blood to us, He imparts His life to us. Let's look further:

> 53 Jesus therefore said to them, "Truly, truly, I say to you, unless you eat the flesh of the Son of Man and drink His blood, you have no life in yourselves.
> 54 "He who eats My flesh and drinks My blood has eternal life, and I will raise him up on the last day.
> 55 "For My flesh is true food, and My blood is true drink.
> 56 "He who eats My flesh and drinks My blood abides in Me, and I in him. . . ."
>
> —John 6

Christ said this early in His ministry, long before the last supper—that unless you eat His flesh and drink His blood you have no life in you. I'm not totally sure what this means. I don't think it is talking about communion although it might be. Yet somehow, way before the last supper, Christ was telling the potential followers who had gathered around Him that unless they drank His blood, they would not have life in them. I think that He was saying that they needed to drink in His life, and then they would really have life in them. We too can partake of His life.

There are a couple of things the blood of Christ does which are recorded in Hebrews 9:

> 11 But when Christ appeared *as* a high priest of the good things to come, *He entered* through the greater and more perfect tabernacle, not made with hands, that is to say, not of this creation;
> 12 and not through the blood of goats and calves, but through His own blood, He entered the holy place once for all, having obtained eternal redemption.
> 13 For if the blood of goats and bulls and the ashes of a heifer sprinkling those who have been defiled, sanctify for the cleansing of the flesh,
> 14 how much more will the blood of Christ, who through the eternal Spirit offered Himself without blemish to God, cleanse your conscience from dead works to serve the living God?

Only the blood of Jesus Christ can cleanse your conscience from dead works to serve the living God. Let's read further:

> 24 For Christ did not enter a holy place made with hands, a *mere* copy of the true one, but into heaven itself, now to appear in the presence of God for us;
> 25 nor was it that He should offer Himself often, as the high priest enters the holy place year by year with blood not his own.
> 26 Otherwise, He would have needed to suffer often since the foundation of the world; but now once at the consummation of the ages He has been manifested to put away sin by the sacrifice of Himself.
>
> —Hebrews 9

Christ sacrificed Himself; He gave His blood, His life, so that you and I could put away sin. So part of the way that we overcome the evil one is by putting away sin. We need to ask God to purify and cleanse us of all the rubbish in our lives which does not glorify Him. We need to have Him take it all away and make us pure by the blood of Christ and then we need to walk in that holiness. Leviticus 11:44 says we are to "sanctify ourselves" *(KJV)*.

Often when we are engaged in struggles against demonic or satanic forces, we bind them in the name of Jesus Christ. Where does the blood fit in? We also need to ask God to cover us with the blood of Jesus Christ in such situations. The blood of Christ is our protection. The way we overcome the evil one is by the blood of the Lamb, according to what we read in Revelation 12:11. We need to plead the blood of Christ over us so that Satan cannot attack us. We also need to ask God for a covering of the blood of Christ over whoever we are praying for; then he can be cleansed from sin. We can't cleanse anybody. Only the blood of Christ can. It is an integral part of our offensive in defeating the evil one.

## The Word of Our Testimony

The second way that the believers we read about in Revelation 12 overcame Satan was by the word of their testimony. I do not think this means testimony in the sense we normally think of that word. I will share with you what the Lord has shown me so far, beginning by looking at Revelation 19. Here John is trying to worship the angel; this is what happens:

**10** And I fell at his feet to worship him. And he said to me, "Do not do that; I am a fellow servant of yours and your brethren who hold the testimony of Jesus; worship God. For the testimony of Jesus is the spirit of prophecy."

—Revelation 19

When the angel said, "the testimony of Jesus is the spirit of prophecy," I do not think he was talking about the gift of prophecy. What the Lord has shown me is that there is testimony and there is *anointed* testimony. The anointing comes from the same spirit that controls a Christian and causes him to speak in tongues or to prophesy. You can give a testimony in the flesh, or you can give a testimony that is somewhat "spiritual," but rarely do most of us give an anointed testimony. Times are coming when we will need to defeat the evil one, and we must use this anointed testimony in order to do so. We must speak the strong words of Jesus Christ under the anointing of the Holy Spirit.

Having this kind of anointed testimony in times of persecution can get one in trouble. We know that in Revelation there are many beheaded because of their testimony for Jesus Christ. Revelation 1 tells us that John was on the Island of Patmos, probably in exile, because of his testimony for Jesus Christ:

**9** I, John, your brother and fellow partaker in the tribulation and kingdom and perseverance *which are* in Jesus, was on the island called Patmos, because of the word of God and the testimony of Jesus.

—Revelation 1

There may be a time coming in the United States when many will be imprisoned or killed because of their anointed testimony of Jesus Christ.

I am a person who likes to be free. The thing that used to petrify me was not dying for Christ, but I would have hated to go to jail. That would have been just about the end of the world for me. One day I realized that the fear of prison was not of God. With all my heart I asked God to remove that fear. I can't explain how or why it left, because that fear had been with me nearly all of my life, but it was gone in an instant! Jail has no fear for me now. Absolutely none! Being imprisoned would give me time to worship and praise the Lord and to witness to other inmates. It would be a great experience. However, a year ago I could not have made that statement. If you have a fear of dying, of prison or anything else, ask the Lord to take it away.

Some people are prophesying about Russia invading the U.S. I am not saying they are or are not of God, but if Russian or Chinese soldiers did come through, we should look at them as prospects for conversion, not as somebody to fear. Do good to them. Return good for their evil. If they come into your house and want to take your grandfather clock or your favorite lamp, help them carry it out! Don't resist them. Why would you resist? If you resist, you are going to get shot and are not going to get shot for Christ but because of the lust of the eyes. That would be a tough way to go.

If you can't speak the language of such invaders, talk to them anyhow. Perhaps the Holy Spirit will give you the gift of speaking in their language. Give them a hug and say "God bless you!" They would know that there is something different about you. There is a day coming when you may have to put on the line all of the things I am saying. I personally want to give an anointed testimony to such soldiers or anyone else persecuting me; I want to love them with the love of the Lord. If they kill me for the testimony of Christ, that's okay. In fact, that's great, because it is in that way that we are going to overcome Satan.

### Love Not Your Life More Than Christ

We also read in Revelation 12:11 that those believers overcame Satan because they did not love their life even to death. Mark 8 expands on this concept:

34 And He summoned the multitude with His disciples, and said to them, "If anyone wishes to come after Me, let him deny himself, and take up his cross, and follow Me.

35 "For whoever wishes to save his life shall lose it; but whoever loses his life for My sake and the gospel's shall save it. . . ."

—Mark 8

At the time this was written, the cross was an instrument of execution. It would be like saying today, "Take up your electric chair, or gas chamber and follow Me." Let me reemphasize: Christ is saying, "If you want to follow me, you need to deny yourself, take up your firing squad (be willing to physically die) and follow Me."

When persecution comes, if we try to hold on to our lives and avoid dying for Christ, in the end we are going to lose our lives. It would be a sad state to be physically alive but spiritually dead. Christ admonishes us to lose our lives for His sake and for the sake of the gospel; if we do this, in the end we will save our lives. What does it profit a man to gain the whole world but forfeit his own soul? (Matthew 16:26). If we are willing to lay down our lives for Christ, He will give us the strength to do so when the time comes.

Let's look at another passage in Revelation:

> 9 And when He broke the fifth seal, I saw underneath the altar the souls of those who had been slain because of the word of God, and because of the testimony which they had maintained;
> 10 and they cried out with a loud voice, saying, "How long, O Lord, holy and true, wilt Thou refrain from judging and avenging our blood on those who dwell on the earth?"
> 11 And there was given to each of them a white robe; and they were told that they should rest for a little while longer, until *the number of* their fellow servants and their brethren who were to be killed even as they had been, should be completed also.
>
> —Revelation 6

In verse 9 we see that many will be slain because of the word of God and because of the anointed testimony which they maintain. You and I may be part of that crowd that is being described here in Revelation. If we are, praise God! It will be glorious to lay down our lives for the Lord, because in the end we will save our spiritual lives and really have true life.

To show you how important the word of our testimony is I would like to relate an example that occurred shortly after the communists took over mainland China. One of the people arrested was a Chinese bishop. This Chinese bishop was being interrogated day after day by a couple of guards. They told him that if he denied Christ, they would let him go and if he did not, they would eventually kill him.

The bishop thought that it wouldn't hurt anything just to deny Christ in front of those two Chinese soldiers. He would then be free to go out and work for the Lord and to encourage and help other Christians. This was his thinking, erroneous as it was. So he did deny Christ in front of those two soldiers, and he was released.

About twenty years later, on his death bed, he wrote a one-page memo. He said that in the twenty years since he had denied Christ and was released from prison, he had lived in total spiritual blackness, with no joy, no peace, and no sense of the presence of God or the love of God. He said how much he wished that he had not denied Christ and that he had been killed, rather than to live for twenty years in hell on earth in such spiritual blackness.

Nothing is worth denying Christ. No matter if you think it is totally inconsequential, it can have eternal consequences. We are going to defeat Satan with the word of our anointed testimony and, in an anointed testimony, we could never deny our precious Savior.

## SUMMARY AND CONCLUSION

We have looked at overcoming evil, overcoming the world, and overcoming Satan himself. In the next chapter we will more closely examine Satan and our battle with him. We *can* overcome him! Praise the Lord! In James there are several good clues as to how to overcome Satan:

7  Submit therefore to God. Resist the devil and he will flee from you.

8  Draw near to God and He will draw near to you. Cleanse your hands, you sinners; and purify your hearts, you double-minded.

9  Be miserable and mourn and weep; let your laughter be turned into mourning, and your joy to gloom.

10  Humble yourselves in the presence of the Lord, and He will exalt you.

—James 4

These are all things that we are to do: submit to God, draw near to God, cleanse our hands, purify our hearts, humble ourselves and resist Satan. If we do these things, God has promised that Satan will flee from us.

There are many people preaching today that we are to be afraid of witchcraft, satanism, demons, Satan himself, and so on. I believe this is not good teaching. We are to resist Satan and he will flee from us. There have been some who say that if you have certain books, records, or kinds of jewelry, you had better get rid of them because Satan and demons will attack and harass you because of them. A Christian could walk in fear following this type of teaching. We do not have to get rid of those objects unless God tells us to. We can command any demonic or satanic influence to get out in the name of Jesus Christ. Satan will flee. We don't have to walk in fear. Praise God! Through the power and the blood of Jesus Christ we can overcome.

In our weakness the power of God can be manifested through us—the same power that raised Christ from the dead:

> **4 For indeed He was crucified because of weakness, yet He lives because of the power of God. For we also are weak in Him, yet we shall live with Him because of the power of God *directed* toward you.**
>
> **5 Test yourselves *to see* if you are in the faith; examine yourselves! . . .**
>
> **—2 Corinthians 13**

Verse 5 says that we are to examine ourselves. I would encourage you to do that. Say: "God, where am I? Where do You want me to be?" Perhaps God has already spoken to you and has shown you where you are, and you need to take the next step. Perhaps you are a born-again Christian and you need to be baptized in the Spirit. Maybe you have been baptized in the Spirit but you need to get off of your plateau and become an overcomer. Through the power of Christ, you can overcome evil, you can overcome the world and you can overcome Satan. Praise the Lord!

Lord God, I pray that every person who reads these words will be taught by the Holy Spirit, who alone can take the word of God and make it alive to their hearts. I pray that the Holy Spirit might show each person clearly where he is and where he should be going. If there is anything hindering these precious brothers and sisters from moving on and becoming victorious, overcoming Christians, we bind that evil force in the name of Jesus Christ and by the blood of Christ. We loose these precious brothers and sisters to move into the position of overcomers. We pray this not in our own righteousness or in our own name, but we come hidden behind Jesus Christ, wrapped in the robe of His righteousness. We ask you, Father, in the name of Jesus, to do a work in the heart of every individual who reads these words, to the glory of Christ. In the beautiful name of Christ, Amen.

## ADDED NOTE

There is one verse that might imply that all Christians are overcomers. Before dealing with that verse, we need to examine a principle in looking at the Scriptures. A good example to take is the subject of prayer.

If we were to take any one verse on prayer and base our teaching on prayer solely on that one verse, we could wind up with an incorrect picture of prayer. For example, in John 14 Jesus says:

14   "If you ask Me anything in My name, I will do *it*. . . ."

There are no other conditions given in this verse to Christ granting our requests other than asking in His name. If we were to base our entire thinking on prayer on this verse, our concept would be distorted. Asking in His name is *one condition* to having our prayers answered but *not the only condition*. We see another condition laid down by Jesus in Matthew 21:

22   "And all things you ask in prayer, believing, you shall receive."

If we were to base our entire theology about prayer on this verse, we would think that the only condition for receiving our requests is believing. Having faith is *a condition* but *not the only condition.*

From the Lord's prayer and 1 John 5:14, we learn that another condition is asking "in God's will." Other Scriptures give other conditions to answered prayer and additional insights to prayer. To get the true picture of what the Bible says about prayer and the requirements for our prayers to be answered, we must look at all of the conditions, not just one.

Now let us look at what John has to say about overcomers in John 5:

**4 "For whatever is born of God overcomes the world; and this is the victory that has overcome the world—our faith.**

**5 And who is the one who overcomes the world, but he who believes that Jesus is the Son of God?**

In these two verses we see two conditions for being an overcomer—believing in Christ and having faith—but these are *not the only conditions* for being an overcomer. If we were to base our thinking on overcomers on these two verses alone, we would fall into the same pit as one trying to base one's thinking concerning prayer on just one or two verses.

As we have seen in this chapter, in addition to these two verses in 1 John, there are many other aspects of being an overcomer. We need to look at the totality of what the Bible teaches on what we overcome and how we overcome, in order to have a complete picture of what God desires us to be.

# 9

# THE ENEMY AND THE BATTLEGROUND

We have just seen that God has a desire to have an army of overcomers. One of the major things that we are to overcome is Satan. There are so many misconceptions about who Satan is and about the war that we are in against him that I felt a need to devote this chapter to looking at Satan, his army and where the battle is actually taking place.

We are all used to conflicts, even organized ones. We see this particularly in team sports such as basketball and, even more so, in hockey and football. I think that everyone would agree that the annual Thanksgiving Cotton Bowl game or the Super Bowl are definitely conflicts or battles.

As you probably guessed, I'm a football fan. I played a little football in high school and in the service. In the pro games and even in college football, if you come against an opponent that you know nothing about you are likely to get slaughtered. That is why teams scout their opponents beforehand.

We need to know something about our enemy; therefore, we need to "scout" him. We need to know who Satan is and something about his kingdom. We do not want to become overly concerned about him, but we do need to know something about our opponent and his tactics if we are going to fight a successful battle or warfare. The first thing we should realize is found in 1 Peter 5:

> 8  Be of sober *spirit,* be on the alert. Your adversary, the devil, prowls about like a roaring lion, seeking someone to devour.
> 9  But resist him, firm in *your* faith, knowing that the same experiences of suffering are being accomplished by your brethren who are in the world.

If a 1,000-pound roaring lion who hadn't eaten in a week came in the back door of your church on a Sunday morning, guess what would happen to the crowd. They would all be exiting out the front door en masse! If you were there, your adrenaline would flow and you would be geared for either "fight" or "flight." You would be vitally concerned, to say the least.

Satan is walking about as a roaring lion, on the spiritual level, and he is just as real as a physical lion is on the physical level. Satan wants to devour you spiritually. He is seeking to devour Christians, according to the Scripture we just read. He already has the unbelievers on his team; he doesn't have to worry about them. Should we be just as concerned on the spiritual level as we would on the physical level, if a lion were to walk into a room where we were? I believe that we should be, and I also believe that most Christians are not. Therefore, the lion—Satan—takes nips out of us and scratches us with his giant claws because we are not ready or prepared to do the spiritual warfare for which we should be prepared. If he is walking about seeking to devour us, as the Bible says he is, then we need to be aware of this and be prepared to do battle.

Now let's see with whom we are doing battle; it is not just Satan:

10 Finally, be strong in the Lord, and in the strength of His might.

11 Put on the full armor of God, that you may be able to stand firm against the schemes of the devil.

12 For our struggle is not against flesh and blood, but against the rulers, against the powers, against the world forces of this darkness, against the spiritual *forces* of wickedness in the heavenly *places*.

13 Therefore, take up the full armor of God, that you may be able to resist in the evil day, and having done everything, to stand firm.

—Ephesians 6

There is a lot that we could discuss in these verses. One of the things that we need to realize is that this was written to Christians. Paul says to put on the armor of God. It is something that we can decide to do or not do. Therefore we must conclude that all Christians do not have on the armor of God. This is something that Paul is recommending that Christians do because of the spiritual war that is going on. Verse 12 tells us about the spiritual war. We wrestle against rulers, powers, world forces of darkness and spiritual forces of wickedness in the heavenly places. Notice that Paul uses the term "struggle," or in the *King James Version* "wrestle," which implies hand-to-hand combat.

If we drew an organizational chart of our enemy based on Ephesians 6, Satan would be at the top as president or commander in chief. Under him would be "generals," "lieutenants," "sergeants" and "privates." There is a whole hierarchy of satanic, evil forces against which we are battling. To help you understand this battle, let me use an example. If you and I got in a fight and you hit me and I took a baseball bat and hit your shadow what would you think of me? If you hit me again and again and I took my baseball bat and hit your shadow, and each time you hit me, I hit your shadow harder, this would make me look pretty dumb, wouldn't it? The reason is that I would not be wrestling with the real thing (you) but with your shadow.

Remember that we wrestle not against flesh and blood but we do wrestle against spiritual beings. The spiritual beings are the reality and the flesh and blood is the shadow. For example, if you have a neighbor, somebody at work or perhaps your boss who is bugging you and you ask the Lord to help you be tolerant of that person, you are hitting the shadow. We wrestle not against flesh and blood (that's the shadow). If you want to wrestle *effectively*, you need to come against the evil, satanic forces which are causing that person to behave as he or she does. That is the only way in which you will be able to win that spiritual battle. You have to come against the real thing, which is the evil spirits or satanic forces of the opposing army. We need to realize what we are wrestling against in order to be able to do so in a way that will lead to victory.

We will have more to say later about *how* to fight effectively and win, but first we need to know more about our enemy.

## WHO IS SATAN?

If you were to ask most Christians who Satan is, they would respond that he is a fallen angel, in fact a fallen angel leader. If you were to ask them when he was kicked out of heaven, they might respond with anything from "during the Old Testament times" or "prior to the garden of Eden" to "he will be kicked out of heaven sometime in the future during the Tribulation."

I have asked many Christians for their biblical basis for believing that Satan is who they think he is and for believing what they do about when he was, or will be, kicked out of heaven. I have found almost no one who had a scriptural basis for what he or she believed. Take yourself as an example. You probably believe that Satan is a fallen angel. On what Scripture do you base that?

I don't mean to put you on the spot, but it is likely that you are repeating what you have heard someone else say. We know from past experience that basing our beliefs on anything but the Scriptures can lead to all sorts of confusion and even error. Why is there so much confusion concerning who Satan is and what his present status is? I believe it is because Satan is the great deceiver, the author of confusion, and the father of all lies. He tries to get Christians to believe false things about himself and to bring confusion anywhere he can. The Lord being my guide and my protection, I would like to share with you some things that the Bible does say about Satan.

Let us first tackle the question of who Satan is. I cannot find a Scripture that says Satan is a fallen angel, although that is what I had been taught all my life. He *might* indeed be a fallen angel; there is nothing in the Scriptures that says he could not be. However, there is nothing in the Scriptures that says that he is. In fact, I do not see in the Bible a clear statement of who he is, although it does give us some good insights.

First let's look at some of the Scriptures that people might use to conclude that Satan is a fallen angel. The first of these is 2 Corinthians 11:

> **13  For such men are false apostles, deceitful workers, disguising themselves as apostles of Christ.**
> **14  And no wonder, for even Satan disguises himself as an angel of light.**

15 Therefore it is not surprising if his servants also disguise themselves as servants of righteousness; whose end shall be according to
their deeds.

We can see that Satan is not called an angel in this passage,
but rather it says that he *disguises* himself as one. Another verse
about him is found in Matthew 25:

41 "Then He will also say to those on His left, 'Depart from Me,
accursed ones, into the eternal fire which has been prepared for the
devil and his angels; . . .'"

Here we learn that eternal fire has been prepared for "the
devil and his angels." Yet Christ also had angels who could protect Him if He jumped off the pinnacle of the temple (Luke 4:
9-11), but that did not make him an angel. This passage no
more makes Satan an angel than the fact that Christ had angels
to serve Him made Christ an angel. Let's look further:

7 And there was war in heaven, Michael and his angels waging
war with the dragon. And the dragon and his angels waged war,
8 and they were not strong enough and there was no longer a
place found for them in heaven.

—Revelation 12

These verses depict a war in heaven between Michael and
his angels and Satan and his angels. This could possibly imply
that Satan and Michael were on equivalent levels, although it
does not necessarily imply this. This is probably the strongest
verse that could lead one to conclude that Satan was an angel,
but it is far from conclusive.

Now let us examine some things that might lead us to believe that Satan might not be a fallen angel. But before we look
at the next passage of Scripture, we should recognize that there
are three types of sons of God in the Bible:

1. Begotten Son of God (Jesus Christ is the *only one* of
   these)

2. Created sons of God (Adam and possibly others fall
   into this category)

3. Adopted sons of God (believers in Jesus Christ are in
   this category)

Let's now look at two passages from Job that talk about sons of God—created sons of God, I believe:

6 Now there was a day when the sons of God came to present themselves before the LORD, and Satan also came among them.

7 And the LORD said to Satan, "From where do you come?" Then Satan answered the LORD and said, "From roaming about on the earth and walking around on it."

8 And the LORD said to Satan, "Have you considered My servant Job? For there is no one like him on the earth, a blameless and upright man, fearing God and turning away from evil."

9 Then Satan answered the LORD, "Does Job fear God for nothing?

10 "Hast Thou not made a hedge about him and his house and all that he has, on every side? Thou hast blessed the work of his hands, and his possessions have increased in the land.

11 "But put forth Thy hand now and touch all that he has; he will surely curse Thee to Thy face."

12 Then the LORD said to Satan, "Behold, all that he has is in your power, only do not put forth your hand on him." So Satan departed from the presence of the LORD.

—Job 1

1 Again there was a day when the sons of God came to present themselves before the LORD, and Satan also came among them to present himself before the LORD.

2 And the LORD said to Satan, "Where have you come from?" Then Satan answered the LORD and said, "From roaming about on the earth, and walking around on it."

3 And the LORD said to Satan, "Have you considered My servant Job? For there is no one like him on the earth, a blameless and upright man fearing God and turning away from evil. And he still holds fast his integrity, although you incited Me against him, to ruin him without cause."

4 And Satan answered the LORD and said, "Skin for skin! Yes, all that a man has he will give for his life.

5 "However, put forth Thy hand, now, and touch his bone and flesh; he will curse Thee to Thy face."

6 So the LORD said to Satan, "Behold, he is in your power, only spare his life."

7 Then Satan went out from the presence of the LORD, and smote Job with sore boils from the sole of his foot to the crown of his head.

—Job 2

A very interesting question arises from these two passages: Who are these sons of God? "Sons" is plural, so we know it cannot be speaking of multiple Christs, because the Bible clearly says that Christ is the *only* begotten Son of God (John 3:16). Back in Job's time there were not yet any "adopted sons of God," because believing in Christ is a prerequisite to being an adopted son of God (Galatians 3:26, 4:4–7). We know that these "sons of God" are not angels:

> 5 For to which of the angels did He ever say,
> "THOU ART MY SON,
> TODAY I HAVE BEGOTTEN THEE"?
> And again,
> "I WILL BE A FATHER TO HIM,
> AND HE SHALL BE A SON TO ME"?
> 6 And when He again brings the first-born into the world, He says,
> "AND LET ALL THE ANGELS OF GOD WORSHIP HIM."
> 7 And of the angels He says,
> "WHO MAKES HIS ANGELS WINDS,
> AND HIS MINISTERS A FLAME OF FIRE."
> 8 But of the Son *He says,*
> "THY THRONE, O GOD, IS FOREVER AND EVER,
> AND THE RIGHTEOUS SCEPTER IS THE SCEPTER OF HIS KINGDOM.
> 9 "THOU HAST LOVED RIGHTEOUSNESS AND HATED LAWLESSNESS;
> THEREFORE GOD, THY GOD, HATH ANOINTED THEE WITH THE OIL OF GLADNESS ABOVE THY COMPANIONS."
>
> —Hebrews 1

We see in verse 5 that God has never called an angel "son" or promised an angel that He would be his Father. Therefore, one must conclude that these are sons of God that were directly created by God, such as Adam.

We need to digress for just a moment here. God's universe is incredibly vast. I do not know whether or not there is life on other planets that revolve around other suns—that is in God's province. He has not chosen to clearly reveal to us much about that yet.

However, scientists have done some interesting estimating concerning the possibility of life on planets that revolve around other suns. They estimate that if one out of every ten suns had planets, and one out of every ten suns that had planets had one that would be able to support life, and one out of every ten planets that could support life actually had life, then there would be ten trillion inhabited planets in the universe.

God could have that many, or even a few inhabited planets. Some of C. S. Lewis' books depict life on other planets. I think that any open-minded person would admit that there *could* be life on other planets. It is possible that the sons of God spoken of in Job were ones that God created on some other planets. Whether this is the explanation or there is some other, the book of Job twice states that the sons (plural) of God were gathered together before God. It is also interesting to note that both of these passages say that Satan was "among them" (among the sons of God gathered before Him). There is nothing to imply that Michael or Gabriel or any of the other angel leaders were there, so one might conclude that Satan was one of these created sons of God.

## SATAN IS A FALLEN CHERUB?

To examine the possibility that Satan might be a fallen cherub, we need to look at Ezekiel 28. In the first ten verses of Ezekiel 28, the word of the Lord came through Ezekiel to the "leader of Tyre." But then, beginning in verse 11, the word of the Lord comes to the "king of Tyre." It is possible that the first ten verses are talking about the human leader of Tyre while the remaining verses of that chapter deal with Satan, the ruler or power behind that leader. Let's read those verses and then we will see why they are possibly talking about Satan.

11 Again the word of the LORD came to me saying,
12 "Son of man, take up a lamentation over the king of Tyre, and say to him, 'Thus says the Lord God,
"You had the seal of perfection,
Full of wisdom and perfect in beauty.

13 "You were in Eden, the garden of God;
   Every precious stone was your covering:
   The ruby, the topaz, and the diamond;
   The beryl, the onyx, and the jasper;
   The lapis lazuli, the turquoise, and the emerald;
   And the gold, the workmanship of your settings and sockets,
   Was in you.
   On the day that you were created
   They were prepared.

14 "You were the anointed cherub who covers,
   And I placed you *there*.
   You were on the holy mountain of God;
   You walked in the midst of the stones of fire.

15 "You were blameless in your ways
   From the day you were created,
   Until unrighteousness was found in you.

16 "By the abundance of your trade
   You were internally filled with violence,
   And you sinned;
   Therefore I have cast you as profane
   From the mountain of God.
   And I have destroyed you, O covering cherub,
   From the midst of the stones of fire.

17 "Your heart was lifted up because of your beauty;
   You corrupted your wisdom by reason of your splendor.
   I cast you to the ground;
   I put you before kings,
   That they may see you.

18 "By the multitude of your iniquities,
   In the unrighteousness of your trade,
   You profaned your sanctuaries.
   Therefore I have brought fire from the midst of you;
   It has consumed you,
   And I have turned you to ashes on the earth
   In the eyes of all who see you.

19 "All who know you among the peoples
   Are appalled at you;
   You have become terrified,
   And you will be no more.'"

                                                    —Ezekiel 28

It is possible that this is not talking about Satan, because in verses 18 and 19 God says that He will consume this being and that he will "be no more." We know from Christ's teaching that Satan has not ceased to exist, so it is possible that this is not talking about Satan.

However, one thing that would lead us to think that this likely is talking about Satan is found in verse 13, where God says, "You were in Eden, the garden of God." There is further evidence that this may be talking about Satan in verse 14, where God says, "You were the anointed cherub" and, "You were on the holy mountain of God; You walked in the midst of the stones of fire." To understand this part about walking in the midst of the stones of fire we must first turn back to Chapter 10 of Ezekiel, where we get a description of the cherubim. (Cherubim is plural for cherub.)

8  And the cherubim appeared to have the form of a man's hand under their wings.

9  Then I looked, and behold, four wheels beside the cherubim, one wheel beside each cherub; and the appearance of the wheels *was* like the gleam of a Tarshish stone.

10  And as for their appearance, all four of them had the same likeness, as if one wheel were within another wheel.

11  When they moved, they went in *any of* their four directions without turning as they went; but they followed in the direction which they faced, without turning as they went.

12  And their whole body, their backs, their hands, their wings, and the wheels were full of eyes all around, the wheels belonging to all four of them.

13  The wheels were called in my hearing, the whirling wheels.

14  And each one had four faces. The first face *was* the face of a cherub, the second face *was* the face of a man, the third the face of a lion, and the fourth the face of an eagle.

15  Then the cherubim rose up. They are the living beings that I saw by the river Chebar.

16  Now when the cherubim moved, the wheels would go beside them; also when the cherubim lifted up their wings to rise from the ground, the wheels would not turn from beside them.

17  When the cherubim stood still, the wheels would stand still; and when they rose up, the wheels would rise with them; for the spirit of the living beings *was* in them.

18 Then the glory of the LORD departed from the threshold of the temple and stood over the cherubim.

19 When the cherubim departed, they lifted their wings and rose up from the earth in my sight with the wheels beside them; and they stood still at the entrance of the east gate of the LORD'S house. And the glory of the God of Israel hovered over them.

20 These are the living beings that I saw beneath the God of Israel by the river Chebar; so I knew that they *were* cherubim.

21 Each one had four faces and each one four wings, and beneath their wings *was* the form of human hands.

22 As for the likeness of their faces, they were the same faces whose appearance I had seen by the river Chebar. Each one went straight ahead.

—Ezekiel 10

From this description of cherubim we see that they each had four faces, they had wings and underneath the wings were hands, like the hands of a man. In verse 22, Ezekiel says that these were the same beings that he saw by the river Chebar. That vision we find back in Ezekiel 1:

2 (On the fifth of the month in the fifth year of King Jehoiachin's exile,

3 the word of the LORD came expressly to Ezekiel the priest, son of Buzi, in the land of the Chaldeans by the river Chebar; and there the hand of the LORD came upon him.)

4 And as I looked, behold, a storm wind was coming from the north, a great cloud with fire flashing forth continually and a bright light around it, and in its midst something like glowing metal in the midst of the fire.

5 And within it there were figures resembling four living beings. And this was their appearance: they had human form.

6 Each of them had four faces and four wings.

7 And their legs were straight and their feet were like a calf's hoof, and they gleamed like burnished bronze.

8 Under their wings on their four sides *were* human hands. As for the faces and wings of the four of them,

9 their wings touched one another; their *faces* did not turn when they moved, each went straight forward.

10 As for the form of their faces, *each* had the face of a man, all four had the face of a lion on the right and the face of a bull on the left, and all four had the face of an eagle.

182 CHAPTER 9 . . .

11 Such were their faces. Their wings were spread out above; each had two touching another *being,* and two covering their bodies.

12 And each went straight forward; wherever the spirit was about to go, they would go, without turning as they went.

13 In the midst of the living beings there was something that looked like burning coals of fire, like torches darting back and forth among the living beings. The fire was bright, and lightning was flashing from the fire.

14 And the living beings ran to and fro like bolts of lightning.

—Ezekiel 1

In verse 13 of this passage we see that these living beings had in their midst coals of burning fire. This ties back to "You walked in the midst of the stones of fire" in Ezekiel 28:14. Verse 14 of Ezekiel 1 also says that the cherubim ran back and forth like bolts of lightning. At one point Christ said that He saw Satan fall from heaven like lightning (Luke 10:18). This might be further evidence that the being talked about in the last half of Ezekiel 28 is indeed Satan.

One thing is clear: if the last half of Ezekiel 28 is talking about Satan, then Satan is no fallen angel. Cherubim are something totally different from angels, with a different function. We know from Revelation 4:4–8 that there are four of these cherubim. They are unique and are definitely not angels.

I do not believe that the Bible tells us explicitly and clearly who Satan is, but it seems to me that the best indications are that he is a fallen cherub, and not a fallen angel, nor a fallen created son of God.

There is one difficulty that we need to address. In Ezekiel 28 we have read that Satan was created beautiful and blameless and later unrighteousness was found in him. However, two verses in the New Testament state that Satan was bad from the beginning. These two passages are:

7 Little children, let no one deceive you; the one who practices righteousness is righteous, just as He is righteous;

8 the one who practices sin is of the devil; for the devil has sinned from the beginning. The Son of God appeared for this purpose, that He might destroy the works of the devil.

—1 John 3

44 "You are of *your* father the devil, and you want to do the desires of your father. He was a murderer from the beginning, and does not stand in the truth, because there is no truth in him. Whenever he speaks a lie, he speaks from his own *nature;* for he is a liar, and the father of lies. . . ."

—John 8

I do not have a good explanation for how these two verses fit in with the previous picture we have had of Satan, unless perhaps when it says he was a "murderer from the beginning" it is talking about from the beginning of the earth. Or perhaps he sinned immediately after he was created and unrighteousness increased in him from that point on. I don't think it really matters. The main thing is what Satan is right now, and that is evil. He is a liar, a murderer and a thief; he is rebellious and he is seeking to destroy any Christian that he can.

Whether Satan is a fallen cherub, a fallen created son of God, a fallen angel or something else, the verses in Job tell us that he had been roaming about the earth and walking around on it. So he had access both to the earth and to God's throne room. This is still true today, as we will see. Satan has access to the earth and yet he has access to the throne of God, because the Bible says that he accuses the brethren night and day before the throne of God:

9 And the great dragon was thrown down, the serpent of old who is called the devil and Satan, who deceives the whole world; he was thrown down to the earth, and his angels were thrown down with him.

10 And I heard a loud voice in heaven, saying,

"Now the salvation, and the power, and the kingdom of our God and the authority of His Christ have come, for the accuser of our brethren has been thrown down, who accuses them before our God day and night.

—Revelation 12

This is part of one of John's visions of things yet to come. In verses such as the following, we also find that Satan is the ruler of this world:

30 "I will not speak much more with you, for the ruler of the world is coming, and he has nothing in Me; . . ."

—John 14

11 and concerning judgment, because the ruler of this world has been judged.

—John 16

Satan is also said to be the ruler of the "air," which is the space between sea level and the clouds (we will have more to say about that later in this chapter). The fact that he is the prince (ruler) of the air is found in these passages:

1 And you were dead in your trespasses and sins,
2 in which you formerly walked according to the course of this world, according to the prince of the power of the air, of the spirit that is now working in the sons of disobedience.

—Ephesians 2

12 For our struggle is not against flesh and blood, but against the rulers, against the powers, against the world forces of this darkness, against the spiritual *forces* of wickedness in the heavenly *places*.

—Ephesians 6

We also know that Satan has power and authority, because he gives these to the first beast in Revelation 13:

1 And he stood on the sand of the seashore.
And I saw a beast coming up out of the sea, having ten horns and seven heads, and on his horns *were* ten diadems, and on his heads *were* blasphemous names.
2 And the beast which I saw was like a leopard, and his feet were *like those* of a bear, and his mouth like the mouth of a lion. And the dragon gave him his power and his throne and great authority.

In spite of his power and authority, Satan does not have many of the attributes of God that he would like to have. For example, he is not omnipresent; that is, he cannot be present everywhere at once. He can only be one place on the earth at a time.

## SATAN'S WAR IN HEAVEN

We know that Satan has access to the earth and to the air, that he has had this dual access at least since the garden of Eden and that he still has it today. We also know that back in the time of Job, he also had access to God's throne room in heaven and he still has that access today. However, there will be a time when Satan will be kicked out of heaven, following a war with Michael and his angels, after which Satan will no longer have access to heaven, but will only have access to earth.

You may be saying, "Wait a minute, Jim. I thought that the battle in heaven has already occurred and Satan has already been cast out of heaven." I would be delighted if someone could give me a passage of Scripture to base that on, but you may have a bit of difficulty in finding one. I did.

This is one subject that always confused me; my "teachers" talked about Satan being kicked out of heaven in a passage back in Isaiah, yet I saw him being kicked out of heaven in Revelation and I could not reconcile the two, I could not figure out if this event had already occurred, if the expulsion from heaven was going to happen in the future, or if it was going to happen twice. Upon doing further research, I found that the passage many people refer to in Isaiah is probably not talking about Satan at all. To begin our search for truth on this subject, let's turn to Isaiah 14. We need to read a long passage from this chapter to get the context, so please be patient and read it all carefully:

3 And it will be in the day when the LORD gives you rest from your pain and turmoil and harsh service in which you have been enslaved,

4 that you will take up this taunt against the king of Babylon, and say,

"How the oppressor has ceased,
*And how* fury has ceased!

5 "The LORD has broken the staff of the wicked,
The scepter of rulers

6 Which used to strike the peoples in fury with unceasing strokes,
Which subdued the nations in anger with unrestrained persecution.

7 "The whole earth is at rest *and* is quiet;
They break forth into shouts of joy.

8 "Even the cypress trees rejoice over you, *and* the cedars of Lebanon, *saying,*
'Since you were laid low, no *tree* cutter comes up against us.'

9 "Sheol from beneath is excited over you to meet you when
   you come;
   It arouses for you the spirits of the dead, all the leaders of the
   earth;
   It raises all the kings of the nations from their thrones.

10 "They will all respond and say to you,
   'Even you have been made weak as we,
   You have become like *us*.

11 'Your pomp *and* the music of your harps
   Have been brought down to Sheol;
   Maggots are spread out *as your bed* beneath you,
   And worms are your covering.'

12 "How you have fallen from heaven,
   O star of the morning, son of the dawn!
   You have been cut down to the earth,
   You who have weakened the nations!

13 "But you said in your heart,
   'I will ascend to heaven;
   I will raise my throne above the stars of God,
   And I will sit on the mount of assembly
   In the recesses of the north.

14 'I will ascend above the heights of the clouds;
   I will make myself like the Most High.'

15 "Nevertheless you will be thrust down to Sheol,
   To the recesses of the pit.

16 "Those who see you will gaze at you,
   They will ponder over you, *saying,*
   'Is this the man who made the earth tremble,
   Who shook kingdoms,

17 Who made the world like a wilderness
   And overthrew its cities,
   Who did not allow his prisoners to *go* home?'

18 "All the kings of the nations lie in glory,
   Each in his own tomb.

19 "But you have been cast out of your tomb
   Like a rejected branch,
   Clothed with the slain who are pierced with a sword,
   Who go down to the stones of the pit,
   Like a trampled corpse.

20  "You will not be united with them in burial,
Because you have ruined your country,
You have slain your people.
May the offspring of evildoers not be mentioned forever. . . ."
—Isaiah 14

Who would you say this passage in Isaiah is talking about? Some people say that it is talking about Satan, because they read only verses 12–15. But if you read the whole thing in context, I believe you will see that it is clearly talking about a king of Babylon. This is a taunt that the children of Israel were to take up against the king of Babylon when he was defeated and they were set free. Verse 17 says that this king overthrew cities and wouldn't let prisoners go home; verses 19–20 say that he is going to go down into a pit like someone who has been stoned to death and he will not have a nice tomb, because he ruined his country and slew his people. I'm not sure how people justify applying the middle part of this taunt to Satan, and using it to "prove" that he has already been cast out of heaven; personally I cannot find any justification for that. Let's now turn to another passage on the fall of Satan:

17  And the seventy returned with joy, saying, "Lord, even the demons are subject to us in Your name."
18  And He said to them, "I was watching Satan fall from heaven like lightning.
19  "Behold, I have given you authority to tread upon serpents and scorpions, and over all the power of the enemy, and nothing shall injure you.
20  "Nevertheless do not rejoice in this, that the spirits are subject to you, but rejoice that your names are recorded in heaven."
—Luke 10

Here Christ says that He was watching Satan fall from heaven like lightning. This could have a number of interpretations. One is that the battle in heaven occurred and Satan was kicked out at that point in time. Another is that Christ, in a visionary way, was looking back to a pre-Adamic event or forward to the battle and expulsion from heaven of Satan spoken of in Revelation. Probably a more plausible interpretation is that, as the seventy went out and conquered demons in the name of Christ, Satan fell from "heaven," which is another name for the "air," and did battle against them.

There is another passage of Scripture that *might* imply that the war in heaven has already occurred:

> 4 For if God did not spare angels when they sinned, but cast them into hell and committed them to pits of darkness, reserved for judgment; . . .
>
> —2 Peter 2

However, upon closely examining this verse you see that it says nothing about Satan or about any war in heaven. I believe this is talking just about individual angels that sinned.

Now let's look at the passage that describes an event involving Satan that we are pretty sure still lies in the future:

> 7 And there was war in heaven, Michael and his angels waging war with the dragon. And the dragon and his angels waged war,
>
> 8 and they were not strong enough, and there was no longer a place found for them in heaven.
>
> 9 And the great dragon was thrown down, the serpent of old who is called the devil and Satan, who deceives the whole world; he was thrown down to the earth, and his angels were thrown down with him.
>
> 10 And I heard a loud voice in heaven, saying,
>
> "Now the salvation, and the power, and the kingdom of our God and the authority of His Christ have come, for the accuser of our brethren has been thrown down, who accuses them before our God day and night.
>
> 11 "And they overcame him because of the blood of the Lamb and because of the word of their testimony, and they did not love their life even to death.
>
> 12 "For this reason, rejoice, O heavens and you who dwell in them. Woe to the earth and the sea, because the devil has come down to you, having great wrath, knowing that he has only a short time."
>
> —Revelation 12

Here we see the first mention of a "war" in heaven, as a result of which Satan is "thrown down" to the earth and evidently no longer allowed access to God's throne. When this happens, Satan will realize that he has only a little while left, and so he will release his full wrath upon the earth (verse 12).

I therefore have to conclude that the actual war in heaven, when Satan is cast down to the earth and no longer allowed access to God's throne, is yet in the future. When that does occur, the persecution of Christians and spiritual warfare will get incredibly intense.

Even though this war is probably still in the future, we know that Satan is evil and he tries to destroy Christians. We have seen that Satan is likely not a fallen angel but a unique fallen cherub. We have also seen that individual angels have sinned (fallen), but the big rebellion of angels is yet ahead of us. When it does occur, we know that it will fail. The victory belongs to God!

## THE BATTLEGROUND

Now that we have seen a little about who Satan is, we need to look at *where* the battle is taking place. As Bible scholars realize, there are at least three heavens. One of these heavens is where the spiritual warfare is going on. Genesis 1 tells us where that heaven is:

> 6 Then God said, "Let there be an expanse in the midst of the waters, and let it separate the waters from the waters."
> 7 And God made the expanse, and separated the waters which were below the expanse from the waters which were above the expanse; and it was so.
> 8 And God called the expanse heaven. . . .

The easiest way to think of this heaven is to think of the area that separates the oceans and the clouds. There is a concentric sphere around the earth touching it at all points between here and the cloud level. That is the heavenly place where the spiritual warfare is going on. This is not the heaven where God is; we read about that heaven in 2 Corinthians 12:

> 2 I know a man in Christ who fourteen years ago—whether in the body I do not know, or out of the body I do not know, God knows—such a man was caught up to the third heaven.
> 3 And I know how such a man—whether in the body or apart from the body I do not know, God knows—

4 was caught up into Paradise, and heard inexpressible words, which a man is not permitted to speak.

—2 Corinthians 12

This is the same heaven that John was caught up into in Revelation where the throne and altar of God and the heavenly temple of God existed (Revelation 4:1, 2; 7:15; 8:3).

We do not know where the second heaven is, but it must be somewhere between the first heaven, which immediately surrounds the earth, and the third heaven, where God's throne is. Some people contend that the second heaven is the realm where Satan reigns and that is why we know nothing about it, but that is purely speculation. The main thing we need to recognize here is that, as we walk on the earth, we are physically in the first heaven where the spiritual war is taking place.

## SATAN'S ARMY

We are at spiritual war with Satan. But don't forget that he is also the commander in chief of an evil army. Since Satan and his army are seeking to devour us (1 Peter 5:8), we need to know something about his army too. We need to know who is in his army and what they do, as well as knowing about Satan himself.

There are basically three groups of beings in Satan's kingdom and army, as we will see. These are:

1.  Demons
2.  Fallen angels
3.  All non-Christians

This list might be a bit confusing to you if you thought that fallen angels and demons were the same thing. Don't feel badly; I thought so too until recently. However, as I studied the subject, I began to realize that they are quite different in nature.

First, to refresh your memory, there are some Scriptures that tell us there are fallen angels:

4  For God did not spare angels when they sinned, but cast them into hell and committed them to pits of darkness, reserved for judgment; . . .

—2 Peter 2

Matthew 25 tells us that Satan has angels:

41  "Then He will also say to those on His left, 'Depart from Me, accursed ones, into the eternal fire which has been prepared for the devil and his angels; . . .'"

—Matthew 25

I can find no evidence in the Scriptures of any angel, either good or fallen, ever seeking to indwell the body of a human being. They evidently have bodies of their own that can be materialized when necessary. For example, the two angels who went to get Lot and his family out of Sodom had their own bodies (Genesis 19:1-16).

On the other hand, demons evidently do not have bodies of their own and they seek diligently and intensely for a body in which they can dwell. You could call these "disembodied evil spirits." The Bible makes numerous references to demons (called "devils" in the *KJV*), sometimes referred to as evil or unclean spirits. These many references inform us that these unclean spirits can indwell a person; such a person is said to be "demon-possessed" (see Mark 5:8, 12, 13, 15, for example).

However, the Bible is silent about the origin of demons and thus one can only speculate about how they came to exist. Robert Peterson, in his book, *Are Demons for Real?*, has this to say about the origin of demons:

Down through the ages, amid much speculation some absurd theories have been advanced regarding the origin of demons. This has been partly due to the definite reserve of Scripture concerning their genesis, a silence which surely suggests that the important thing is not where the demons come from, but that they do actually exist, and that a ceaseless warfare must be waged against them. Nevertheless the question is legitimate and one that is often asked.

Dr. Bancroft says, " Demons are an order of spirit beings apparently distinct and separate from angels, and which from the intimations of certain passages of Scripture (Matt. 12:43, 44; Mark 5:10-14) seem to be in a disembodied state, having existed in some previ-

192 CHAPTER 9 . . .

ous period and place in bodily form." He suggests that the disembodied spirits are *from a pre-Adamite race,* but this must remain in the realm of theory, for the suggestion has no Scriptural support.

Dr. Chafer advances the theme that demons were probably created as subjects of Satan in his original angelic glory. Then when Satan fell, he drew them after him (John 8:44; II Pet. 2:4; Jude 6). This hypothesis is known as the *"fallen angel theory,"* and it divides the fallen angels into two classes; those that are free and those that are bound. The free are the demons, while the bound are those angels guilty of such enormous wickedness that they are confined to pits of darkness awaiting judgment (II Pet. 2:4; Jude 6).

The picture becomes more confused when equally able teachers affirm that demons resulted from the union between "sons of God" (fallen angels) and daughters of men. This is *"the monstrous offspring of angels and antediluvian women theory."* Dr. De Haan is of the opinion that "The sons of God in this passage were none other than fallen angels who caused a supernatural union with the daughters of man, with the resultant birth of these monstrosities." This theory is open to serious doubts that cannot be satisfactorily answered.

These three propositions are the ones most commonly accepted among evangelicals, but the silence of Scripture makes them nothing more than theoretical hypotheses. Others only show how far man can go in absurdity: for example, that demons are the personifications of violent and incurable diseases, or that they are the spirits of the wicked dead as held by the Jewish historian Josephus.

—Moody Press, p. 113-115

As you can see from what Peterson had to say, there is a wide divergence of opinions as to the origin of demons. However, I do believe that it is fairly safe to say that they are indeed different from fallen angels, because fallen angels do not need a body nor seek one, whereas demons evidently need a body in which to dwell and they seek to possess one.

## DEMONS ARE PART OF SATAN'S ARMY

Let's now take a look at the first group of beings in connection with Satan's army, the demons:

22  Then there was brought to Him a demon-possessed man *who was* blind and dumb, and He healed him, so that the dumb man spoke and saw.

23  And all the multitudes were amazed, and *began* to say, "This *man* cannot be the Son of David, can he?"

24  But when the Pharisees heard it, they said, "This man casts out demons only by Beelzebul the ruler of the demons."

25  And knowing their thoughts He said to them, "Any kingdom divided against itself is laid waste; and any city or house divided against itself shall not stand.

26  "And if Satan casts out Satan, he is divided against himself; how then shall his kingdom stand?

27  "And if I by Beelzebul cast out demons, by whom do your sons cast them out? Consequently they shall be your judges.

28  "But if I cast out demons by the Spirit of God, then the kingdom of God has come upon you. . . ."

—Matthew 12

Here we see that the demonic world has a ruler and the ruler is Beelzebul, another name for Satan. We also see that Christ can command these demons and cast them out, but He does so by the power of the kingdom of God.

Satan cannot be everywhere at once. God is omnipresent, but Satan is not. Satan can only be in one place on the earth at a time. Therefore he has to have a giant communication network, probably of demons who relay his messages and communicate to him what is happening.

Most people who think that they have been attacked by Satan really haven't been attacked by him personally. It is rare that he would pick your town and your house. A few years ago, many people in Colombia, South America, had a sense that Satan had come to that country. Hundreds and hundreds of Christians simultaneously had that sense. However, most of what we think of as attacks by Satan are really attacks by demons, who are a part of his kingdom.

Do you remember the television ads where a lady is shown talking to herself and then the two images are merged back into one person? Even though a Christian can be attacked by demons and possibly indwelt by one, I do not believe he can be

194 CHAPTER 9 . . .

demon possessed. I look at demon possession as occurring when a demon merges with a person and controls him. This is usually at the person's invitation. Demon possession almost always involves multiple evil spirits indwelling a person. These demons of Satan will try to deceive people into thinking that they are "red buzz bombs" or "huge black monsters" to be greatly feared, but they are not. They are evil spirits, part of Satan's army, but we can come against them and command them to go, in the name of Jesus, and—praise the Lord—they must obey! In His name and by the power of His blood we have authority over them.

## FALLEN ANGELS ARE PART OF SATAN'S ARMY

We know that fallen angels are part of Satan's kingdom and army for we read about it earlier in this passage from Revelation:

> 3 And another sign appeared in heaven: and behold, a great red dragon having seven heads and ten horns, and on his heads *were* seven diadems.
> 4 And his tail swept away a third of the stars of heaven, and threw them to the earth. . . .
> 7 And there was war in heaven, Michael and his angels waging war with the dragon. And the dragon and his angels waged war,
> 8 and they were not strong enough, and there was no longer a place found for them in heaven.
> 9 And the great dragon was thrown down, the serpent of old who is called the devil and Satan, who deceives the whole world; he was thrown down to the earth, and his angels were thrown down with him.
>
> —Revelation 12

In this passage we see that Satan gathers together about a third of the angels (this is probably going to happen sometime in the future) and rebels against God. He wants to be like God in every way and to be worshiped like God. Satan and his angels lose the battle and they are thrown down to the earth.

## NON-CHRISTIANS ARE IN SATAN'S ARMY

Jesus informs us of another group that is part of Satan's kingdom. He had the following to say when talking to the Pharisees, the religious leaders who obeyed the Jewish laws but were not willing to receive Jesus Christ as the Messiah:

> 44 "You are of *your* father the devil, and you want to do the desires of your father. He was a murderer from the beginning, and does not stand in the truth, because there is no truth in him. Whenever he speaks a lie, he speaks from his own *nature;* for he is a liar, and the father of lies. . . ."
>
> —John 8

According to this, even good, moral religious leaders who do not know and follow Christ are part of Satan's organization and he is their father. Remember, Christ was talking to leaders of the Jews. It is hard for us to visualize a sweet, moral rabbi, who just couldn't believe that Jesus was the Messiah, as being in Satan's kingdom. But Christ said that he was.

Also as part of Satan's kingdom is *anyone* who does not know Jesus Christ—no matter how "spiritual" he might be. Let's read about it:

> 7 Little children, let no one deceive you; the one who practices righteousness is righteous, just as He is righteous;
> 8 the one who practices sin is of the devil; for the devil has sinned from the beginning. The Son of God appeared for this purpose, that He might destroy the works of the devil.
> 9 No one who is born of God practices sin, because His seed abides in him; and he cannot sin, because he is born of God.
> 10 By this the children of God and the children of the devil are obvious: anyone who does not practice righteousness is not of God, nor the one who does not love his brother.
>
> —1 John 3

We see that anyone who does not *practice* righteousness and love is of Satan. Just to be sure that we're together, let me reemphasize: *everyone* that practices sin is of the devil. This means that all non-Christians are of Satan's kingdom, period. No matter if someone is the world's nicest religious leader or your fiancé or business partner; according to the Bible, anyone who does not recognize and accept Jesus Christ as Savior and Lord is part of Satan's kingdom.

Would you want your child to marry or go into business with a communist? "No way! That's ridiculous! Communists have vowed to bury us in America. Their goal is still world domination," you might reply. Wouldn't it be even worse to have your son or daughter marry someone who is part of Satan's kingdom? Satan too has vowed to destroy us. Yet I see Christians, because they are lonely or for other reasons, marrying non-Christians. They should realize that they are marrying a person who is part of a kingdom that is trying to destroy them!

If I start a business and my partner is not a Christian, I should realize he is taking instructions from his king, Satan, who will influence him. His king has vowed to try to destroy me. Any Christian who gets involved with a non-Christian to the extent that the decisions of that non-Christian can affect his life is asking for constant spiritual battles. We can be friends with and reach out to non-Christians, but even being "best friends" implies a commitment. How can you have a best friend who is in the opposing army and is trying to destroy you? Just wait until the persecution of Christians begins in this country and see how much of a "best friend" that person is.

On the other hand, the verses we read in 1 John 3 say that the one that is of God is the one that practices righteousness. I believe there are a lot of misconceptions about what righteousness is. The Lord is calling us to righteousness today. However, many people feel righteousness is a list of rules and regulations, such as: don't drink, don't smoke, don't dip snuff, and go to meetings several times a week. That is being put under the law and under bondage. That is not righteousness.

I would have to say that getting up and going to work without asking God about it is not righteousness. God may want you to go to work 199 days out of 200. But there may be a day when He wants you to stay home to either minister to your wife or just spend a day with Him. I think a person should get up and ask God what He wants him to do that day. Someday He may want you to stay home, but if you don't ask Him, you won't hear His voice. *Righteousness is doing the will of God.* Jesus Christ was righteous; He did God's will perfectly. He also happened to drink wine, yet some people would say that that is not a righteous act. Forget the rules and regulations, and *just follow Jesus and obey God.* To see about the effectiveness of such rules, let's look at Colossians:

> **20 If you have died with Christ to the elementary principles of the world, why, as if you were living in the world, do you submit yourself to decrees, such as,**
> **21 "Do not handle, do not taste, do not touch!"**
> **22 (which all *refer to* things destined to perish with the using)— in accordance with the commandments and teachings of men?**
> **23 These are matters which have, to be sure, the appearance of wisdom in self-made religion and self-abasement and severe treatment of the body, *but are* of no value against fleshly indulgence.**
> —Colossians 2

You can submit to all the rules and regulations you want to, but they are of no value in checking the indulgences of the flesh. The way you check the indulgences of the flesh is by drawing close to God and by doing His will, whatever it is. At times He may lead you to do some things that may seem strange to you. However, doing His will, regardless, assures that you are on the right side.

Now let's see where we have come. We have seen that the kingdom of Satan includes fallen angels, demons, and non-Christians—anyone who has not received Jesus Christ as his Savior and Master and acknowledged Him as God. These are all part of Satan's kingdom and Satan is their king and commander in chief. He uses them to get at you spiritually. If you are going to win in this spiritual war, you first need to recognize who your enemy is. Christ instructed us to love our enemies and to pray for those who despitefully use us. We can pray for our enemies and try to win them over to Jesus Christ's side of the war, but we should not be involved with them in such a way that they can determine our lives.

## SUMMARY AND CONCLUSION

We have covered a great deal in this chapter. Some of it may be new thoughts to many Christians. However, with my whole heart I have tried to lay aside any preconceived ideas and just see what the Bible has to say about the topics we have discussed.

We looked at who Satan is. It is possible that he is a fallen angel leader, although the Bible does not state this explicitly. It is also possible that he is one of the created sons of God, who has turned evil. However, it is most likely that he is a fallen cherub.

We saw that Satan has a kingdom and an army. There are three basic groups of beings in Satan's kingdom and army: demons, fallen angels, and all non-Christians, no matter how moral or religious they may be.

We saw that the battleground of the spiritual war that we are in is in the first heaven. This first heaven is roughly the space between sea level and the clouds in a concentric sphere around the earth touching it at all points.

This is a chapter I would have preferred not to have written, but realistically we need to look at our enemy if we are going to effectively fight against him. Now let's turn to the positive side and look at Christ's army and at how we can better fight against Satan and his troops and win!

# 10

# SPIRITUAL WARFARE

We have just looked at Satan, his kingdom, and his army. We now need to turn our attention to the positive side and to look at Jesus Christ and His army.

The first thing we will be looking at is the angels who are part of Christ's army. There are two errors that we can make concerning angels. One is to be overly concerned about them, even going to the extreme of seeking an encounter with an angel. The other error is to totally ignore them. We will try to very briefly put angels in their proper perspective in the spiritual warfare.

## ANGELS ARE PART OF CHRIST'S ARMY

Just as Satan has fallen angels who are actively involved in his warfare, we also have good angels on our side:

> 10 "See that you do not despise one of these little ones, for I say to you, that their angels in heaven continually behold the face of My Father who is in heaven. . . ."
>
> —Matthew 18

The Bible says that the little children have angels in heaven looking out for them. There are angels of God in this spiritual warfare, who are very real and more powerful than any demon, who are there to protect and care for our children. God loves the children and provides special protection for them.

Now let's look at Psalm 91, part of which is applied to Christ, but I believe it also applies to you and me.

1 He who dwells in the shelter of the Most High
   Will abide in the shadow of the Almighty.
2 I will say to the LORD, "My refuge and my fortress,
   My God, in whom I trust!"
3 For it is He who delivers you from the snare of the trapper,
   And from the deadly pestilence.
4 He will cover you with His pinions,
   And under His wings you may seek refuge;
   His faithfulness is a shield and bulwark.

5 You will not be afraid of terror by night,
   Or of the arrow that flies by day;
6 Of the pestilence that stalks in darkness,
   Or of the destruction that lays waste at noon.
7 A thousand may fall at your side,
   And ten thousand at your right hand;
   *But* it shall not approach you.
8 You will only look on with your eyes,
   And see the recompense of the wicked.
9 For you have made the LORD, my refuge,
   *Even* the Most High, your dwelling place.
10 No evil will befall you,
    Nor will any plague come near your tent.
11 For He will give His angels charge concerning you,
    To guard you in all your ways.
12 They will bear you up in their hands,
    Lest you strike your foot against a stone.
13 You will tread upon the lion and cobra,
    The young lion and the serpent you will trample down.

—Psalm 91

This is applied to Christ in Luke 4:9–12 and legitimately so, but it also legitimately applies to you and me. God gives His angels charge over us to guard and protect us (verses 11–12).

Let's now look at a couple of places in the Bible where angels really do look out after God's children.

9 But Michael the archangel, when he disputed with the devil and argued about the body of Moses, did not dare pronounce against him a railing judgment, but said, "THE LORD REBUKE YOU."

—Jude

Here Michael is warring against Satan over the dead body of Moses. How much more must Michael have fought for Moses while he was alive! Keep in mind that Michael, in all his power, came against Satan in the name of the Lord. If we are effectively going to do battle against wickedness, we too must rebuke Satan in the name of the Lord.

Let's read about an angel that did battle on Daniel's behalf:

1  In the third year of Cyrus king of Persia a message was revealed to Daniel, who was named Belteshazzar; and the message was true and *one of* great conflict, but he understood the message and had an understanding of the vision.

2  In those days I, Daniel, had been mourning for three entire weeks.

3  I did not eat any tasty food, nor did meat or wine enter my mouth, nor did I use any ointment at all, until the entire three weeks were completed.

4  And on the twenty-fourth day of the first month, while I was by the bank of the great river, that is, the Tigris,

5  I lifted my eyes and looked, and behold, there was a certain man dressed in linen, whose waist was girded with *a belt of* pure gold of Uphaz.

6  His body also was like beryl, his face had the appearance of lightning, his eyes were like flaming torches, his arms and feet like the gleam of polished bronze, and the sound of his words like the sound of a tumult.

7  Now I, Daniel, alone saw the vision, while the men who were with me did not see the vision; nevertheless, a great dread fell on them, and they ran away to hide themselves.

8  So I was left alone and saw this great vision; yet no strength was left in me, for my natural color turned to a deathly pallor, and I retained no strength.

9  But I heard the sound of his words; and as soon as I heard the sound of his words, I fell into a deep sleep on my face, with my face to the ground.

10  Then behold, a hand touched me and set me trembling on my hands and knees.

11  And he said to me, "O Daniel, man of high esteem, understand the words that I am about to tell you and stand upright, for I have now been sent to you." And when he had spoken this word to me, I stood up trembling.

12  Then he said to me, "Do not be afraid, Daniel, for from the first day that you set your heart on understanding *this* and on humbling yourself before your God, your words were heard, and I have come in response to your words.

13  "But the prince of the kingdom of Persia was withstanding me for twenty-one days; then behold, Michael, one of the chief princes, came to help me, for I had been left there with the kings of Persia.

14  "Now I have come to give you an understanding of what will happen to your people in the latter days, for the vision pertains to the days yet *future.*"

—Daniel 10

Daniel had prayed for God to help him understand his vision. On that very day his prayer was heard and an angel messenger was started toward Daniel with the interpretation of the vision. Evidently one of the princes of Satan (the prince of Persia) withstood him for twenty-one days. Finally Michael had to come and battle the prince of Persia so that this angel messenger could go on to Daniel. That is a picture of the spiritual warfare that is going on even today and is affecting you and me. It affected Daniel, didn't it? We need to be well aware of this very real war that is going on even at this very moment.

While the battle in heaven was going on, Daniel was fasting and praying for three weeks. I wonder what would have happened if after one week Daniel had given up? I really don't know. But Daniel persisted, so the victory was won in the heavenlies, in the spiritual warfare. I think that we often ask God for something once or twice and then we stop seeking and asking. Since we don't know what is going on in this spiritual warfare, many times we need to press in and continue in prayer. If we really want something, perhaps we need to fast for a day or even for three weeks like Daniel did. Perhaps Daniel wanted spiritual guidance a lot worse than we do. He came out the victor in the spiritual warfare. We might lose out on the victory, if we don't have his type of resolve.

Remember we said that angels are part of God's kingdom and that angels are given charge over us. We see that illustrated in this passage from Daniel. An angel was looking after Daniel and he had to call another angel to help. Angels are concerned about God's people, about protecting us and about being involved in the battle against the satanic angels and demons. God's angels are on our side!

There are not just one or two angels looking out after us. There frequently are many, as we will see in the following passage from 2 Kings. In the beginning of this passage, God supernaturally—by a word of knowledge—tells Elisha where the enemy army is going to be, so Elisha goes to the king and tells him to go the other way:

> 8 Now the king of Aram was warring aginst Israel; and he counseled with his servants saying, "In such and such a place shall be my camp."
>
> 9 And the man of God sent *word* to the king of Israel saying, "Beware that you do not pass this place, for the Arameans are coming down there."
>
> 10 And the king of Israel sent to the place about which the man of God had told him; thus he warned him, so that he guarded himself there, more than once or twice.
>
> 11 Now the heart of the king of Aram was enraged over this thing; and he called his servants and said to them, "Will you tell me which of us is for the king of Israel?"
>
> 12 And one of his servants said, "No, my lord, O king; but Elisha, the prophet who is in Israel, tells the king of Israel the words that you speak in your bedroom."
>
> 13 So he said, "Go and see where he is, that I may send and take him." And it was told him, saying, "Behold, he is in Dothan."
>
> 14 And he sent horses and chariots and a great army there, and they came by night and surrounded the city.
>
> 15 Now when the attendant of the man of God had risen early and gone out, behold, an army with horses and chariots was circling the city. And his servant said to him, "Alas, my master! What shall we do?"
>
> 16 So he answered, "Do not fear, for those who are with us are more than those who are with them."
>
> 17 Then Elisha prayed and said, "O LORD, I pray, open his eyes that he may see." And the LORD opened the servant's eyes, and he saw; and behold, the mountain was full of horses and chariots of fire all around Elisha.
>
> 18 And when they came down to him, Elisha prayed to the LORD and said, "Strike this people with blindness, I pray." So He struck them with blindness according to the word of Elisha.

19  Then Elisha said to them, "This is not the way, nor is this the
city; follow me and I will bring you to the man whom you seek."
And he brought them to Samaria.

20  And it came about when they had come into Samaria, that
Elisha said, "O LORD, open the eyes of these *men,* that they may
see." So the LORD opened their eyes, and they saw; and behold,
they were in the midst of Samaria.

—2 Kings 6

God's army of angels were interested in Elisha's well-being,
as we see in verse 17. There was an entire mountain full of warrior angels ready to fight. Don't underestimate that powerful
force. At times when you feel spiritually overpowered by the
forces of evil, ask God to open your eyes to let you see His
hosts that surround you. You may not physically see them. You
may see them in a vision or you may just sense their presence,
but they are there, ready to fight for you! Praise God!

You might be thinking, "Well, that was great back in the
Bible times, but these things are not really happening today." I
would like to quote from Billy Graham's book, *Angels: God's
Secret Agents:*

Dr. S. W. Mitchell, a celebrated Philadelphia neurologist, had gone
to bed after an exceptionally tiring day. Suddenly he was awakened
by someone knocking on his door. Opening it he found a little girl,
poorly dressed and deeply upset. She told him her mother was very
sick and asked him if he would please come with her. It was a bitter-
ly cold, snowy night, but though he was bone tired, Dr. Mitchell
dressed and followed the girl.

As *Reader's Digest* reports the story, he found the mother des-
perately ill with pneumonia. After arranging for medical care, he
complimented the sick woman on the intelligence and persistence of
her little daughter. The woman looked at him strangely and then
said, "My daughter died a month ago." She added, "Her shoes and
coat are in the clothes closet there." Dr. Mitchell, amazed and per-
plexed, went to the closet and opened the door. There hung the
very coat worn by the little girl who had brought him to tend to her
mother. It was warm and dry and could not possibly have been out
in the wintry night.

Could the doctor have been called in the hour of desperate need
by an angel who appeared as this woman's young daughter? Was
this the work of God's angels on behalf of the sick woman?

The Reverend John G. Paton, a missionary in the New Hebrides Islands, tells a thrilling story involving the protective care of angels. Hostile natives surrounded his mission headquarters one night, intent on burning the Patons out and killing them. John Paton and his wife prayed all during that terror-filled night that God would deliver them. When daylight came they were amazed to see the attackers unaccountably leave. They thanked God for delivering them.

A year later, the chief of the tribe was converted to Jesus Christ, and Mr. Paton, remembering what had happened, asked the chief what had kept him and his men from burning down the house and killing them. The chief replied in surprise, 'Who were all those men you had with you there?" The missionary answered, "There were no men there; just my wife and I." The chief argued that they had seen many men standing guard—hundreds of big men in shining garments with drawn swords in their hands. They seemed to circle the mission station so that the natives were afraid to attack. Only then did Mr. Paton realize that God had sent His angels to protect them. The chief agreed that there was no other explanation. Could it be that God had sent a legion of angels to protect His servants, whose lives were being endangered?

—Doubleday and Company, Inc.,<br>Pocket Book Edition, p. 14-15

We see by this quote from Billy Graham's book that even today God is using His angels to care for and protect His people.

## The Power of Angels

As we try to comprehend the power of an angel, it might help if we first remind ourselves of the incredible power of the sun around which the earth rotates. Pause for a minute and think of the immensity of the power of the nuclear reactions going on there. Even at our distance, millions of miles away, we cannot bear to look straight at it. Yet, remember, our sun is simply a star. Thus, legitimately we could say that each star has that same incredible power.

Did you know that angels are often equated to stars in the Scriptures? One example of this is in Revelation 1:

20 "As for the mystery of the seven stars which you saw in My right hand, and the seven golden lampstands: the seven stars are the angels of the seven churches, and the seven lampstands are the seven churches. . . ."

We could think of an angel as having the same power in the spiritual realm as the sun (our star) has in the physical realm. (You could think of the battles between Satan's angels and God's angels as the only real and legitimate "star wars.")

Right now the angels are only to do the bidding of God the Father. When He tells them to protect us, they must do this. We could never order an angel about. It is meaningless to even attempt to request that an angel do something. It is legitimate, however, to ask God to have his angels protect you.

Hebrews tells us that, at present, we are in a state a little lower than angels:

6 But one has testified somewhere, saying,
"WHAT IS MAN, THAT THOU REMEMBEREST HIM?
OR THE SON OF MAN, THAT THOU ART CONCERNED
ABOUT HIM?
7 "THOU HAST MADE HIM FOR A LITTLE WHILE LOWER
THAN THE ANGELS;
THOU HAST CROWNED HIM WITH GLORY AND HONOR,
And hast appointed him over the works of Thy hands;
8 THOU HAST PUT ALL THINGS IN SUBJECTION UNDER
HIS FEET."
For in subjecting all things to him, He left nothing that is not subject to him. But now we do not yet see all things subjected to him.
—Hebrews 2

However, the Bible tells us that eventually the angels will be our servants (ministers):

13 But to which of the angels has He ever said,
"SIT AT MY RIGHT HAND,
UNTIL I MAKE THINE ENEMIES
A FOOTSTOOL FOR THY FEET"?
14 Are they not all ministering spirits, sent out to render service for the sake of those who will inherit salvation?
—Hebrews 1

Here we see that the angels are serving spirits, sent out for the sake of those who are going to inherit salvation.

We can legitimately appreciate and be thankful that God loves us and has given His powerful angels charge to guard over us. However, when the ultimate kingdom of God is revealed, they will be our servants and, therefore, we should not worship them, give them any undue honor or become overly enamored with them.

Angels are part of God's army and I praise God for them, but they are not the most significant part of God's army, as we will soon see.

## ALL CHRISTIANS SHOULD BE IN CHRIST'S ARMY

Christians have the privilege of entering God's army, but I do not believe that all Christians are a part of God's army. Spiritual birth, being "born again," is the first prerequisite and it must occur before we can even "see" the kingdom of God, much less be part of it or of God's army:

> 3 Jesus answered and said to him, "Truly, truly, I say to you, unless one is born again, he cannot see the kingdom of God."
> —John 3

God has recently shown me something different than what I had always taught. I previously taught that all Christians were in God's army. I no longer think that this is true. Let's look at 2 Timothy 2:

> 3 Suffer hardship with *me,* as a good soldier of Christ Jesus.
> 4 No soldier in active service entangles himself in the affairs of everyday life, so that he may please the one who enlisted him as a soldier.

Paul is saying here that being a good soldier is something that we are to do. I believe that God wants every Christian to be a soldier in His army, but as I look at Christendom, I see many spiritual civilians who enjoy the blessings of God and the nice times of fellowship, but they are not out battling evil and trying to defeat the enemy. They enjoy "a nice cozy fire in the home country" while the battle is going on someplace else. There are

Christians who once were soldiers but who are now AWOL (absent without leave). Perhaps they think they have been soldiering long enough and feel that they need to take care of themselves for a while. I think there are also traitors in God's army: anyone who aids and abets the enemy is becoming involved in an act of treason. You can probably think of many things Christians do that help Satan and his cause.

There are many ways that Satan can use Christians. In a physical war, if your buddy gets wounded out in the battlefield, a real friend would risk his own life to try to save him. Christians, however, are frequently like vultures. A brother gets wounded and rather than concentrating on how much we love him and how much he needs our help, we often "kick him while he's down." If a brother in a fellowship gets wounded spiritually, loses a battle or gets a spiritual arm or a leg shot off, our response needs to be one of love and restoration, because we need his strength in this spiritual warfare. The Bible has some clear things to say about what to do if we cannot salvage such a brother or if that person refuses to listen when we try to help him, but that's no excuse for not trying, is it?

In the story that Christ told of the shepherd that had ninety-nine sheep in the fold and one that was lost, the shepherd left the ninety-nine and went after the one (Matthew 18: 12–13). How many pastors I have seen in my years as a Christian who have let people go who are mad or upset! That is not a shepherd's heart. If somebody is spiritually wounded and limping, our reaction should not be "to heck with him"; rather we should yearn to go out and bring him back to the fold, as the shepherd did with the one lost sheep in Christ's parable. There may be a day when the situation will be reversed and that person will be carrying you. As you treat other people, someday you will be treated the same way.

As I said earlier, however, if a brother is wounded in the spiritual warfare but does not want any help, the Bible has some strong things to say about what we should do. Let's look at this in Matthew 18. The main point of this passage is the attempt to restore our brother.

15 "And if your brother sins, go and reprove him in private; if he listens to you, you have won your brother.

16 "But if he does not listen *to you,* take one or two more with you, so that BY THE MOUTH OF TWO OR THREE WITNESSES EVERY FACT MAY BE CONFIRMED.

17 "And if he refuses to listen to them, tell it to the church; and if he refuses to listen even to the church, let him be to you as a Gentile and a tax-gatherer. . . ."

—Matthew 18

This is the only place in the New Testament where Christ told the "ekklesia," which is the Greek word for church, how to behave in the future. He could have told them how to organize or how to have church meetings, but this is the only thing that He said concerning how He wanted the church to operate. If a brother offends you (sins against you), you are to go to him. (I believe that offense here refers to anything that breaks your fellowship with him.) If he listens, then you have won a brother and restored your fellowship. It does not say that he has to change—only "listen." ("If he listens" I believe means if he will seriously go to God and seek God's will on the matter.) However, if he refuses to "listen," then you should go to him again with two or three witnesses; if he still won't listen he should be brought before the entire church and given one more opportunity. If he still will not listen, he should then be cast out and treated like a pagan.

You might say: "Wait a minute, Jim. We're not supposed to judge one another." That is *not true.* We are not to judge non-Christians, as we will see in a moment; that is God's domain. However, the Bible clearly says that we are to judge those in our fellowship who claim to be Christians:

9 I wrote you in my letter not to associate with immoral people:

10 I *did* not at all mean with the immoral people of this world, or with the covetous and swindlers, or with idolaters; for then you would have to go out of the world.

11 But actually, I wrote to you not to associate with any so-called brother if he should be an immoral person, or covetous, or an idolater, or a reviler, or a drunkard, or a swindler—not even to eat with such a one.

12  For what have I to do with judging outsiders? Do you not judge those who are within *the church?*

13  But those who are outside, God judges. REMOVE THE WICKED MAN FROM AMONG YOURSELVES.

—1 Corinthians 5

We should try to restore a wounded brother or one who is living in sin. If he will not be restored, then, according to the passage we just read, we should not even eat with him. If such a person asks to have lunch with you, you should say, "No, not if you are continuing to live in this sin," or something to that effect. We are not to judge outsiders, but we must judge those who are in the body of believers in order to be able to "remove the wicked man from among ourselves."

Even though 1 Corinthians says to cast out the Christian who is living in sin, we must remember that 2 Corinthians says that if he repents we are to receive him back. Some Christians are quick to practice the "casting out" of 1 Corinthians, but unfortunately they forget about 2 Corinthians. If we practice 1 Corinthians, we must be sure also to receive a brother back into full fellowship as soon as he repents. I knew a pastor once who committed an immoral act. God convicted him and he immediately repented. Half of the church accepted his repentance and remained. The other half left the church. God blessed those who remained. I believe those who left were wrong. They were not willing to accept the brother, even though he had repented.

Let me give you another example on the other side. A couple years after I finished college, a Bible study still met in my home which was composed of mostly college students. There was a girl who attended who was sleeping with her boyfriend. We knew it and she knew that we knew it. After they had broken up, the Lord began to teach us the above principle. This girl said, with tears in her eyes, "Oh how I wish you would have applied that principle to me. As long as I could have both my boyfriend and my Christian fellowship, I would take both. But if I had had to choose, I would have chosen the Christian fellowship." We did her a bad disservice in not really drawing the line and forcing her to choose. If she had chosen sleeping with her boyfriend instead of the Christian fellowship, we would not even have been able to eat with her, according to 1 Corinthians 5.

The passage we read from Matthew 18 is the only thing that Christ taught about the operation of the church, and it is probably one thing that churches rarely practice today. This command from Christ—to go directly to your brother if he offends you—is for the purifying of the body and to help us encourage one another to be good soldiers.

In judging the brothers who are in our local fellowship, we have to be careful not to "accuse" them. Let's see why:

> 9  And the great dragon was thrown down, the serpent of old who is called the devil and Satan, who deceives the whole world; he was thrown down to the earth, and his angels were thrown down with him.
> 10  And I heard a loud voice in heaven, saying,
> "Now the salvation, and the power, and the kingdom of our God and the authority of His Christ have come, for the accuser of our brethren has been thrown down, who accuses them before our God day and night. . . ."
>
> —Revelation 12

Here we see that the accuser of our brethren is Satan. When we accuse a brother, whose team are we playing on? We are playing on Satan's team! Usually the accusing is done with a more or less well-meaning intention of "warning weaker brothers." For example, I have heard some people say of one outstanding Christian leader, "Well, his teachings used to be good, but he is off on this bad tangent now." What are they doing when they say things like that? They are really accusing one of the brethren. The Bible clearly says we are not to do that. We are to go to that Christian brother, if he has offended us (Matthew 18:15), or keep our mouths shut.

I have even found this to be a problem in my own situation. There have been some false rumors started about me that had no basis in truth whatsoever. As these were passed from mouth to mouth, these people were guilty of "accusing" me and thus were playing on Satan's ball team. They were also guilty of breaking one of the ten commandments for they were "bearing *false witness*" against me. Only two Christians ever came to me and asked me about the rumors; we were able to clear it up instantly. It was only by a caring brother coming to me that I even came to know about the false rumors that were circulating.

Whether it be a national Christian leader, someone in your own fellowship, or even your pastor, if you hear anything negative spoken about that person, either go to him or dismiss it from your mind and keep quiet about it; otherwise *you* will be guilty of acting as a traitor and fighting in Satan's army rather than in God's army.

### Are You In or Out?

I would hope that you will examine yourself as to whether you are a spiritual civilian, enjoying God's blessings and Christian fellowship but not really battling Satan and the evil forces, or whether you are a soldier involved in spiritual warfare. If you find yourself in a position other than that of an active soldier, God is asking you to volunteer for His army.

You may have been a good soldier at one time but have gone AWOL, for whatever reason. God is asking you to come back. He will pardon the offense and you can get on with the spiritual warfare.

You may occasionally be committing acts of treason in your closet when you don't think anyone knows. Everyone in the spiritual heavenlies knows, so you are only fooling yourself. I think that we all need to examine our hearts afresh to see where we stand.

Remember, a soldier is much like a slave. When you join God's army, you give up all of your rights. However, once you join, God provides all that you need. One of His major provisions we will examine next.

### THE ARMOR OF GOD

One of the most significant things that God gives to His soldiers is the armor of God. You may be thinking: "Ho hum!

The armor of God again. I've heard this over and over." Yet I have found that most people who speak or teach on the armor of God do so incorrectly. I have heard ministers preach on the armor of God who say: "Here's the shield of faith. We need to have more faith. Here's the breastplate of righteousness. We need to do more righteous acts. Here's the helmet of salvation, which means the born again experience." Many of the things they say might be true, but this is not what Paul is talking about in Ephesians 6. We do need to live more righteously, but that is not the helmet of salvation. We do need to have faith, but that is not the shield of faith. Let's begin by reviewing what Paul had to say on this subject in Ephesians:

> 10 Finally, be strong in the Lord, and in the strength of His might.
> 11 Put on the full armor of God, that you may be able to stand firm against the schemes of the devil.
> 12 For our struggle is not against flesh and blood, but against the rulers, against the powers, against the world forces of this darkness, against the spiritual *forces* of wickedness in the heavenly *places*.
> 13 Therefore, take up the full armor of God, that you may be able to resist in the evil day, and having done everything, to stand firm.
> 14 Stand firm therefore, HAVING GIRDED YOUR LOINS WITH TRUTH, and HAVING PUT ON THE BREASTPLATE OF RIGHTEOUSNESS,
> 15 and having shod YOUR FEET WITH THE PREPARATION OF THE GOSPEL OF PEACE;
> 16 in addition to all, taking up the shield of faith with which you will be able to extinguish all the flaming missiles of the evil *one*.
> 17 And take THE HELMET OF SALVATION, and the sword of the Spirit, which is the word of God.
>
> —Ephesians 6

Did you notice in verse 11 that this is not our armor, but that it is *God's armor*. Ministers frequently teach this as though we have to create our own armor. However, we must realize that it is not our armor, but God's. This armor totally exists in a complete form right now; all we have to do is to put it on. This is taught clearly in Isaiah 59. In this passage, God sees the wickedness and the injustice in Israel. He doesn't find anyone who is interceding because of all this wickedness and injustice. Let's read what He does about it:

> 15  . . . Now the LORD saw,
>       And it was displeasing in His sight that there was no justice.
> 16  And He saw that there was no man,
>       And was astonished that there was no one to intercede;
>       Then His own arm brought salvation to Him;
>       And His righteousness upheld Him.
> 17  And He put on righteousness like a breastplate,
>       And a helmet of salvation on His head;
>       And He put on garments of vengeance for clothing,
>       And wrapped Himself with zeal as a mantle.
> 18  According to *their* deeds, so He will repay,
>       Wrath to His adversaries, recompense to His enemies;
>       To the coastland He will make recompense.
>
> —Isaiah 59

In these verses we see God putting on His armor. When God sees that no one is doing anything about the wickedness and the injustice, He puts on the helmet of salvation (helmet of "deliverance" is a better translation) and the breastplate of righteousness, and He intervenes to take care of the situation. This is *His* armor. It already exists and it is perfect.

God also puts on two other things. One is the clothing that goes under armor: the garment of vengeance. You would expect that this would be omitted in Ephesians 6, because we should never take vengeance ourselves. "Vengeance is mine, I will repay," says the Lord (Romans 12:19b). If your neighbor throws rocks in your yard, you shouldn't throw them back. If you are taking vengeance, on any level, God will not bless it. Vengeance is the Lord's, so we do not wear the garment of vengeance.

In Old Testament times, soldiers put a mantle over the suit of armor. Isaiah 59 also says that God put on zeal as a mantle. I think that God does want us to add a mantle of zeal to our armor. Remember that Christ was zealous for the house of the Lord (John 2:17).

Let's look in more detail at the Lord's armor, beginning with the shield of faith.

## The Shield of Faith

The shield is part of God's armor listed in Ephesians 6. We will need to wear this armor if we are going to be good and victorious soldiers. We find out something interesting about the shield of faith in Genesis 15:

> 1  After these things the word of the LORD came to Abram in a vision, saying,
>     "Do not fear, Abram,
>     I am a shield to you;
>     Your reward shall be very great."

God is telling Abraham that *He* is his shield. Now look at Psalm 3:

> 3  But Thou, O LORD, art a shield about me,
>     My glory, and the One who lifts my head.

God is a shield that surrounds us. Also, in Psalm 5 we read:

> 12  For it is Thou who dost bless the righteous man, O LORD,
>      Thou dost surround him with favor as with a shield.

If God Himself is my shield, and He surrounds me all the way around—front and back  if Satan throws a fiery dart at me, who must he go through to get to me? He has to go through God the Father. Can Satan get through God to get at me? No way!

What is our problem then if we are being hit by Satan? We are outside of God. We have stepped outside of His armor and have gone our own way. We are doing our own thing and suddenly find ourselves battling Satan and the fiery darts begin to sting. We find ourselves sinning and displeasing God. What's the solution? Immediately hop back inside of God, who is our shield. Where faith comes in is that once we step back inside the Lord's shield, we need to have faith that Satan cannot get through to us. That is a very easy thing to have faith about. If you find yourself being clobbered by Satan, the first thing to do is get back inside the shield of God Himself, which should be around you.

It is exciting to recognize that the New Testament depicts a similar concept.

> **13** No temptation has overtaken you but such as is common to man; and God is faithful, who will not allow you to be tempted beyond what you are able, but with the temptation will provide the way of escape also, that you may be able to endure it.
>
> —1 Corinthians 10

In southern California there are what are called "walled communities." These are communities that have a wall built all the way around them and there is a gate at the front with a guard. If you want to visit somebody who lives within one of these walled communities, you approach the guard and tell him who you are and who you wish to see. He then phones that person and if he says it is all right to let you in, then you can go in; otherwise you are turned away.

God has similarly built a wall around you and me, and *He* is the guard at the gate. If a temptation "wants to visit you," God will not allow that temptation to come to you if it is beyond what you are able to handle. If the temptation is too strong for you, God turns it away. Nothing can get at you that 'God does not allow. God is a shield about you and nothing will get inside that shield that He has not allowed. Anytime you are tempted of anything, you can know that it has passed God's inspection and that He has confidence that you can handle it. It might give you a little extra strength to know that He is counting on you.

Back in Chapter 4 of this book, we talked about Christ being tempted in all areas as we are. To review, Hebrews 4 says:

> **15** For we do not have a high priest who cannot sympathize with our weaknesses, but one who has been tempted in all things as *we are, yet* without sin.

Satan has confused people with what is a temptation and what is a sin. As I said earlier in this book, if a thought comes into our minds, that thought is not a sin; it is a temptation. It is only if I harbor that thought and begin to nurture it and enjoy it mentally that it becomes a sin in my heart, which frequently then leads to overt sin. Rarely is there any sin that we commit that we have not already enjoyed in our mind many times over. The first thought is not a sin, but a temptation. I believe that Christ had some tempting thoughts, such as to bust a Pharisee in the mouth, but he did not yield to that temptation. If Satan can get you to thinking that that first thought is sin, he will have you constantly churned up and feeling guilty. He will remind you of all the terrible thoughts that you are having which make you so rotten and filthy that the Lord could never use you. That is a lie of Satan! Christ was tempted in every point like we are, but He was without sin.

God tests us and tries us, but He never tempts us. Let's look in Hebrews, where we see that God tested Abraham:

> 17 By faith Abraham, when he was tested, offered up Isaac; and he who had received the promises was offering up his only begotten *son;*
>
> 18 *it was he* to whom it was said, "IN ISAAC YOUR DESCENDANTS SHALL BE CALLED."
>
> 19 He considered that God is able to raise *men* even from the dead; from which he also received him back as a type.
>
> —Hebrews 11

Let's also look at 1 Peter 1:

> 6 In this you greatly rejoice, even though now for a little while if necessary, you have been distressed by various trials,
>
> 7 that the proof of your faith, *being* more precious than gold which is perishable, even though tested by fire, may be found to result in praise and glory and honor at the revelation of Jesus Christ;
>
> 8 and though you have not seen Him, you love Him, and though you do not see Him now, but believe in Him, you greatly rejoice with joy inexpressible and full of glory,
>
> 9 obtaining as the outcome of your faith the salvation of your souls.

This passage says that God brings trials and testings but, remember, God never brings temptation. When you have something come into your life and you wonder whether it is a testing of God or a temptation, look at the end result. Is it something that will not glorify God, in which case it is a temptation;

or will it glorify God, in which case it is a trial or a testing from the Lord? But, praise the Lord, none of these—trials, testings, or temptations—can get to you if you are within the shield of God, unless God has approved it.

In Ephesians 6, where it says that we are to take up the shield of faith, all we have to do is to reach out and take God's shield, which is God Himself. Nothing that Satan throws at us can penetrate that shield!

Martin Luther must have had this in mind when he wrote that great hymn, "A Mighty Fortress Is Our God." God is a *fortress* about us—you could think of it as a shield perhaps 100 feet thick. When we are inside the shield or the fortress of God Himself, Satan cannot get at us.

### The Breastplate of Righteousness

As we begin to look at God's breastplate of righteousness, we need to remind ourselves of Isaiah 64:6, which says that all our righteousness is like filthy rags. How much would a breastplate of filthy rags protect us from the enemy? Not much. That's not to say we are not to live righteously—we are called to righteousness (1 Timothy 6:11). But in looking at God's armor, we are not putting on our righteousness as a breastplate; we are putting on the breastplate of God's righteousness. Can a sword penetrate God's righteousness? No!

> 10  I will rejoice greatly in the LORD,
>       My soul will exult in my God;
>       For He has clothed me with garments of salvation,
>       He has wrapped me with a robe of righteousness, . . .
>
> —Isaiah 61

All of the righteousness of Jesus Christ is imputed to me. God looks at all of Christ's righteous acts as though I did them! All of the sins that I have done, God looks at as though Jesus Christ did them. *That* is the righteousness that protects us.

Now let's look at Galatians 2:

> 21  "I do not nullify the grace of God; for if righteousness *comes* through the Law, then Christ died needlessly."

The law says that I should do certain things and that I should abstain from other things. Can any person become righteous by doing good things and not doing bad things? No. If they could, this passage says that the death of Christ would have been a needless thing. If we put our faith in Jesus Christ, His righteousness is counted or "reckoned" to us as though it were our own. *This* is the way we become righteous. It's *God's* righteousness that we have confidence in, not our own.

Lest you might think that I am saying we do not need to be righteous, let's look briefly at the righteousness we are to pursue:

> 9 And this I pray, that your love may abound still more and more in real knowledge and all discernment,
> 10 so that you may approve the things that are excellent, in order to be sincere and blameless until the day of Christ;
> 11 having been filled with the fruit of righteousness which *comes* through Jesus Christ, to the glory and praise of God.
> —Philippians 1

God wants us to be filled with the fruit of righteousness, which is the fruit of the Holy Spirit—love, joy, peace, longsuffering, and so forth (Galations 5:22, 23). This is something that we are to do. The breastplate is on the outside. We are to be filled on the inside with the fruit of righteousness. The breastplate of righteousness on the outside is God's righteousness, which He has given to us. When Satan accuses us of being filthy and good for nothing, we can count on God's righteousness to protect our hearts. Praise the Lord!

### The Helmet of Deliverance

The helmet of deliverance or salvation cannot be the salvation experience, because in Isaiah 59 God put it on and He certainly did not need "saving from sin." To put on any of the armor of God, you must have already had the salvation experience. This is God's helmet of "deliverance," a better translation than "salvation." What is God delivering Christians from? Let's take a look at a couple of things, starting with Psalm 34:

4  I sought the LORD, and He answered me,
And delivered me from all my fears.

God is in the deliverance business. One of the things that
He delivers us from is fear. What are people afraid of today?—
nuclear war, an economic collapse, that their spouse might die,
to name just a few. Seek the Lord and He will answer you and
deliver you from *all* your fears. He has the helmet of deliverance. Our fears exist in our minds. That is why it is the *helmet*
of deliverance. God wants to deliver our minds from all the
fear, anxieties, corruption, and misconceptions that we have.

If we get worried about persecution or people doing painful things to us physically, the Lord will deliver us from these
fears and even from the fear of death. The helmet of deliverance protects our minds from those things that Satan would
bring against us. Fear, anxiety and depression exist in our minds
and God is perfectly able to deliver us from them. One way
that we are to be an overcomer and victorious in the spiritual
warfare is by putting on the helmet of His deliverance. If we do
that, Satan cannot penetrate that helmet of deliverance and get
at our minds.

## The Shoes of The Preparation of The Gospel

The shoes of the preparation of the gospel are part of
God's armor, listed in Ephesians 6, that a soldier of God is to
put on. I don't have great insight into this, but I will share with
you what I have found.

Back in Exodus when Moses saw the burning bush, what
did God tell him to do? . . . To take off his shoes for he was
standing on holy ground. In another instance, the captain of
the Lord's host told Joshua to remove his sandles for he was
standing on holy ground (Joshua 5:15). We need to take off our
old shoes before we can put on new ones. We take off our old
shoes to go into the presence of the Lord and, in prayer and
supplication with thanksgiving, we make our requests known
to God and He will answer. That is the preparation part of it.

We then put on some new shoes to go out and do battle with Satan and to help win people into God's kingdom. Eventually, those shoes are going to play a part in the victory:

> 20 And the God of peace will soon crush Satan under your feet. . . .
>
> —Romans 16

God is eventually going to crush Satan under *our* feet! It doesn't say under God's feet or under Christ's feet, but God is going to crush Satan under *our* feet and we will be wearing the shoes that we put on as part of the full armor of God.

## Having Our Loins Girded With Truth

The girdle of truth is a significant part of the armor of God in Ephesians 6. Back in the days when the New Testament was written, it was from the girdle that the sword in the armor hung. According to Ephesians 6:14, we are to have a girdle of truth. The battle is over truth, as we will see in the next chapter. Satan is the father of lies. Everything he says is a lie. Everything that a demon says is a lie. If a demon tells you that he is tall, that is a lie. If he tells you that he is red, that is a lie. All that comes from them are lies.

One of Satan's best tactics against us is to get us to lie, either to other people or to ourselves. I think often we lie more to ourselves than we do to other people. The way in which we will defeat Satan is by having our loins girded with truth. Many people, including Christians, tend to lie on their income tax forms. They think that since they got $25 from helping Joe, for example, it doesn't need to be reported. God wants to deliver you from even "little white lies" and the rationalization that goes with them.

Speaking of truth, this takes us to a concept that I feel God wants us to deal with here, and that is keeping our word. I have had so many Christians tell me that they were going to do something and then not do it or that they would pick me up at a certain time and be an hour late. Their word has begun to mean very little to me. In the Old Testament times, a person's word could be relied upon totally.

In Joshua 9, Joshua and the army of Israel were conquering city after city. The people in the next city knew that they were soon going to be conquered and they thought they had better do something about it. So they got some old clothes, old shoes, old bread and old wine skins and circled around behind Joshua and his army. They told Joshua that they had come from a long distance and wanted to make a peace treaty. Joshua didn't ask counsel of God but took everything at face value and made a covenant with them to let them live. When he found out that they were the people from the next city, he didn't kill them, even though God had told him to do so. In our thinking, we would say that the contract was based on a lie and so Joshua should have gone ahead and killed them. But Joshua had made a covenant with them, and his word and the word of the children of Israel was so important that even if somebody else had deceived them, they would not break their word. In Psalm 15 we read:

> 4   In whose eyes a reprobate is despised,
>     But who honors those who fear the LORD;
>     He swears to his own hurt, and does not change; . . .

Here in Psalms it says that if a righteous man gives his word and it proves to be to his disadvantage, he will still keep his word. In the early days of our country, a man's word was as good as his bond—just as though he had put up $5,000. If two men shook hands in the evening in agreement about the selling of a horse to be picked up in the morning, and the horse died during the night, the buyer would go ahead and pay the seller for the horse anyhow, because he had given his word. It was just as if it had been a signed and sealed contract.

I think we Christians in general treat our word too lightly. We agree to something but all too often we don't come through. Christ says to let our "yes" mean "yes" and our "no" mean "no" and anything else is sin (Matthew 5:37). If we tell someone we will be at his house at 7:30, we need to realize that we have given our word and we should not wander in at 8:00.

If you begin to get a reputation among your non-Christian friends that your word doesn't mean much, how are they going to rely on your word when you tell them about Christ? I really believe we need to sharpen up on the keeping of our word and treat it as a valuable commodity. As I said, I have had many Christians tell me that they were going to do something and it never happened; frequently there was never even an apology. That is not having our loins girded with truth, is it? We need to watch our word so that when we speak and commit to something, people know that they can absolutely count on it. One of the reasons I say this is because I believe times of persecution are coming for Christians and we really have to know whom we can count on and whom we cannot. Now is the time to be able to begin to count on one another's word.

It is important that the sword hangs from the girdle of truth. You will not be able to use the word of God, the sword of the Spirit, unless you have a girdle, the truth of your own lips, to hang it on. If people cannot trust what you say, neither will they believe you when you talk about Christ.

## The Sword of The Spirit—The Word of God

The sword of the Spirit is the only *offensive* weapon in the armor of God. All of the other pieces listed are *defensive*. But whose sword is it? Yours? Definitely not. The Bible says that it is the sword of the Holy Spirit.

I have seen people hold up their Bibles and say, "I have 'my sword' with me." There is no way that the Bible can be "your" sword. It is the sword of the Holy Spirit. As the Holy Spirit uses the word of God, Satan will surely be defeated because the Holy Spirit is so much more powerful than Satan.

Even though it is the sword of the Spirit, He uses our mouths to give forth the word of God, but it must be empowered by the Holy Spirit. This was pointed out very vividly to me in a book that I read shortly after I became a Christian. This book was by R. A. Torrey, and he was recounting the experience he had had in an evangelistic meeting in England. This series of meetings went on for a number of days. After each meeting he invited people to come to a counseling room if they wanted to receive Christ.

On this particular evening, a number of people had come to the counseling room and one by one they had received Christ. As the people gradually drifted out of the room, there was only one inquirer left. Talking to him was R. A. Torrey's senior, number-one counselor. Finally this counselor called Dr. Torrey over and asked if he would talk to this inquirer, because he didn't seem to be able to get through to him. R. A. Torrey sat down, went over a few verses of Scripture, and the person decided to pray and receive Jesus Christ as his Savior.

After the new convert had left, the counselor asked Dr. Torrey what the difference was, because Dr. Torrey had used the same verses of Scripture that the counselor had been going over. Dr. Torrey's answer was that he knew that if his counselor couldn't lead that man to the Lord, he couldn't either. So he breathed a prayer and asked the Holy Spirit to make the verses that he would be using alive and real to the inquirer's heart. Do you see that the counselor was trying to use the sword himself, whereas Dr. Torrey was being used of the Holy Spirit to speak the words, but the Holy Spirit was the One using the sword. The sword of the Spirit is powerful if we allow Him to use it.

To see how powerful the sword of the Spirit is, consider what occurs at Christ's return. When Christ returns at the battle of Armageddon, He will slay the armies gathered against Him and the only weapon that He will use will be the words of His mouth (the sword proceeds out of His mouth). His word is the most powerful weapon in the universe.

We could spend a lot more time on the armor of God; it is such an exciting subject. But the main thing to remember is that it is *His* armor. *He* is our shield. It is *His* righteousness that protects our hearts. It is His helmet of deliverance that will deliver our minds from fear and other attacks. The Holy Spirit is available to use His sword on our behalf. God's armor is available to us now. All we have to do is put it on. If you haven't done that, you are really not a soldier or you are AWOL without a uniform on. I would encourage you to make that decision to become a soldier. Put on the armor of God. Get into the battle and the victory *will* be yours in Christ Jesus.

In summary, we see that part of the army of Christ are those Christians who have volunteered to become soldiers of Jesus Christ, who have given up all rights of their own, and who are not entangled in the affairs of this world.

We must first become soldiers before we can fight and win, and thus become overcomers. But don't forget, becoming a bondslave is the doorway to entering the overcomer realm. I believe that becoming a bondslave and volunteering to be a soldier are really the same act of the will.

## OUR COMMANDER IN CHIEF, JESUS CHRIST

In looking at Christ's army, we see the host of warrior angels, and the host of Christians who have volunteered to be bondslaves, soldiers and overcomers. However, by far the single most important person in this army is our Commander in chief, Jesus Christ.

No one can stand against the incredible power of Jesus Christ. We know that when Christ returns at the battle of Armageddon, He will slay the armies gathered against Him. As we mentioned earlier, the only weapon He will use, and the only one He needs, is the words of His mouth. The spoken words that proceed out of His mouth will obliterate the armies, for His word is the most powerful weapon in existence.

In the next chapter, we will look more at our Commander in chief and at the ultimate victory that is ours through Him.

## SUMMARY AND CONCLUSION

We have discussed the army of Jesus Christ. There are two main components of His army, one being His angel warriors, who are incredibly powerful and whose job it is to protect and care for the truly dedicated Christians.

The other part of Christ's army consists of those Christians who have volunteered to become bondslaves or soldiers. Not every Christian is a soldier or we would not be encouraged to "put on" the whole armor of God or to "become a soldier."

To be an effective soldier we must put on the armor of

God. We saw that we do not create this armor but that it has existed from time immemorial. All that we have to do is to put it on and learn to use it. However, we do not wield the sword, the word of God. That is the Holy Spirit's weapon and one of God's gifts to us, for the Holy Spirit lives within us and fights alongside us and He wields that weapon to put Satan to flight.

Of course, by far the single most important person in this army is our Commander in chief, Jesus Christ. As we follow close behind Him, we are absolutely guaranteed a victory, as we already know that He will be the ultimate victor.

# 11

# THE BATTLE AND THE VICTORY

We have looked at Satan's army and Christ's army. Hopefully by now you have decided to become a soldier in Christ's army. I pray that you have decided to put on God's armor and not rely on your own armor or your own strength.

Now if we are truly going to be overcomers or victors in this spiritual warfare, we need to take a closer look at the battle itself. But even as we look at the battle, we should keep our eyes on our Commander in chief, Jesus Christ, and the ultimate victory that will be His.

## THE BASIC BATTLE IS OVER TRUTH

We know that the battle is not over power:

18 And Jesus came up and spoke to them, saying, "All authority has been given to Me in heaven and on earth. . . ."

—Matthew 28

All power or all authority has been given to Christ in heaven and on earth. Since He has all power and authority, the battle cannot be over power.

The battle is also not over ownership, since Psalm 24 records the fact that God owns the earth and all that dwells in it.

1 The earth is the LORD'S, and all it contains,
The world, and those who dwell in it.

—Psalm 24

What is the battle over then? To answer this, we must first examine several things. In the Scriptures, Christ is called the morning star or the morning light (a star being a source of light):

16    "I, Jesus, have sent My angel to testify to you these things for the churches. I am the root and the offspring of David, the bright and morning star."

—Revelation 22

This next verse from Job lets us know that there are other beings referred to as morning stars:

7    When the morning stars sang together,
And all the sons of God shouted for joy?

—Job 38

Often in the Scriptures, angels are referred to as stars. For example, Revelation 12:4 says that the dragon (Satan) "swept away a third of the stars of heaven, and threw them to earth."

When the fifth trumpet is sounded in the book of Revelation, we see Satan also referred to as a star:

1    And the fifth angel sounded, and I saw a star from heaven which had fallen to the earth; and the key of the bottomless pit was given to him.

—Revelation 9

If indeed the long passage that we read in Chapter 9 from Isaish 14 is applicable to Satan, as well as to the king of Babylon, then Satan, too (as well as Christ), is called the morning star or the morning light (verse 12). Christ is the true morning star and Satan is the false morning star.

## LIGHT EQUALS TRUTH

Today light is often equated to truth. People today often say things such as, "Don't keep me in the dark," or "Can you shed some light on the subject?" In these cases, they are equating light to truth. What they really mean is, "Can you give me some truth on the subject?"

The Bible also equates light and truth. For example, from the Psalms:

3    O send out Thy light and Thy truth, let them lead me;
Let them bring me to Thy holy hill,
And to Thy dwelling places.

—Psalm 43

105 Thy word is a lamp to my feet,
And a light to my path.

—Psalm 119

In the New Testament, we also see truth and light equated:

19 . . . you yourself are a guide to the blind, a light to those who are in darkness,
20 a corrector of the foolish, a teacher of the immature, having in the Law the embodiment of knowledge and of the truth, . . .

—Romans 2

7 Therefore do not be partakers with them;
8 for you were formerly darkness, but now you are light in the Lord; walk as children of light
9 (for the fruit of the light *consists* in all goodness and righteousness and truth),
10 trying to learn what is pleasing to the Lord.

—Ephesians 5

We read in 1 John that God is light:

5 And this is the message we have heard from Him and announce to you, that God is light, and in Him there is no darkness at all.

—1 John 1

Jesus is also described as being the true light in numerous verses in the book of John:

4 In Him was life, and the life was the light of men.
5 And the light shines in the darkness, and the darkness did not comprehend it. . . .

9 There was the true light which, coming into the world, enlightens every man. . . .

17 For the Law was given through Moses; grace and truth were realized through Jesus Christ.

—John 1

12 Again therefore Jesus spoke to them, saying, "I am the light of the world; he who follows Me shall not walk in the darkness, but shall have the light of life."

—John 8

5  "While I am in the world, I am the light of the world."

—John 9

But of course the Bible also talks about Christ being truth. It is interesting that when Christ was talking about being "the way" and "the life," He could have chosen to add that He was "love," or "power," or many other things. But rather, this is what He said:

6  Jesus said to him, "I am the way, the truth, and the life; no one comes to the Father, but through Me. . . ."

—John 14

Christ chose to say that He was the way, the *truth* and the life. Another passage that we are all familiar with is this one from John 8:

31  Jesus therefore was saying to those Jews who had believed Him, "If you abide in My word, *then* you are truly disciples of Mine;
32  and you shall know the truth, and the truth shall make you free."

How will Christ's truth set us free? Free from what? Free from believing the lies of Satan and being in bondage to Satan. More exciting passages about this are the following:

15  "I do not ask Thee to take them out of the world, but to keep them from the evil *one.*
16  "They are not of the world, even as I am not of the world.
17  "Sanctify them in the truth; Thy word is truth.
18  "As Thou didst send Me into the world, I also have sent them into the world.
19  "And for their sakes I sanctify Myself, that they themselves also may be sanctified in truth. . . ."

—John 17

36  Jesus answered, "My kingdom is not of this world. If My kingdom were of this world, then My servants would be fighting, that I might not be delivered up to the Jews; but as it is, My kingdom is not of this realm."
37  Pilate therefore said to Him, "So You are a king?" Jesus answered, "You say *correctly* that I am a king. For this I have been born, and for this I have come into the world, to bear witness to the truth. Everyone who is of the truth hears My voice."

—John 18

The next verse tells us that one of the Holy Spirit's major tasks is to guide us into truth, and thus protect us from Satan's lies:

> 13 "But when He, the Spirit of truth, comes, He will guide you into all the truth; for He will not speak on His own initiative, but whatever He hears, He will speak; and He will disclose to you what is to come. . . ."
>
> —John 16

In contrast, we know that there is no truth in Satan and that he is the father of lies.

> 44 "You are of *your* father the devil, and you want to do the desires of your father. He was a murderer from the beginning, and does not stand in the truth, because there is no truth in him. Whenever he speaks a lie, he speaks from his own *nature;* for he is a liar, and the father of lies. . . ."
>
> —John 8

Do you see that the battle is really over who has the truth: Christ or Satan? If you can grasp this it will make an incredible difference in your life.

If you stop to think about it, this has really been the battle from the beginning. When Eve was tempted in the garden of Eden, Satan came to her and asked her what God had told her. She told him and then, in effect, he said: "That really isn't the truth; I have the real truth. The real truth is that when you eat of this fruit you will be wise like God."

Eve then voluntarily chose to believe Satan's "truth" rather than God's truth. By believing him, you could say that she followed him and gave her allegiance to him rather than to God, and the fall of man resulted.

Similarly, we find that Abraham believed God (believed that God had the truth) and because of that he was accounted as righteous:

> 3 For what does the Scripture say? "AND ABRAHAM BE-LIEVED GOD, AND IT WAS RECKONED TO HIM AS RIGH-TEOUSNESS." . . .

13 For the promise to Abraham or to his descendants that he would be heir of the world was not through the Law, but through the righteousness of faith.

—Romans 4

Do you believe that this same battle is going on even in your own life today? It most assuredly is! God will tell you something, in His word or through direct revelation. Satan then comes and whispers in the other ear, "Well, that's not quite the truth. The real truth is that everyone is doing it and it really wouldn't hurt you spiritually." At that moment you are engaged in a spiritual battle over who actually has the truth; if you yield to Satan you are giving him your allegiance and are preferring him over God.

## Our Thoughts

We often talk about saving somebody's "soul." What is a person's soul? According to the Bible, it is the seat of one's will and emotions. What is the best equivalent word that we would have for this today? I believe that the best term would be "mind." It is in our minds (the seat of the will) that we make our decisions and it is in our minds that we experience emotions. Thus, when we talk about saving somebody's soul, in today's terms it would be more accurate to describe it as saving someone's mind.

Once the mind is saved, the battle is not over. It goes on, but it is possible to win in this battle of the mind. The goal is set out before us in 2 Corinthians 10:

3 For though we walk in the flesh, we do not war according to the flesh,

4 for the weapons of our warfare are not of the flesh, but divinely powerful for the destruction of fortresses.

5 *We are* destroying speculations and every lofty thing raised up against the knowledge of God, and *we are* taking every thought captive to the obedience of Christ,

6 and we are ready to punish all disobedience, whenever your obedience is complete.

Isn't that incredible! We are to bring "every thought captive to the obedience of Christ." That is our goal and, if it were not possible, God would not expect it of us. Oh God, help me and each reader of this book to yearn to truly bring every thought into the captivity and control of Christ and of the Holy Spirit.

The Bible has much to say about the mind and our thinking. One of the most beautiful exhortations is found in Philippians:

> 8 Finally, brethren, whatever is true, whatever is honorable, whatever is right, whatever is pure, whatever is lovely, whatever is of good repute, if there is any excellence and if anything worthy of praise, let your mind dwell on these things.
>
> —Philippians 4

Here in Philippians we are adminished to let our minds dwell on things that are:

- true
- honorable
- right
- pure
- lovely
- of good repute
- excellent
- praise worthy

You might examine your own thinking pattern of yesterday. Did the things that you thought about fit these criteria? Perhaps Philippians 4:8 would be a good verse to memorize.

## Light of the World

Have you ever wondered what Christ meant when He talked about us being the "light of the world" or "letting our light shine"? I wonder if He was telling us that we have the truth and that we are to give it to the world. Perhaps this is substantiated in Matthew:

CHAPTER 11 ...

14  "You are the light of the world. A city set on a hill cannot be hidden.

15  "Nor do *men* light a lamp, and put it under the peck-measure, but on the lampstand; and it gives light to all who are in the house.

16  "Let your light shine before men in such a way that they may see your good works, and glorify your Father who is in heaven. . . ."

—Matthew 5

We know that Christ came into the world as the light of the world and to give the truth of God to the world:

46  "I have come *as* light into the world, that everyone who believes in Me may not remain in darkness. . . ."

—John 12

We read earlier (John 8:44) that Satan is a liar and does not stand in the truth. Although he is the father of all lies and there is no truth (light) in him, Satan *disguises* himself as an angel of light:

14  And no wonder, for even Satan disguises himself as an angel of light.

—2 Corinthians 11

Satan dwells in darkness and is the ruler over darkness (lies or non-truth). However, Satan disguises himself as a truth bearer, a messenger of light. So here again we see that the basic battle is over the minds of men. Satan is trying to convince people that he has the truth and God longs for us to know that the truth is found in Him alone and in His Son, Jesus Christ.

The mind is so very, very important. Here's one reason why:

7  For as he thinketh in his heart, so *is* he: Eat and drink, saith he to thee; but his heart *is* not with thee.

—Proverbs 23, *KJV*

As we think in our heart, so we actually become—"as a man thinketh in his heart, so is he." This is why the Bible admonishes us to renew our minds, to think on things that are excellent, and to bring every thought into the captivity of Jesus Christ. If we do this, our actions will be perfect as a result.

## OUR GOAL IS TO BE PERFECT

Christ gave an incredible command. It is not a suggestion. It is not a recommendation. It is a command. We know that He would not command us to do anything that was not possible. This startling command is found in Matthew 5:

> 48 "Therefore you are to be perfect, as your heavenly Father is perfect. . . ."

Christ commands us to be perfect, just like our heavenly Father is perfect. I believe that Satan has convinced Christians that this is an impossible goal, that it cannot be achieved, and therefore they shouldn't even try, since they obviously can't achieve it. Do you agree with Satan on this score?

If not, then you are saying that what Christ commanded us to do is achievable and we should be straining every ounce of our energy toward attaining that goal. We should be able to say at least what Paul said when he wrote to the church at Philippi:

> 7 But whatever things were gain to me, those things I have counted as loss for the sake of Christ.
>
> 8 More than that, I count all things to be loss in view of the surpassing value of knowing Christ Jesus my Lord, for whom I have suffered the loss of all things, and count them but rubbish in order that I may gain Christ,
>
> 9 and may be found in Him, not having a righteousness of my own derived from *the* Law, but that which is through faith in Christ, the righteousness which *comes* from God on the basis of faith,
>
> 10 that I may know Him, and the power of His resurrection and the fellowship of His sufferings, being conformed to His death;
>
> 11 in order that I may attain to the resurrection from the dead.
>
> 12 Not that I have already obtained *it,* or have already become perfect, but I press on in order that I may lay hold of that for which also I was laid hold of by Christ Jesus.
>
> 13 Brethren, I do not regard myself as having laid hold of *it* yet; but one thing *I do:* forgetting what *lies* behind and reaching forward to what *lies* ahead,
>
> 14 I press on toward the goal for the prize of the upward call of God in Christ Jesus.
>
> 15 Let us therefore, as many as are perfect, have this attitude;

and if in anything you have a different attitude, God will reveal that also to you;

16   however, let us keep living by that same *standard* to which we have attained.

—Philippians 3

I want to encourage you to go back and reread that passage at least once more, and maybe two or three times, and ask God to speak to your heart. We see that Paul, a bondslave of God, counted everything as loss that he might attain the prize of God in Christ Jesus. In verse 15 he also claimed to be perfect, didn't he? Even though he counted himself as perfect, he was still striving to know the power of Christ's resurrection and he was pressing forward toward the goal of his calling in Christ Jesus.

God is calling us to be holy, righteous, and—yes—even perfect. That is our goal. We need to quit believing Satan's lie that perfection is unattainable. If he can convince us of that, he can convince us that we don't need to try. If we set our sights on the highest star and only get three-quarters of the way there, we are far better off than if we said, "There's no need shooting for the highest star. I can't make it anyway." An old saying goes, "He who shoots at nothing, usually hits it."

Let me share with you a little example I heard once that helped me to understand how we can be perfect in God's sight and that our definition of perfection is not always the same as God's.

Someone once used the analogy of an apple tree to express God's view of perfection. God created the apple tree perfectly and with everything it needs to please and glorify Him. When a blossom comes out, it is *perfect* in God's sight, for it is exactly what God created it to be. That blossom then changes and becomes a little green apple which slowly matures to a bright, perfect red apple. But at each stage in that process, God sees that apple as perfect.

Relating this to you and me, even as little green apples, imperfect in our own sight, we can be perfect in God's sight, *if* we are walking in obedience to Him and our hearts are right with Him in all areas. That example made me love God all the more when it was shared with me and I hope it does the same for you.

We are not shooting at nothing. We are aiming for the perfection of God in Christ Jesus. It *is* attainable or Christ wouldn't have commanded us to be perfect. Paul and others have become overcomers and have even become perfect in times past. God wants you to attain perfection and to bend every effort toward it.

I feel like pausing and praying now. If you do also, just lay this book down and talk to the Lord.

Now that we have considered the primary battle, which is the battle over truth that takes place in our minds (souls), we need also to look at the battle involving our physical bodies.

## THE BATTLE OF THE BODY

Satan can attack us in our bodies, but not all sickness comes from Satan. We can bring sickness upon ourselves by getting overtired, worrying constantly, not eating properly, and in other ways. We can also be exposed to a contagious disease, like mumps. However, Satan *can* attack our bodies. God is not always going to heal every Christian. Otherwise no Christian would ever die. There will be times when He wants to heal somebody and times when He does not. We have to know the mind of the Lord to discern when He wants to do a healing. Once we know that God is really telling us that He wants to heal us, then we can step out in faith and with confidence.

There are two types of healing that I see in the Bible. The first is apostolic healing. When the shadow of Peter would pass over people, they would be healed, for example (Acts 5: 12–15). I think that even today God is giving that miraculous type of healing gift to a few people. At times it takes discernment to know to whom He has given this gift and to whom He hasn't, because there are counterfeits and phonies who can mislead even Christians.

The other, more common form of healing described in the Bible is as follows:

13 Is anyone among you suffering? Let him pray. Is anyone cheerful? Let him sing praises.

14 Is anyone among you sick? Let him call for the elders of the church, and let them pray over him, anointing him with oil in the name of the Lord;

15 and the prayer offered in faith will restore the one who is sick, and the Lord will raise him up, and if he has committed sins, they will be forgiven him.

16 Therefore, confess your sins to one another, and pray for one another, so that you may be healed. The effective prayer of a righteous man can accomplish much.

—James 5

I believe that this is the type of healing that God expects as a norm for the local body. The key is in verse 16. To help you understand this, I would like to tell you about a blind man in a fellowship in Detroit. I believe that he had been blind since birth and he was a part of that fellowship for years. Finally one day he came to the elders and said, "I want you to pray for my eyes to be healed." They began to search the Scriptures and the Lord made James 5:16 very real to them.

As a result, they set aside a Saturday and all morning the elders and the blind man confessed before one another every sin, every piece of garbage and pent-up jealousy, and the Lord forgave it all. Then and only then did they anoint the blind man with oil and pray for him. The results? He received his sight! Praise the Lord!

I think the healing of the sick, in a body of believers, by the laying on of hands by the elders is used by God for the purification of the church. It involves confession and cleansing of sin. I would not want to pray for somebody to be healed if God is allowing that illness so that person might give up some sin in his heart or get rid of something in his life. For me to try and get that person healed without God doing the work that He wants to do in his life would really be an error on my part. If you have an illness, you should do some searching to find out if there is something that God is trying to purge out of you and determine if He is using this as a red flag to tell you to draw close to Him and "clean up your act."

## THE BATTLE WITH SATAN

Now let us turn to direct warfare with Satan. To start with, we should look at John 10. Here Christ is contrasting Himself with Satan.

> 10 "The thief comes only to steal, and kill, and destroy; I came that they might have life, and might have *it* abundantly.
>
> —John 10

Satan comes to steal, to kill, and, if he can, to destroy. The killing and the destroying we more readily understand, but what is he stealing from Christians? Satan loves to steal a Christian's peace, joy, love, patience and so forth. If he steals your peace (one of his favorite things to steal) and takes it to his house, how do you get it back? Matthew 12 tells us how:

> 25 And knowing their thoughts He said to them, "Any kingdom divided against itself is laid waste; and any city or house divided against itself shall not stand.
>
> 26 "And if Satan casts out Satan, he is divided against himself; how then shall his kingdom stand?
>
> 27 "And if I by Beelzebul cast out demons, by whom do your sons cast them out? Consequently they shall be your judges.
>
> 28 "But if I cast out demons by the Spirit of God, then the kingdom of God has come upon you.
>
> 29 "Or how can anyone enter the strong man's house and carry off his property, unless he first binds the strong *man?* And then he will plunder his house...."
>
> —Matthew 12

If Satan, who is the strong man, has carried off your peace to his house, you cannot go into that house and get your peace back until Satan is bound. The question then becomes, how do we bind Satan? To find out, let's look at Matthew 18. Remember, this spiritual warfare is taking place in heaven (the first heaven), which is a concentric sphere around the earth.

> 18 "Truly I say to you, whatever you shall bind on earth shall be bound in heaven; and whatever you loose on earth shall be loosed in heaven...."
>
> —Matthew 18

This passage says that whatever I bind in prayer here on the earth is going to be bound in this heaven where the spiritual warfare is taking place. If I bind Satan on my knees in prayer, in the name of Christ and by the blood of Christ, he is bound in the heavenly warfare. If I then loose my peace in the name of Jesus Christ, as I am on my knees in prayer here on the earth, then it will be loosed in the heavenly warfare. To repeat, whatever I bind on earth will be bound in this heaven and whatever I loose on earth will be loosed in the heavenly warfare. I do this on my knees in prayer in the name of Jesus Christ.

To show you how this works, I'll take an example from my own life. Not long ago I was driving into town and I suddenly felt a lack of peace. Right then, through the power of Christ, I bound Satan and claimed my peace back, and I got it! There was only about sixty seconds or so when I didn't have peace. You might ask if it was my lust or Satan that caused my peace to go. I don't care *what* the cause was. All I knew was that my peace was gone and I wanted it back! Christ gave me His peace. It is rightfully mine and I don't want to live even a minute without it.

When we bind Satan and claim back what he has stolen from us, in the name and by the power of Jesus Christ, we have won a victory in the spiritual warfare. Once our joy is gone, in its place comes depression. Once our peace is gone, in its place comes anxiety. When I sense this happening, right then I bind Satan and loose whatever he has stolen, so that it can return to me.

Don't make the error of waiting; bind Satan immediately. Some may think that they will wait until they finish what they are doing or until evening to pray about it. They may forget and live several days in depression or anxiety. I believe this is a mistake. Stop whatever you are doing and bind Satan right away and loose your joy or peace to return to you. Why wait? If someone came up to you and started hitting you, would you wait until evening to do something about it and let that person keep hitting you all day? Of course not! This spiritual battle is *real.* When Satan starts hitting you, don't wait, fight back immediately.

If a Christian close to you is anxious, before you even try to analyze what is going on, together go to the Lord in prayer. Bind Satan in the heavenlies and loose the other person's peace and it will return.

Let's review how real and how critical this battle and struggle is. Remember the passage we read in an earlier chapter from Ephesians 6?

> 10 Finally, be strong in the Lord, and in the strength of His might.
>
> 11 Put on the full armor of God, that you may be able to stand firm against the schemes of the devil.
>
> 12 For our struggle is not against flesh and blood, but against the rulers, against the powers, against the world forces of this darkness, against the spiritual *forces* of wickedness in the heavenly *places*.
>
> 13 Therefore, take up the full armor of God, that you may be able to resist in the evil day, and having done everything, to stand firm.

In verse 12, the *King James Version* says that we "wrestle" not against flesh and blood, which implies that we do wrestle against spiritual forces. Wrestling indicates a hand-to-hand combat. We are to resist and stand firm in the Lord and we are to be strong in *His* might. The spiritual wrestling match we are involved in is very, very real.

In 1 Peter the admonition to resist Satan is repeated:

> 6 Humble yourselves, therefore, under the mighty hand of God, that He may exalt you at the proper time,
>
> 7 casting all your anxiety upon Him, because He cares for you.
>
> 8 Be of sober *spirit,* be on the alert. Your adversary, the devil, prowls about like a roaring lion, seeking someone to devour.
>
> 9 But resist him, firm in *your* faith, knowing that the same experiences of suffering are being accomplished by your brethren who are in the world.
>
> 10 And after you have suffered for a little while, the God of all grace, who called you to His eternal glory in Christ, will Himself perfect, confirm, strengthen *and* establish you.
>
> —1 Peter 5

Praise God! Even though Satan is like a lion trying to devour us Christians, if we resist him, verse 10 tells us that God will perfect, confirm, strengthen and establish us. We can cast all of our anxiety on Him, because we know that He cares for us! The victory will be ours!

## RUN SILENT, RUN WEAK

After writing this book and going back and rereading it, I felt the Lord wanted me to add this section. Unfortunately we won't have the space to develop it as much as I would like, but I feel that the concept is important.

God can read our minds. We can silently pray and God hears us and understands. However, there are times in the spiritual warfare that we must speak out loud with our mouths. The reason for this is that neither Satan, the fallen angels, nor the demons can read our minds. If you stop to think about it for a moment, we can be very glad that they cannot read our minds and our thoughts like God can. In a war, it would be terrible for our enemy to be able to know our thoughts and our plans.

We know from the Scriptures that we have authority over the forces of evil, including Satan. We can actually command them. However, our commands must be out loud and not silent, spoken only in our minds. If I am praying and asking God to bind Satan, I can do that silently. On the other hand, if I address Satan himself, and say, "Satan, in the name of Jesus Christ I bind you," that must be spoken out loud, because Satan cannot read our thoughts.

The Lord convinced me afresh of this one night recently when I felt incredible attacks of Satan at about 2:00 a.m., while I was in bed with my wife. I started doing spiritual battle silently because I didn't want to awaken my wife. That is when the Lord reminded me afresh that Satan could not hear the silent commands that I was trying to give to him. So I got up, went into the bathroom, shut the door and then audibly spoke the commands to Satan. When we command him or his demonic forces, in the name of Christ, to leave us alone they *must* obey. They have no other choice. Once I did this *out loud,* even though it was in a quiet voice, the spiritual battle was won to the glory of Christ!

So you can see that when we pray to God, we can pray silently because He knows our thoughts and our hearts. However, when we take dominion over Satan and his evil forces and command them, this must be done with spoken words. I think this is possibly why so many Christians feel demonic attacks after they are in bed and have been asleep for awhile. If Satan can catch them where they are not inclined to fight back orally, he has a much easier time winning a victory than if he attacks them when they are driving in their car and they can shout at him, in the name of Christ, to get out and leave them alone.

I am sorry that I do not have the space to go into a biblical basis for this concept, but I want to encourage you to pray about it, search out Scriptures on the subject, and let God speak to your heart about it.

## THE VICTORY

If the United States had a war with Russia, we would not know who would win. In the war between Christ and Satan, we *know* that Jesus Christ will be the victor. He is the King and every knee will eventually bow to Him. He *will* conquer all enemies. I would like to take six passages of Scripture about His victory and coming kingship.

> 35 Who shall separate us from the love of Christ? Shall tribulation, or distress, or persecution, or famine, or nakedness, or peril, or sword?
> 36 Just as it is written, "FOR THY SAKE WE ARE BEING PUT TO DEATH ALL DAY LONG: WE WERE CONSIDERED AS SHEEP TO BE SLAUGHTERED."
> 37 But in all these things we overwhelmingly conquer through Him who loved us.
>
> —Romans 8

We don't just barely conquer, leaving us drained of strength. We *overwhelmingly* conquer, and we still have strength and power in the Lord to do what He has for us to do next. To see the scope of this victory, let's read this passage from 1 Corinthians:

23  But each in his own order: Christ the first fruits, after that those who are Christ's at His coming,

24  then *comes* the end, when He delivers up the kingdom to the God and Father, when He has abolished all rule and all authority and power.

25  For He must reign until He has put all His enemies under His feet.

26  The last enemy that will be abolished is death.

27  For HE HAS PUT ALL THINGS IN SUBJECTION UNDER HIS FEET. But when He says, "All things are put in subjection," it is evident that He is excepted who put all things in subjection to Him.

28  And when all things are subject to Him, then the Son Himself also will be subjected to the One who subjected all things to Him, that God may be all in all.

—1 Corinthians 15

God will be all in all. At that point, God will fill the universe, including us. There will be no evil or anything unrighteous left. Wow! It will be incredible! In Ephesians 1, which is Paul's prayer for the Ephesians, we read:

18  *I pray that* the eyes of your heart may be enlightened, so that you may know what is the hope of His calling, what are the riches of the glory of His inheritance in the saints,

19  and what is the surpassing greatness of His power toward us who believe. *These are* in accordance with the working of the strength of His might

20  which He brought about in Christ, when He raised Him from the dead, and seated Him at His right hand in the heavenly *places,*

21  far above all rule and authority and power and dominion, and every name that is named, not only in this age, but also in the one to come.

22  And He put all things in subjection under His feet, and gave Him as head over all things to the church,

23  which is His body, the fulness of Him who fills all in all.

—Ephesians 1

God the Father is going to put all enemies in subjection under Christ's feet. Christ and His body (the church) will receive the fulness of Him who fills all in all. Philippians tells us of the universal worship of Christ that is coming:

9  Therefore also God highly exalted Him, and bestowed on Him the name which is above every name,

10  that at the name of Jesus EVERY KNEE SHOULD BOW, of those who are in heaven, and on earth, and under the earth,

11  and that every tongue should confess that Jesus Christ is Lord, to the glory of God the Father.

—Philippians 2

Someday our conquering King will come and every knee *(every* knee—no exceptions) will bow and *every* tongue will confess Him as Lord. If you do not know Jesus Christ as your Savior and Lord, sooner or later you are going to say that Jesus is Lord anyhow. If you voluntarily make Him Lord of your life now, you will have eternal life and will enjoy the inheritance of Christ. If you wait until you are forced to admit that Jesus Christ is Lord, you will spend eternity away from the presence of God and the joy of the Lord. Eventually *every person* will acknowledge Jesus as Lord.

Let's look at 1 John for our last two passages of Scriptures on victory. First, in chapter 3, we read about the works of Satan being destroyed:

7  Little children, let no one deceive you; the one who practices righteousness is righteous, just as He is righteous;

8  the one who practices sin is of the devil; for the devil has sinned from the beginning. The Son of God appeared for this purpose, that He might destroy the works of the devil.

—1 John 3

Chapter 4 of 1 John assures us that we can overcome the spirits that are not of God:

1  Beloved, do not believe every spirit, but test the spirits to see whether they are from God; because many false prophets have gone out into the world.

2  By this you know the Spirit of God: every spirit that confesses that Jesus Christ has come in the flesh is from God;

3  and every spirit that does not confess Jesus is not from God; and this is the *spirit* of the antichrist, of which you have heard that it is coming, and now it is already in the world.

4  You are from God, little children, and have overcome them; because greater is He who is in you than he who is in the world.

—1 John 4

Greater is the One in us—that is, in Christians—than the one who is in the world! Our victory is certain and sure. Verses 3–4 say that *we will overcome* the spirit of the Antichrist. If we are part of God's army, if we put on God's armor, and if we trust Him to shield us about, we are guaranteed absolute victory in the spiritual warfare!

God is calling us to walk as good soldiers of Jesus Christ. The victory will be ours in the spiritual warfare for we are more than conquerors—we overwhelmingly conquer in the name of Christ!

The victors or the overcomers in this spiritual warfare will be those who have paid a price for being a slave and a soldier. They have counted everything as rubbish for the sake of being a good soldier. As we saw earlier in this book, the overcomers are the only Christians who are promised to be the bride of Christ, to live in the new Jerusalem, and to receive the other rewards promised to overcomers in Christ's letters to the seven churches. However, our motivation to be an overcomer (victor) should not be the rewards. In the next chapter, we will discuss what our motivation should be.

# 12

# THE KEY TO IT ALL

We now come to the last chapter in this book. Hopefully, it has been an exciting and a challenging book for you, and one that will draw you into a deeper commitment to God. My prayer is that God will speak many valuable things to your heart that will prepare you for the days of turmoil that lie ahead. I trust that by now you may have made a commitment to God to be a bondslave, to become a soldier, and to move into the overcomer (victor) realm. However, as important as all of these things are, I have saved the very best for this last chapter.

If you and I met and I could only share one thing with you, it would be what is contained in this final chapter of this book. It is without any doubt the singly, most important lesson that God has ever taught me.

This lesson that God taught me is also, as far as I am concerned, the only valid motivation for really wanting to become an overcomer. Our motivation should not be to receive the wonderful rewards that Christ promises to the overcomers, nor to be a part of the bride of Christ, nor to dwell in the new Jerusalem, nor to have our tears wiped away by God's own hand. In this chapter I will share what I believe our motivation must be.

This incredible lesson is recorded in one of my booklets entitled, *Only One Word*. In order to help you understand our true motivation to its fullest, I will simply reprint much of that booklet here.

## ONLY ONE WORD

If you picked up a hitchhiker and led him to Christ or met someone on an airplane or bus and had the privilege of helping him find Jesus Christ as his Savior, and if in parting company you only had time to give him one piece of advice to encourage a good start in his Christian life, what would that piece of advice be?

I have had the privilege of asking that question of a number of Christian groups and I get an amazingly large variety of answers. What would your answer be? What would you tell a brand-new Christian, if you could give him only one piece of advice? (Before you read further, please just close this book and pause for a minute—think through what *your* answer would be.)

From mature, spiritual, wonderful Christians I have received such answers as:

1.   Join a good Spirit-filled church.

2.   Read your Bible daily.

3.   Pray daily.

4.   Share your faith with someone.

5.   Find a good pastor and go talk to him.

6.   Give me your name and address, and I will send you something.

Every one of these are good answers. However, I believe the Scriptures give us an even better answer than any of these. It is found in Matthew 22:

> **34   But when the Pharisees heard that He had put the Sadducees to silence, they gathered themselves together.**
>
> **35   And one of them, a lawyer, asked Him a question, testing Him,**
>
> **36   "Teacher, which is the greatest commandment in the Law?"**
>
> **37   And He said to him, "'YOU SHALL LOVE THE LORD YOUR GOD WITH ALL YOUR HEART, AND WITH ALL YOUR SOUL, AND WITH ALL YOUR MIND.'**
>
> **38   "This is the great and foremost commandment.**

39  "And a second is like it, 'YOU SHALL LOVE YOUR NEIGH-BOR AS YOURSELF.'
40  "On these two commandments depend the whole law and the Prophets."

Here the Lord says that absolutely the most important command (thing for a Christian to do) is to love God with all your heart, soul and mind. The equivalent passage in Mark 12 (verses 28–33), says "with all your heart, and with all your soul, and with all your mind, and with all your strength." Therefore, if I could only tell a new Christian one thing to do, I would be compelled to tell him to love God with all his heart, soul, mind, and strength. (It just so happens, I believe, that if he were to do that, he would then automatically do all of the other things mentioned previously. We will see why in just a moment.)

## FROM THE KNOWN TO THE UNKNOWN

As I began to think through what it was to really love God, He had me first start with a love that I understood: that of a young man for a young woman. There are certain things that are true when a young man falls in love with a young woman. He really wants to get to know her. This causes him to do a number of things, which no one has to tell him to do—they just naturally happen.

*HE WANTS TO BE WITH HER.* In fact, if he really loves her, he would like to be with her twenty-four hours a day. The time that they are apart is sheer agony for him. His mind is so much on her and he so desires to be with her that he even stirs salt into his coffee, because his mind is absent and is present with her! There are times when he enjoys being with her in the presence of other people. There are also times when he wants to be completely alone with her.

*HE WANTS TO TALK TO HER.* He wants to share with her his dreams and aspirations and problems. He wants to share with her his background.

*HE WANTS TO FIND OUT ALL ABOUT HER.* Just as he wishes to share himself with her, he wants to find out all about her—her background and childhood, her dreams, her aspirations, and her desires. If there was a book written about her, he would break his neck to get a copy of it, and not just read it once, but many, many times, until he had almost memorized the pages. Even when he wasn't reading the book, he would frequently be thinking about all the things that he read in the book about her.

*HE WANTS TO PLEASE HER.* He quickly finds out what pleases and displeases her. Because of his deep love for her, he wants to avoid doing things that displease her and wants to do those things that please her and make her happy.

*HE WANTS TO TELL EVERYONE ABOUT HER.* Not only does he tell his family and friends, but those at work, and anybody that will listen. At IBM we had one young man fall in love and all that he could talk about was his girlfriend, until we finally wanted to put a cork in his mouth!

*HE WANTS TO LOVE THOSE THAT SHE LOVES.* Her family may not be the type of people that he would naturally choose as friends. However, because of his deep love for her, he develops a genuine love for her family and her friends.

## IF WE REALLY LOVED GOD,
## WOULD THESE SAME THINGS BE TRUE?

I used to interpret this greatest commandment as loving Christ with all my heart, soul, mind and strength. However, it is obvious that Christ was not giving us a command to love Himself, but He was talking about loving His heavenly Father, the Almighty God. I believe that Christ had this tremendous love relationship with His Father and wanted us to share the joy of loving the Father.

If we really love God, our heavenly Father, then in the same sense as the young man wanting to get to know the young lady, we will really want to get to know God the Father. The following things will naturally occur without anyone having to tell us to do them.

*I WILL WANT TO BE WITH HIM.* Of course, during much of the time that I spend with God, there will be other people around. But if I really love Him, I will also want to spend much time alone with Him. If you have trouble setting aside time for a quiet time with God, that is really not your difficulty. Your difficulty is that you don't love God with all your heart, soul, mind and strength. If you did, you would naturally make time to be alone with Him. Jesus Christ was our supreme example in how to love God the Father. Let's read about some of His habits:

> 35 And in the early morning, while it was still dark, He arose and went out and departed to a lonely place, and was praying there.
>
> —Mark 1
>
> 16 But He Himself would often slip away to the wilderness and pray.
>
> —Luke 5

Here we see that Christ got up a great while before day-break (that probably means several hours), just to spend time alone with the Father. To be sure that He was alone, He went out into the wilderness where there were no distractions. If Christ, God's own Son, needed that kind of time because of His love for the Father, our love too should compel us to have time alone with our loving Father every day.

*I WOULD WANT TO TALK TO HIM.* Here, naturally, we are talking about prayer. If I truly love God, I want to share with Him my dreams, my aspirations, my hopes and my problems (sins and struggles). I want to ask His counsel and thoughts. If you have difficulty putting aside time for prayer (not just riding down the highway, on-and-off type of prayer, but a time devoted solely to talking with God), the difficulty is not with prayer, but that you don't love God enough. If you really loved Him with all your heart, you would naturally set aside time to talk to Him.

*I WOULD WANT TO FIND OUT ALL ABOUT HIM.* There *has* been a book written about Him (and even inspired by Him); it's called the Bible! If you have not been spending much time in the word recently and find it difficult to set aside time for Bible study and Bible reading, your problem isn't with Bible study; it's a problem with loving God. If you really loved Him, you would *want* to read about Him, find out about His character, find out what pleases Him, and displeases Him, and find out about the wonderful things that He has in store for you.

*I WOULD WANT TO PLEASE HIM.* If I really loved God with all my heart, soul, mind, and strength, I would want to avoid doing things that displease Him, and I would want to do the things that please Him. Do you have trouble with obedience? Is there some habit or activity of yours that you know displeases the Father, but you continue to do it anyhow? Your problem really isn't one of obedience—it is one of not loving God enough. You naturally want to do things to please Him, if you really love Him. We read about this in John 14:

15 "If you love Me, you will keep My commandments. . . ."

I wish this were a tape rather than a written manuscript, because the inflection of that verse is very important. I want to try to put that inflection in writing, if I can. Some people read it: "If you love Me, you WILL keep my commandments." They use this as a club to force people into obeying God's commands. The way that I read this verse is: "If you love Me, you will (naturally) keep my commandments." Perhaps you can reread the verse with your own inflection, putting in those two interpretations.

*I WILL WANT TO TELL PEOPLE ABOUT HIM.* Of course not only will I want to tell people about Him, but also about the way in which they too can get to know Him through His Son, Jesus Christ. Do you have trouble with witnessing? That's not your trouble. What is the trouble? By now you know that it is because you don't love God enough. If you loved Him with all of your heart, you would naturally tell people about how wonderful He is. You couldn't help it. In fact, it is interesting to note that the disciples naturally witnessed during the three years that they were with Christ, without any command to do so. We find one record of this in John 1:

40 One of the two who heard John speak, and followed Him, was Andrew, Simon Peter's brother.

41 He found first his own brother Simon, and said to him, "We have found the Messiah" (which translated means Christ).

42 He brought him to Jesus. Jesus looked at him, and said, "You are Simon the son of John; you shall be called Cephas" (which translated means Peter).

The great commission was not given until the very end of the Gospels (Mark 16:15-18). No one should ever need to tell a new Christian to witness. He is naturally going to be excited about what God has done in his heart and life, and he will want to share that with people. In fact, you can't keep him quiet! If you are no longer witnessing, perhaps your love has grown a bit lukewarm, and you are no longer excited about our wonderful, fantastic, transforming heavenly Father.

*I WILL LOVE THOSE WHOM HE LOVES.* What this says is if I obey the greatest commandment—to love God with all my heart, soul, mind, and strength—I will naturally obey the second command to love my neighbor as myself. I will love my neighbor (and we know from the good Samaritan story whom Christ considers our neighbor to be) because God loves my neighbor. "For God so loved the world . . ." (John 3:16). I cannot help but love my neighbor if I really love God and want to love those whom He loves. Do you have trouble loving someone at work, someone in your neighborhood, or perhaps even someone in your own church? That is not really the problem, is it? You've got it—the real problem is that you don't love God the way that He deserves to be loved, because if you did you would love even your enemies.

## ACTIONS SPEAK LOUDER THAN WORDS

I am sure that we have all heard the saying that actions speak louder than words. This usually implies that someone is telling someone that he loves him (or her), but his actions say the opposite. In our earlier example of a young man falling in love with a young woman, what would you think if he said that he loved her, and yet never spent any time alone with her, even when she lived next door? If there was a book written about her and it was lying on his table unread day after day, if he had habits that displeased her that he was making no effort to change, and if he really didn't care about her family or her friends, what would you think of his claim that he loved her deeply? If he only talked about how wonderful she was when he was around people who liked her, but never mentioned her or stood up for her when he was around people who didn't like her, what would you judge to be the quality of his love? If true and deep love is present, love actions will naturally follow. Words without the actions are hollow indeed.

## EVERYTHING FALLS INTO PLACE IF . . .

Can you see that everything falls into place *if* we really love God with all our heart, soul, mind and strength? If I really love Him, my quiet time will be in order; I will take time to pray (alone); I will hunger after the Bible (Psalm 1 says that a righteous man meditates in God's law *day and night);* the sin in my life will give way to obedience; I will witness in a natural, comfortable way; and I will naturally love my neighbors, my co-workers and my brothers and sisters in the church.

If Satan can get us to be all concerned about witnessing or Bible reading or some such thing, and can keep us away from being concerned about the main issue that would set everything in order, then he has the victory. It is a bit like a man in a leaky rowboat. The boat springs a leak, and he sticks a finger into the hole, and another leak springs up, and he sticks a toe into it. Pretty soon he runs out of fingers and toes. Similarly, in getting concerned at various times about obedience or prayer and so forth, we are just chasing symptoms. What we need is a new bottom on the rowboat—not more fingers and toes! Loving God with all your heart, soul, mind and strength is the new bottom on the rowboat. It is the one thing that makes everything else fall perfectly into place. Praise the Lord! It's so simple and so beautiful.

## HOW DO I FALL IN LOVE WITH GOD?

"How do I fall in love with God?" is a very legitimate question. Do I sit on a log and repeat over and over again, "I love God, I love God, I love God . . ."? Do I write "I love God 5,000 times on the blackboard? These might help a little, but I rather doubt it.

The first place to start is to *ask.* "Ye have not, because ye ask not" (James 4:2c *KJV*). Start by asking, not just once a day, but many times a day: "Loving, wonderful Father God, help me to love you with all of my heart, soul, mind, and strength." He will answer that prayer. I know—it happened to me.

Let me relate how this occurred in my own life. I was living in a Navigator home, spending much time studying and memorizing Scriptures (I still love the Navigators and use their memory work). However, it seemed like the more I memorized and studied the Scriptures while living there, the deader I became spiritually. I lost the excitement and zeal and enthusiasm that I had felt for God and for Christ when I first became a Christian. I began to earnestly ask God what was wrong. I told Him that I was memorizing and studying the Scriptures, trying to please Him, and yet it seemed like the more I did this the deader my spiritual life really became. He showed me that I had elevated 2 Timothy 2:15 (study to show thyself approved unto God . . .) above all of the other commands. He then said that I should push that one back down into a place level with all the other commands and elevate the one that God elevated to love Him with all of my heart, soul, mind and strength. Once He showed me this, I began to ask Him often during the day, "God, how do I really fall in love with You?"

He never answered that prayer directly. What He did was to begin to show me how much He loved me. Every time I read a portion of the Scriptures, it was a passage that talked about His incredible love for me! Every time I opened a hymnal, the song was about how much He loved me. One of the songs said that "His love is like a river flowing on eternally." I began to try to imagine how much water would flow through the Mississippi River in billions and billions of years. One day the immensity of His love for me really hit me, and I almost physically staggered backwards, with my mouth open in awe, at how much God loved me. Once I got the impact of His love, I *could not help* but love Him back with all of my being.

In the book *The Gentle Breeze of Jesus* (Creation House, Carol Stream, Illinois), Mel Tari suggests that you imagine yourself to be the only person on Earth and visualize God and Christ sitting in Heaven, occupying twenty-four hours a day thinking of good things to do for you, caring for the hairs on your head, and being concerned about your health, your thought life, your spiritual life and your happiness—just bestowing 100 percent of their love on you. Can you imagine that? Try for a minute.

That really is how much God *does* love you, and how much Christ loves you. Become aware of His immense love and you will naturally love Him. The Bible points this out:

> 7 Beloved, let us love one another, for love is from God; and everyone who loves is born of God and knows God.
>
> 8 The one who does not love does not know God, for God is love.
>
> 9 By this the love of God was manifested in us, that God has sent His only begotten Son into the world so that we might live through Him.
>
> 10 In this is love, not that we loved God, but that He loved us and sent His Son to be the propitiation for our sins.
>
> 11 Beloved, if God so loved us, we also ought to love one another.
>
> 12 No one has beheld God at any time; if we love one another, God abides in us, and His love is perfected in us.
>
> 13 By this we know that we abide in Him and He in us, because He has given us of His Spirit.
>
> 14 And we have beheld and bear witness that the Father has sent the Son to be the Savior of the world.
>
> 15 Whoever confesses that Jesus is the Son of God, God abides in him, and he in God.
>
> 16 And we have come to know and have believed the love which God has for us. God is love, and one who abides in love abides in God, and God abides in him.
>
> 17 By this, love is perfected in us, that we may have confidence in the day of judgment; because as He is, so also are we in this world.
>
> 18 There is no fear in love; but perfect love casts out fear, because fear involves punishment, and the one who fears is not perfected in love.
>
> 19 We love, because He first loved us.
>
> —1 John 4

It says here that we love Him *because He first loved us.* Aren't you glad it starts with Him? Praise You, Father! Therefore, another prayer that you could pray daily is "Father, show me how much You love me." This is guaranteed to increase your love for Him. It was back in 1955 when God first showed me this. I don't believe a day has gone by since then that I haven't asked God at least once that I might love Him with all my heart, soul, mind, and strength. It is so easy to love Him, because He tells me in 1 Corinthians 2:

> 9 . . . "THINGS WHICH EYE HAS NOT SEEN AND EAR HAS HEARD,
> AND *which* HAVE NOT ENTERED THE HEART OF MAN,
> ALL THAT GOD HAS PREPARED FOR THOSE WHO LOVE HIM."

Isn't it fantastic how much He loves us! Wow! Imagine the most beautiful world, the most wonderful paradise that you can think of . . . it would all be garbage compared to what God has prepared for us. We cannot even begin to think of how great it is going to be, and it is not because of our worthiness, but because we have Christ as our Savior and we are cleansed by His precious blood.

My dear brother or sister in Christ, from the depths of my heart I would hope that you too might benefit from this most important lesson that the Lord has taught me. If I can only give you one word of encouragement or advice, it would be to love God with all of your heart, soul, mind and strength. If you do, you are going to be happy and your Christian life, your family life, your finances, and everything else will fall into place. I trust that you will join with me in daily asking the Lord to show you how much He loves you and to give you an exciting and deep love for Him in return.

## MOTIVATION TO BECOME AN OVERCOMER

Do you see now that our only real motivation for wanting to be an overcomer, a bondslave, or a soldier of Jesus Christ is our love for God the Father? Of course we can only come to the Father through Christ, but it is the Father to whom we are to come.

If we love Him, we will want to be His bondslave; in fact, we will really insist on it. If we love Him, we will be willing to die for Him as a good soldier and to not entangle ourselves in the affairs of this life. If we really love Him we are going to want to be as close to Him in eternity as we can possibly be. That is why I want to be an overcomer. I could care less about ruling and reigning over the other nations on the new earth or the other rewards. However, it would break my heart to be able to visit the new Jerusalem just occasionally. I want to dwell there so I can be as close as possible to God the Father and His precious Son, Jesus Christ, who are the light of the new Jerusalem.

I don't believe any amount of resolve, nor gritting the teeth, nor resolutions will in the end prove to be a valid motivation but will leave one falling far short of the overcomer mark. I do believe if your love of God the Father is the key motivating factor, you can joyously give up everything in order to be a bondslave and an overcomer to the glory of God the Father and His Son, Jesus Christ.

## A REVIEW OF WHERE WE HAVE COME

Rather than trying to generalize in a review of this book, I would like to take a chapter at a time:

### Chapter 1: Rewards of the Overcomers

In this chapter, we looked at the incredible rewards that Christ promised to the overcomers in His letters to the seven churches in Revelation 2 and 3. We also looked at Revelation 21 and 22 and saw that it is only to the overcomers that the following things are promised: they will inherit the new Jerusalem and will be the bride of Christ, they will rule and reign with Christ, God will wipe away their tears and He will dwell among them.

### Chapter 2: Why Were You Created?

As we went back to lay a foundation, we saw that we were created to glorify God. We encouraged you to find out what things the Bible says we can do that specifically glorify God. We also pointed out that not glorifying God is the biblical definition of sin: "For all have sinned and fall short of the glory of God" (Romans 3:23).

### Chapter 3: Knowledge of Good and Evil

In this chapter we saw that the reason people do not glorify God is because they choose to follow their own knowledge of good and evil rather than what God tells them to do. The knowledge of good and evil is the one thing that God did not want human beings to have. It still seems to be the thing that causes problems for most people. If they rely on their own knowledge rather than seeking God's will and then doing it, they are living independent of God and thereby cannot please Him.

### Chapter 4: Your Image of Jesus

Most Christians want to become like Christ. However, as we discussed in this chapter, Christians have widely differing views as to what Christ was really like. We went back to the New Testament to try to get a realistic image of Christ in all of His humanity and manliness and we saw that He was tempted in all points as we are. Every tempting thought that we have ever had, Christ had the equivalent of it, and yet He did not yield to that temptation and did not commit even mental sin.

### Chapter 5: Knowing God

To replace the knowledge of good and evil with the knowledge of God, we need to know what God is like. Here we tried to get a realistic view from the Bible of what God is like. God has not changed and the things that He did in the Old Testament still reflect a part of His nature.

In the Old Testament He commanded Joshua and the children of Israel to kill everyone in a town, including little babies and old women. He gave poisoned water to people to drink and He commanded a deliverer that He raised up to actually murder a government official. Yet God is also a Father of love and mercy, as is seen especially in the New Testament. However, during the Tribulation some of the characteristics of God's wrath seen in the Old Testament will become visible once again. Many Christians will be shaken to the core by this, because they do not know God as He truly is, nor do they have a realistic picture of Him. Because of their knowledge of good and evil, many

Christians would refuse to obey God if He asked them to do something like He asked of Joshua and the children of Israel.

We also discussed that God is a loving Father to us, who encourages us and at times is proud of us.

### Chapter 6: The Progression of a Christian

We examined a three-step progression that emerges from the Old Testament. In the tabernacle there was the outer court, the holy place, and the holy of holies. In the Old Testament Feasts, there was the Feast of the Passover, the Feast of Pentecost, and the Feast of Tabernacles. In the New Testament we saw this same pattern: there was a stage of being a brother, a fellow-worker, and finally a fellow-soldier. When one becomes a Christian, he is in the first stage, which is equivalent to the Feast of the Passover and the outer court. When he is baptized (filled) with the Holy Spirit, he is in stage two, or the holy place and the Feast of Pentecost. However, that is only the mid-point and God really desires that Christians go on to the third stage, which is represented by the Feast of Tabernacles and the holy of holies. Christians in this third stage have two names: bondslaves and overcomers.

### Chapter 7: Bondslaves

In this chapter, we looked at what it means to be a bondslave. In the Old Testament times, if for monetary reasons a man had to become a temporary slave of a master, at the end of this time of enslavement he was free to go. However, if he loved the master enough, he could volunteer to become a permanent slave, a bondslave. If he did this, the master would drive an awl through his ear as he stood by the doorpost and pierce his ear, which was the mark of a permanent slave. From then on, this slave had no rights, no property, and had to be willing to die for his master. Becoming a bondslave because of love for our Master is the door through which we enter into the overcomer realm.

### Chapter 8: The Overcomers

Here we looked specifically at the overcomers. Overcoming is a military term used to describe hand-to-hand combat between two soldiers: it is said that one overcomes the other. This involves a fight, a struggle, wrestling and winning. We examined what we are to overcome and saw that there are three major things we are to overcome:

1. evil
2. the world:
   2.1—the lust of the flesh
   2.2—the lust of the eyes
   2.3—the pride of life
3. Satan

We saw that we are to meet these various battles in different ways. We also observed that there have been some Christians through the centuries who have been overcomers.

### Chapter 9: The Enemy and the Battleground
In this chapter we looked at Satan and who he is. We discussed who is in Satan's army, such as demons and fallen angels. We then observed that the battleground is the first heaven, which is the area roughly between sea level and the clouds.

### Chapter 10: Spiritual Warfare
Here we looked at Christ's army, which consists of the angels and of Christians who volunteer to become soldiers. We also looked at the armor that a soldier of God wears, which is God's armor. We saw that this armor already exists. All we have to do is to put it on and use it. The shield of faith is one piece of this armor, which is God Himself, who surrounds us on all sides like a gigantic fortress.

### Chapter 11: The Battle and the Victory
In this chapter we saw that the battle is basically over truth and it involves primarily our minds and our thought lives. However, there are also battles involving our physical bodies and battles against Satan himself. However, because of our incredible Commander in chief, Jesus Christ, we are *sure beforehand* that we will have the victory and that we will overcome, if we march and fight behind Him in this spiritual warfare.

*Chapter 12:  The Key to It All*
We have seen in this chapter that the key to it all is loving
God with all our heart, all our soul, all our mind, and all our
strength. If we do this, everything falls into place. We will obey
God, we will move into the overcomer realm and we will dwell
in the new Jerusalem with Him forever. Praise You, God!

## CONCLUDING THOUGHTS

Well, we have come to the end of this book. I have put a
great deal of my heart and being into it. I believe without any
doubt that this is the most important book I have written to
date and it is likely to be the most important book that I will
ever write. With my whole heart I hope that it has helped you
draw closer to God, to love Him more, and to move on into the
overcomer realm.
If we are to go through battles, the time of birth pangs,
and even the Tribulation before we get to see our precious Savior face to face, then I say: "Let the battle begin. *We will overcome* by the power of Jesus Christ."

## YOUR COMMITMENT

There is a commitment page for overcomers on the next
page of this book. Look for it and use it if God leads you to do
so.

## COMMITMENT TO BE A BONDSLAVE AND AN OVERCOMER
## TO THE GLORY OF GOD THE FATHER,
## AND HIS SON, JESUS CHRIST

TO THE GOD OF ETERNITY,

I am voluntarily becoming a bondslave of Yours. I have no property nor possessions of my own. I have no time nor rights of my own. I am willing to permanently be Your slave.

I am willing to put on Your armor and to fight against Your enemies. I am willing to do absolutely anything You tell me to do, even if it goes against my knowledge of what is good. I am willing to die for You. Nothing is more important than doing Your will—not my family, my (former) possessions, my job, nor even my own life.

Through Your power I will be an overcomer, not to my glory, but only to Your glory and the glory of Your Son and my Savior, Jesus Christ.

I make this lifetime commitment, not because I have to, nor because of rewards. I make it because of my love for You, because I desire to please You, and because I want to be as close to You as possible throughout eternity.

Signed _____ Date _____

Witness _____ Date _____

- - - - - - - - - - - - - - - - - - - - - - - - - - - - - - - - - - - -

## JOIN WITH US

If you would like to join with other committed bondslaves to keep in touch and to possibly help each other, send us a copy of this page. We feel that the Lord is raising up an army and we want to be part of His special troops. Perhaps this part of God's army will become known as "The Omega Force." At some point, we may have a conference just for bondslaves that will not be announced to anyone else.

We are going to need each other when persecution starts. Let's help one another to be good soldiers for Jesus Christ.

To: Jim McKeever, P.O. Box 4636, Medford, Oregon 97501

☐ Yes, I would like to keep in touch with others who have also made a commitment to be a bondslave and an overcomer.

Name _____

Address _____

City _____ State _____

Zip _____ home phone ( ) _____

Occupation _____ business phone ( ) _____

# APPENDIX A

# HOW TO BECOME A CHRISTIAN

If you are reading this I am assuming that you are not sure that you have received Jesus Christ as your personal Savior. Not only is it possible to know this for sure, but God *wants* you to know. This is what 1 John 5:11-13 has to say:

11 And the witness is this, that God has given us eternal life, and this life is in His Son.
12 He who has the Son has the life; he who does not have the Son does not have the life.
13 These things I have written to you who believe in the name of the Son of God, in order that you may know that you have eternal life.

These things are written to us who believe in the name of the Son of God, so that we can *know* that we have eternal life. It is not a "guess so," or "hope so" or "maybe so" situation. It is so that we can *know* for certain that we have eternal life. If you do not have this confidence, please read on.

In order to get to the point of knowing that we have eternal life, we need to first go back and review some basic principles. First, it is important to note that all things that God created (the stars, trees, animals, and so on) are doing exactly what they were created to do, except man. Isaiah 43 indicates why God created us:

> 7   ". . . Everyone who is called by My name,
>     And whom I have created for My glory,
>     Whom I have formed even whom I have made."

Here it says that humans were created to glorify God. I am sure that neither you nor I have glorified God all of our lives in everything that we have done. This gives us our first clue as to what "sin" is. We find more about it in Romans 3:

> 23   . . . for all have sinned and fall short of the glory of God . . .

This says that we have all sinned and that we all fall short of the purpose for which we were created—that of glorifying God. I have an even simpler definition of sin. I believe that sin is "living independent of God." A young person out of high school can choose which college to attend. If he makes this decision apart from God, it is "sin." This was the basic problem in the garden of Eden. Satan tempted Eve to eat the fruit of the tree of "the knowledge of good and evil." He said that if she would do this, she would know good from evil and would be wise like God. This would mean that she could make her own decisions and would not have to rely on God's wisdom and guidance. Since you and I fit in the category of living independent of God and not glorifying Him in everything we do, we need to look at what the results of this sin are.

First let me ask you what "wages" are. After thinking about it, because you probably receive wages from your job, you will probably come up with a definition something like "wages are what you get paid for what you do." That is a good answer. Now let's see what the Bible has to say concerning this, in Romans 6:

> 23   For the wages of sin is death, but the free gift of God is eternal life in Christ Jesus our Lord.

Here we see that the wages of sin is death—spiritual, eternal death. Death is what we get paid for the sin that we do. Yet this passage also gives us the other side of the coin: that is, that through Jesus Christ we can freely have eternal life, instead of eternal death. Isn't that wonderful?!

But let's return for a moment to this death penalty that

the people without Christ have hanging over their heads, because of the sin that they live in. In the Old Testament God made a rule: "The soul who sins will die" (Ezekiel 18:4). If we were able to live a perfect, sinless life, we could make it to heaven on our own. If we live anything less than a perfect life, according to God's rule, we will not make it to heaven, but instead will be sentenced to death. All through the Bible we find no one living a good enough life to make it to heaven.

This brings us to the place where Jesus Christ fits into this whole picture. His place was beautifully illustrated to me when I was considering receiving Christ as my Savior, by a story about a judge in a small town.

In this small town, the newspapermen were against the judge and wanted to get him out of office. A case was coming up before the judge concerning a vagrant—a drunken bum—who happened to have been a fraternity brother of the judge when they were at college. The newspapermen thought that this was their chance. If the judge let the vagrant off easy, the headlines would read, "Judge Shows Favoritism to Old Fraternity Brother." If the judge gave the vagrant the maximum penalty, the headlines would read, "Hardhearted Judge Shows No Mercy to Old Fraternity Brother." Either way they had him. The judge heard the case and gave the vagrant the maximum penalty of thirty days or $300 fine.

The judge then stood up, took off his robe, laid it down on his chair, walked down in front of the bench and put his arm around the shoulders of his old fraternity brother. He told him that as judge, in order to uphold the law, he had to give him the maximum penalty, because he was guilty. But because he cared about him, he wanted to pay the fine for him. So the judge took out his wallet and handed his old fraternity brother $300.

For God to be "just," He has to uphold the law that says "the soul who sins will die." On the other hand, because He loves us He wants to pay that death penalty for us. I cannot pay the death penalty for you because I have a death penalty of my own that I have to worry about, since I, too, have sinned. If I were sinless, I could die in your place. I guess God could have sent down millions of sinless beings to die for us. But what God chose to do was to send down *one* Person, who was equal in value, in God's eyes, to all of the people who will ever live, and yet who would remain sinless. Jesus Christ died physically and spiritually in order to pay the death penalty for you and me. The blood of Christ washes away all of our sins, and with it the death penalty that resulted from our sin.

The judge's old fraternity brother could have taken the $300 and said thank you, or he could have told the judge to keep his money and that he would do it on his own. Similarly, each person can thank God for allowing Christ to die in his place and receive Christ as his own Savior, or he can tell God to keep His payment and that he will make it on his own. What you do with that question determines where you will spend eternity.

Referring to Christ, John 1:12 says:

12  **But as many as received Him, to them He gave the right to become children of God,** *even* **to those who believe in His name** . . .

John 3:16 says:

16  **"For God so loved the world, that He gave His only begotten Son, that whoever believes in Him should not perish but have eternal life. . . ."**

Here we see that if we believe in Christ we won't perish, but we will have everlasting life and the right to become children of God. Right now you can tell God that you believe in Christ as the Son of God, that you are sorry for your sins and that you want to turn from them. You can tell Him that you want to accept Christ's payment for your sins, and yield your life to be controlled by Christ and the Holy Spirit. (You must accept Christ as your Savior *and your MASTER.*)

If you pray such a prayer, Christ will come and dwell within your heart and you will *know for sure* that you have *eternal life.*

If you have any questions about what you have just read, I would encourage you to go to someone that you know, who really knows Jesus Christ as his Savior, and ask him for help and guidance. After you receive Christ, I would encourage you to become a part of a group of believers in Christ who study the Scriptures together, worship God together and have a real love relationship with each other. This group (body of believers) can help nurture you and build you up in your new faith in Jesus Christ.

If you have received Christ as a result of reading these pages, I would love to hear from you. My address is at the end of this book.

Welcome to the family of God.

Jim McKeever

# APPENDIX B
# MEET THE AUTHOR

Jim McKeever

Jim McKeever has been a regular guest on Pat Robertson's "700 Club" and on other Christian television programs. He is in demand as a speaker at major Full Gospel Businessmen's (FGBMFI) meetings. In speaking at Christian rallies, fairs and conventions, he has shared the program with the following: Josh McDowell, Dr. Bill Bright, Terry Bradshaw, Dr. Walter Martin, Phil Keaggy, Leon Patillo, Paul Little, Dr. Ted Engstrom, Dr. Carlton Booth, Bob Turnbull, Andre Kole, Dr. Raphy Byron, and many other outstanding men of God.

Mr. McKeever is president of Ministries of Vision, which is a nonprofit organization established under the leading of the Holy Spirit to minister to the body of Christ by the traveling ministry of many anointed men of God, through books, cassettes, seminars, conferences, and the newsletter, *End-Times News Digest.* The various ministries of Ministries of Vision are supported by the gifts of those who are interested.

Mr. McKeever is rapidly becoming one of America's well-known Christian authors. Among his books and booklets are: *Chirstians Will Go Through the Tribulation—and How to Prepare for It, Now You Can Understand the Book of Revelation, Close Encounters of the Highest Kind, The Almighty and the Dollar, You Can Overcome, Only One Word, Why Were You Created?,* and *Knowledge of Good and Evil.*

Mr. McKeever makes his living as an international consulting economist, lecturer, author, world traveler, and Bible teacher. His financial consultations are utilized by scores of individuals from all over the world who seek his advice on investment strategy and international affairs. He has spoken at monetary, gold and tax haven conferences in London, Zurich, Bermuda, Amsterdam, and Hong Kong, as well as all over the North American continent and Latin America.

As an economist and futurist, he has shared the platform with such men as Ronald Reagan, Gerald Ford, William Simon, William Buckley, Harry Browne, Harry Schultz, Philip Crane, Alan Greenspan, heads of foreign governments and many other outstanding thinkers. As a money manager, he manages millions of dollars for his clients.

Mr. McKeever is the editor and major contributing writer of *The McKeever Strategy Letter (MSL).* He was formerly editor of *Inflation Survival Letter.* For five years after completing his academic work, Mr. McKeever was with a consulting firm which specialized in financial investments in petroleum. Those who were following his counsel back in 1954 invested heavily in oil.

For more than ten years he was with IBM, where he held several key management positions. During those years, when IBM was just moving into transistorized computers, he helped that company become what it is today. With IBM, he consulted with top executives of many major corporations in America, helping them solve financial, control and information problems. He has received many awards from IBM, including the "Key Man Award" and the "Outstanding Contribution Award." He is widely known in the computer field for his books and articles on management, management control and information sciences.

After leaving IBM, Mr. McKeever founded and was president of his own consulting firm. In addition to directing the activities of more than 100 employees, he personally gave consultation to the chief executives of client organizations. Some of the men who sought his counsel were Dr. Bill Bright, Nicky Cruz, Dr. Ted Engstrom, Dr. Lloyd Hubbard, Josh McDowell, and Dr. Stanley Mooneyham.

In 1972, Mr. McKeever sold his interest in this consulting firm and resigned as president in order to devote his "business" time to writing, speaking and consulting.

In addition to this outstanding business background, Mr. McKeever is an ordained minister. He has been a Baptist evangelist, pastor of Catalina Bible Church for three and a half years (while still with IBM) and a frequent speaker at Christian conferences. He has the gift of teaching and an in-depth knowledge of the Bible.

# APPENDIX C

# CONTACT THE AUTHOR

The following pages give information on other books and services by the author. If you are interested in these or in any of the teaching cassettes, we have included a coupon that you can mail in.

If you would like to contact Jim McKeever, see the last page in this book.

## *YOU CAN OVERCOME*
### by Jim McKeever

Now that you have read this thought-provoking book, why not send copies to your loved ones, so that it might be a blessing to them too?

If you would like to give away some copies, we could mail them directly to your friends, with a card saying that the book is a gift from you, or we could send them all to you to distribute personally.

- - - - - - - - - - - - - - - - - - - - - - - - - - - - - - - - - -

Omega Publications                                            BC-911
P.O. Box 4130
Medford, OR 97501

I am enclosing the amount shown below for additional copies of *YOU CAN OVERCOME.*

(      ) _____ Copies of hardback at $10.95 each =      $_____
(      ) _____ Copies of softback at $ 6.95 each =     $_____
Please add $.50 per book for postage and handling.     $_____
Send these copies to:                        TOTAL   $_____

My Name _____
My Address_____
City, State _____ Zip _____

Gift to: _____
Address _____
City, State _____ Zip _____

Gift to: _____
Address _____
City, State _____ Zip _____

Gift to: _____
Address _____
City, State _____ Zip _____

Gift to: _____
Address _____
City, State _____ Zip _____

# CHRISTIANS WILL GO THROUGH THE TRIBULATION
## —And how to prepare for it
### by Jim McKeever

This book could affect every major decision that you make!

Most Christians have only heard about a pre-Tribulation Rapture, and probably believe in it because they have not heard a viable alternative presented intelligently. This book is solidly based on the word of God and shows clearly why Christians will go through all, or at least part, of the Tribulation.

If a Christian believes that we are indeed going through the Tribulation, the next question is, how near is it? If the Tribulation is thousands of years away, there is no need to prepare for it. On the other hand, if we are living in the end times, preparation to go through the Tribulation is essential.

This book goes on to discuss both physical and spiritual preparation for the Tribulation. It gives practical, "how to" suggestions for preparation.

### PRAY ABOUT ORDERING THIS VITAL BOOK

In times past God did not remove His people from trials, but allowed them to go through them victoriously (Daniel in the lion's den, the three Hebrews in the fiery furnace, the children of Israel in the Egyptian plagues). It is possible that you will go through the Tribulation. The Holy Spirit can use this book to help you understand and prepare.

- - - - - - - - - - - - - - - - - - - - - - - - - - - - - - - - -

Omega Publications                                                    BC-911
P.O. Box 4130, Medford, OR 97501

I am enclosing the amount shown below for _____ copies of *CHRISTIANS WILL GO THROUGH THE TRIBULATION—And how to prepare for it:*

| | | |
|---|---|---|
| _____ Copies of hardback at $10.95 each = | $ | _____ |
| _____ Copies of softback at $ 5.95 each = | $ | _____ |
| Please add $.50 postage and handling per book. | $ | _____ |
| TOTAL | $ | _____ |

Name _____

Address _____

City _____ State _____ Zip _____

## NOW YOU CAN UNDERSTAND THE BOOK OF REVELATION

### by Jim McKeever

At last! . . . A clear, readable study of the Book of Revelation, geared for plain folks.

In past times, understanding the book of Revelation was almost optional. But, in the light of recent world events, the understanding of this essential book is urgently needed.

God says, "Blessed is he who heeds the words of the prophecy of this book." (Revelation 22:7) And if we are to heed the words we must understand them. God would not ask you to heed them unless it were possible.

Satan wants you not to read the book of Revelation. He wants you to be confused by the conflicting interpretations of it. But God wants you to read it, to understand it, *and to act on what it says.*

McKeever makes Revelation an exciting and understandable book, and an essential guide to survival in these end times.

— — — — — — — — — — — — — — — — — — — — — — — — — — —

Omega Publications                                          BC-911
P.O. Box 4130, Medford, OR 97501

I am enclosing the amount shown below for _____ copies of
*Now You Can Understand the Book of Revelation:*

| | |
|---|---|
| _____ Copies of hardback at $10.95 each = | $_____ |
| _____ Copies of softback at $ 5.95 each = | $_____ |
| Please add $.50 postage and handling per book. | $_____ |
| TOTAL | $_____ |

Name _____

Address _____

City _____ State _____ Zip _____

## *THE ALMIGHTY AND THE DOLLAR*
### by Jim McKeever

This book is a must for anyone interested in being a good steward over the assets that God has entrusted to him. Being written from a biblical perspective by a noted free-market economist and investment counselor, this book is one of a kind and it is filled with valuable information.

The forms in this book will help you analyze your present financial status, factoring in inflation, so as to enable you to intelligently plan and invest.

The chapter titles are as follows:

1. The Foundation is First
2. Three Critical Trends
3. Hurricane Inflation
4. How to Get Money to Invest
5. Developing Your Plan of Action
6. Saving versus Investing
7. Real Estate
8. Gold and Silver
9. Collectibles
10. Stocks and Bonds
11. Commodities
12. Tax Considerations
13. Insurance, Wills, and Your Estate
14. The Multinational Individual
15. Prayer, Planning, Prayer, Action
16. Tyranny of the Urgent

- - - - - - - - - - - - - - - - - - - - - - - - - - - - - - - -

Omega Publications                                        BC-911
P.O. Box 4130, Medford, OR 97501

I am enclosing the amount shown below for _____ copies of
*The Almighty and the Dollar:*

_____ Copies of hardback at $10.95 each =           $ _____
_____ Copies of softback at  $ 6.95 each =          $ _____
Please add $.50 postage and handling per book.      $ _____
                                      TOTAL         $ _____

Name _____

Address _____

City _____ State _____ Zip _____

# E ND-TIME
# News
# Digest

The *End-Time News Digest* is a newsletter published by Ministries of Vision, of which Brother McKeever is president, and is printed and distributed by Omega Publications.

The *End-Time News Digest* not only reports the news that is important to Christians, much of which they may have missed in our controlled media, but also gives an analysis of it from the perspective of a Spirit-filled Christian. In addition it suggests actions and alternatives that would be appropriate for a Christian to take.

The *End-Time News Digest* also has a physical preparation section which deals with various aspects of a self-supporting life-style. The spiritual preparation section deals with issues of importance to both the individual Christian and the body of believers.

All of the contributing writers to this newsletter are Spirit-filled Christians. Brother McKeever is the editor and major contributing writer. God gives him insights that will help you, open your eyes to new things and lift you up spiritually.

- - - - - - - - - - - - - - - - - - - - - - - - - - - - - - -

BC-911

Ministries of Vision
P.O. Box 4636
Medford, OR 97501

Please send me information about receiving your newsletter, *End-Time News Digest.*

Name _____

Address _____

City, State _____ Zip _____

## CASSETTES BY JIM McKEEVER

**CASSETTE ALBUMS**

Qty   Contribution

____ $_____   **Becoming an Overcomer** (6 tapes) $24
1. The Future
2. The Overcomers
3. Foundations for Overcomers
4. Spiritual Warfare – Part 1
5. Spiritual Warfare – Part 2
6. The Two Greatest Lessons God Has Taught Me

____ _____   **Now You Can Understand the Book of Revelation**
(16 tapes) $49
1. An Encounter with Jesus (Revelation 1)
2. Letters to the Churches (Revelation 2 & 3)
3. Climax of the Bible (Revelation 4 & 5)
4. The Rapture and the Tribulation
5. Seven Seals and the 144,000 (Revelation 6 & 7)
6. The First Six Trumpets (Revelation 8 & 9)
7. The Little Scroll, the Two Witnesses and the Seventh Trumpet (Revelation 10 & 11)
8. The Woman, Man-Child and the First Beast (Revelation 12 & 13:1-10)
9. The Second Beast and the Second 144,000 (Revelation 13:11-18 & 14)
10. The Seven Angels and the Seven Bowls of Wrath (Revelation 15 & 16)
11. Mystery Babylon (Revelation 17 & 18)
12. Return of Christ and the Millennium (Revelation 19 & 20)
13. The New Heaven and the New Earth
14. Review of Revelation
15. The Overcomers
16. Who is Israel?

____ _____   TOTAL ENCLOSED FOR CASSETTE ALBUMS
____ _____   Additional Gift for Ministries of Vision

- - - - - - - - - - - - - - - - - - - - - - - - - - -

Ministries of Vision                                    BC-911
P.O. Box 4636, Medford, OR 97501

Please ship me the cassettes indicated above.

Name _____
Address _____
City _____ State _____ Zip _____

## TO THE AUTHOR

The various services and materials available from Mr. McKeever are shown in summary form on the reverse side. Please indicate your area of interest, *remove this page and mail it to him*.

Mr. McKeever would appreciate hearing any personal thoughts from you. If you wish to comment, write your remarks below on this reply form.

*Comments:*

TO:

JIM McKEEVER
P.O. Box 4130
MEDFORD, OR 97501

Fold Here

NAME _____ PHONE _____
ADDRESS _____
CITY _____ STATE_____ ZIP _____

Dear Jim,                                                    BC-911

I am enclosing a check (payable to Omega Publications) for:

☐ $_____ for _____ hardback copies of *You Can Overcome*
at $10.95 each.

☐ $_____ for _____ softback copies of *You Can Overcome*
at $6.95 each.

☐ $_____ for ___softback copies of *Christians Will Go Through the
Tribulation—and how to prepare for it* at $5.95 each.

$_____ TOTAL ENCLOSED

Please send me information on:

☐ Cassettes and other books by you.

☐ Your Christian newsletter, *End-Times News Digest (END)*.

☐ Your financial and survival newsletter, *McKeevers' Strategy Letter
(MSL)*.

☐ Your speaking at our church or Christian conference.

☐ Please read the comments on the other side.